KINGDOM LIVING

by

Mike Green

Bless God Publishing
St. Augustine, FL 32086 USA

Bless God Publishing
St. Augustine, FL 32086 USA

Kingdom Living
by Mike Green

Copyright ©2008 by Bless God Ministries

Printed in the United States of America.

Library of Congress Catalog Card Number: pending
International Standard Book Number: 978-0-615-21600-3

Contents

Preface

Jesus Christ had a lot to say about Kingdom living. He came preaching, "Repent for the kingdom is at hand." Matthew 4:17. Later He said, "As you go preach this message, "The Kingdom of heaven is near." Matthew 10:6-8. What did He mean by this? What Kingdom? Where is it? And when or how is it seen? Explaining the concept of the Kingdom is the purpose of this book.

Kingdom Living is a collection of articles written over a period of years. Most of the articles were originally penned as responses to questions raised by the men and women Michele and I mentor. Therefore, Kingdom Living is not a complete treatment of all subjects pertaining to discipleship, but is a work in progress. This first edition is a presentation of the current collection of articles in one volume. We intend to publish future editions.

The articles presented here are not arranged in order of importance. Certainly each subject could be more meaningful for one reader than for another. However, each essay should help the reader understand subjects pertinent to a greater experience of God and His Kingdom on earth. This then is our goal and we pray we have accomplished it. However, the value of our effort will be yours to decide.

We wish to add one caution. All the articles are written from an understandably hazy view of the loftiest of subjects. For how can anyone say truly, "I know God." I can say I know Him better than I did ten years ago. Yet quickly I must add, "But, I know Him less than He truly is, for the chasm that separates the two of us is wide indeed!"

Therefore bear in mind that I write to encourage and to inspire the disciple of Christ to grow in the knowledge of God and in a personal experience with Him. My musings on Scripture are simple, not profound, and should not be confused with cerebral theological treatises written by university scholars. It is a delight to share my insights with you yet I do so self-consciously, aware of the burden of exegetic responsibility as well. Therefore, those seeking the treasure of sophisticated theological research are encouraged to enjoy these articles in spite of their simplicity.

And finally, dear one, read carefully, prayerfully, and even critically, if you must, but extend the author grace in your critique, for he, like you, is continuing to traverse the path of righteousness for His name's sake, and has not yet arrived.

Mike Green
St Augustine, Florida
2008

CHAPTER 1

WHAT IS TRUTH?

John 18:37 Pilate therefore said unto him, "Art thou a king then?" Jesus answered, "Thou sayest that I am a king. To this end was I born, and for this cause came I into the world, that I should bear witness unto the truth. Every one that is of the truth heareth my voice."

John 18:38 Pilate saith unto him, "What is truth?" And when he had said this, he went out again unto the Jews, and saith unto them, "I find in him no fault at all."

Pontius Pilate asked this rhetorical question of Jesus on the day he condemned Jesus to death on the cross. The question was a sign of his frustration. Pilate was growing impatient with the insistent but false accusations of the Jewish leaders. They hated Jesus so much they were trying to convince the Roman government to crucify Him. However, in spite of their insistence, Pilate was not sure Jesus had done anything worthy of crucifixion. Finally, the Jews accused Jesus of being in competition with Caesar, since Jesus had claimed to be King of the Jews. When Pilate asked Jesus to defend or deny this life-threatening accusation Jesus' answer was in the affirmative, it is true, and that He was born for this very purpose; to bear witness of that truth. He added that anyone who believed His claim was also in possession of the truth. At that Pilate retorted, "What is truth?" Pilate was implying that truth is relative, and that each person must make up his own mind regarding the definition and source of truth. His response further implied, since truth was relative, in the end it did not matter what one believed to be true.

Yet, unlike Pilate, Jesus was not speaking of relative truth. He was speaking of the absolute truth. Jesus was not interested in debating philosophy with Pilate, or with the Jews for that matter. His mission on earth was to teach us the truth about the Kingdom of God and to demonstrate a Kingdom lifestyle. The Kingdom of God is governed by the reign absolute truth.

Since that day in Jerusalem, two thousand years ago, the same question has been asked by millions of people around the world. What is truth? Some really do want to know. Others just want to argue or to promote their particular philosophy. But the answer to this question is truly the foundation upon which every philosophical construct stands or falls. And it is the foundation for understanding the Kingdom of God and for enjoying Kingdom life.

Is there a source of absolute truth? If there is, can those who want to, know it? Is knowing the truth really necessary? According to God and His Word, the Bible, yes there is a source of truth, you can know it, and yes your reaction to it will determine the quality of your life now and of your relationship with God now, and after you die.

From a Christian perspective the answer to this perplexing question is found easily in the inspired text of the Bible. According to Jesus, knowing the truth is easy and beneficial. Jesus told Pilate, and anyone else that would listen, He was the truth. At first this statement may seem debatable. However, when beginning to study absolute truth, one needs to accept Jesus' allegedly rash declaration without argument. Why? Since absolute truth originated within the majesty and mystery of God in the dateless past, it is expressed solely through God's flawless eternal will. Thus, absolute truth cannot be known through the intellect. Man may learn about God through the intellect by reading or hearing and then storing information, but he cannot experience God this way. Man's defiled mind cannot grasp the reality of absolute truth. It is a concept that lies beyond the range of his broken intellectual faculties. The mystery and majesty of God's infinitude and perfection is so completely unlike man, that man has nothing with which to compare it. Possibly the most frustrating task imperfect man can undertake is attempting to grasp the concept and personhood of the flawless eternal God.

As we will see in this study, absolute truth is transmitted through, and must be discerned on, the spiritual level.

For this to occur one must be granted the understanding by the Holy Spirit, the Spirit of Truth. Presented below are Bible verses, which reveal the answer to the question, "What is truth?" As we will soon discover Jesus' statement is accurate, absolute truth is tied directly and permanently to Jesus Christ.

Truth According to the Bible

First we will present the verse from the Bible and below it we will offer a brief explanation. We will use the King James Version because it will be easier for the student, if he so desires to follow up using Strong's Concordance. But feel free to read from the Bible of your choice.

John 1:1 In the beginning was the Word, and the Word was with God, and the Word was God.

John 1:12 But as many as received him, to them gave he power (exousia; privileged ability) to become the sons of God, even to them that believe on his name: 13 Which were born, not of blood, nor of the will of the flesh, nor of the will of man, but of God.

John 1:14 And the Word was made flesh, and dwelt among us, (and we beheld his glory, the glory as of the only begotten of the Father,) full of grace and truth.

This passage explains that Jesus Christ was with God before He was born on the earth. He was known as the Word of God, meaning He was the epitome of all God is when He came to be born on earth. Because He was with God, He was, and is, and forever will remain the embodiment of the truth. He was a man because He was born through the birth canal of a woman. But He was from heaven, from God, because He was conceived by the Holy Spirit, not by Joseph, who was married to His mother, Mary. To receive Him means to believe Him to be what and whom God and the Bible say He is. As a result of this belief, or confidence/faith, in His truth, a person is granted a privileged power or ability to know the absolute truth. By this the "enlightened" person is known as a child of God! This is why true Christians are referred to as being "born again." To become born again man must accept the truth of Jesus Christ when he hears it. When a man accepts this truth God's Spirit takes up residence within the man. And it is His Spirit who then leads the born again man, the child of God, into an ever deepening understanding of the truth.

As difficult as this concept might be to understand and accept when one first hears it; it is the truth. And it is vitally important to our discussion for us to accept it as the truth in the beginning of our discussion. As one chooses to accept the truth as God presents it, His Spirit will then guide the continued exploration of His truth. If, on the other hand, we reject the possibility that this is the truth, further discussion is pointless, and our journey is over. Why? Because by rejecting the possibility that His truth is the truth, we reject the One, and only One, who grants us access to the truth. One needs an invitation to get into the Presidential Palace. However, even if you are invited, you will not get in without a presenting your invitation at the door. Shall we go in?

John 1:17 For the law was given by Moses, but grace and truth came by Jesus Christ.

This verse explains the difference between God's dealings with the nation of Israel in the Old Testament, and His dealings with the Church in the New Testament. Since the time of God's creation of Adam and Eve God has wanted a people on earth who were His representatives. In the OT, after the flood of Noah, Abraham became the father of the family that eventually became known as the nation of Israel. The Israelites were to be God's representatives on the earth. They were given the Law at Sinai, through Moses, to govern their lives and to enable them to harmoniously relate to God on His terms. For many reasons to lengthy to be discussed in this article Israel did not follow God's plan successfully. So, for about five hundred years, known as the inter-testament period, God was silent. The silence was broken in 4 B.C. when Jesus Christ was born!

When Jesus Christ (the incarnate Word of God) came to earth God began to build a new family. His church, also known as the body of Christ, would be made up of anyone who professed faith in the atoning work of Jesus Christ on the cross. Men and women from every tribe, tongue, and nation, throughout history from 33 AD to the present time could become members of God's family, the church. How? As John 1:12 reveals, by believing the Truth about Jesus Christ as it is presented in the Bible.

John 3:21 But he that doeth truth cometh to the light, that his deeds may be made manifest, that they are wrought in God.

One who knows the truth lives a life which is pleasing to God and which verifies he is connected to God. Why? Because one cannot live a life in harmony with God without being convinced that He is the originator of absolute truth. No matter how good one is, if he does not believe the truth about Jesus Christ he cannot be connected to God.

John 4:23 But the hour cometh, and now is, when the true worshipers shall worship the Father in spirit and in truth for the Father seeketh such to worship him.

In this verse Jesus was addressing a conflict of theology. He explained to a Samaritan woman that it no longer mattered where one worshipped God, it mattered only that one worship God because God had revealed the truth to him and he agreed with it. The reason the hour had come was because Jesus Christ was the truth and He was on earth. Samaritans were looked upon with disdain by the Jews. They were not allowed to worship in the synagogue or the Temple in Jerusalem because they were not "pure" Jews. Jesus tells her that from this moment forward worship is going to be different. Under the new rules worship by her and her people would be welcomed by God. One did not need to be a Jew, or to worship in a synagogue, or in the temple in Jerusalem. Anyone from any race or ethnic group could worship in any town or nation on earth, if the worship was a reaction to receiving the Holy Spirit's revelation of God, and His atoning sacrifice through Jesus Christ. This is a tremendously liberating concept and declares God's willingness to allow all men everywhere to join God's family, and to receive all the benefits available to His children.

John 4:24 God is a Spirit: and they that worship him must worship him in spirit and in truth.

Here again Jesus is clarifying a theological conflict for the Samaritan woman at the well. And He is doing that today for anyone who reads His words now. The truth is what God says about Himself, and what He says about everything else for that matter. He is a spirit and He made His Spirit available to man in the process of regeneration, by being born again, through faith in Jesus Christ. And it is those who have become children of God through their acceptance of the truth revealed by His Spirit about Jesus Christ that are now able to worship Him the way He desires to be worshipped. Think about it for a moment. If He was a man with a physical body we could see Him. But He isn't and hence, we don't. Being a spirit does not mean He does not have a body, it means we cannot see His glorified (perfected) physical body with our (corrupted) physical eyes. But He promised us that one day, when we had glorified bodies like His, we would see Him, face to face. (1 John 3:2).

John 8:30 As he spake these words, many believed on him. 31 Then said Jesus to those Jews which believed on him, "If ye continue in my word, then are ye my disciples indeed; 32 And ye shall know the truth and the truth shall make you free."

As Jesus disclosed the truth about Himself many Jews believed He was telling them the truth. He said continuing in the truth is what marks you as one of His disciples; not simply being a member of the Jewish nation. This was a big deal! Some of the Jews were beginning to believe He was Messiah. But He exhorted them to continue to learn and continue to believe, for then they would experience true and lasting freedom. He knew unbelievers would criticize them. It always happens. When you believe the truth about Jesus and begin to share that truth with others, you will be criticized. To continue to walk in the truth against the opposing lifestyle and culture of unredeemed men you will need to be strong. The more you read the Bible, the more truth you will possess, and the stronger your faith will become.

The freedom Jesus promised would come by "continuing" is discovered in an ever-deepening relationship with God and a growing awareness of His Kingdom. As a human being pursues God the temporary carnal pleasure of the world around him loses its attractiveness and its devastating impact on his life.

John 8:40 But now ye seek to kill me, a man that hath told you the truth, which I have heard of God: this did not Abraham. (or; Abraham did not do this!) parentheses mine.

Here Jesus is challenging Jews who did not believe He was telling them the truth about Himself. He accuses them of secretly preparing to kill Him for blaspheming against God! Why? Because He was telling them they could be free by believing He was who God said He was.

Abraham, by the way, was considered righteous because he simply believed God. He pre-dated the Jewish culture and religion. New Testament believers are known as children of Abraham regardless of their nation of origin because they have faith in God, like Abraham did. Jesus was telling the Jews, who claimed to be ancestors of Abraham, that when God spoke to Abraham, he believed. By contrast, Jesus says, when I tell you the truth, you try to kill me! It's no wonder they were enraged! They promoted themselves as the people of God and yet they were being accused of trying to kill God! Ironic that it was God Who was accusing them! This certainly shows how one's religion can interfere with one's relationship with God.

> *John 14:6 Jesus saith unto him, I am the way, the truth, and the life: no man cometh unto the Father, but by me.*

This is the most clearly stated truth about Jesus Christ in the Bible. And Jesus said it! If we will believe the truth and the truth will set us free we must believe every word He says. He is the Truth, personified! Here He tells us there is no other way to have eternal peace with God the Father. All who believe must believe God has made the way. And Jesus declares emphatically there is no other way. He says "no man" can come into a right relationship with God except through Jesus. If there was another way, Jesus would tell us, because He always tells us the truth. If it was found that Jesus Christ lied to us or tricked us or said something He did not mean, He would not, He could not be God!

The only way to know the truth and to have eternal life with God is by believing the truth regarding Jesus Christ; including His incredible conception and birth, His sinless life, His horrible yet sacrificial death, and His glorious resurrection.

John 14:17 Even the Spirit of truth; whom the world cannot receive, because it seeth him not, neither knoweth him: but ye know him; for he dwelleth with you, and shall be in you.

The scene is the last supper. Jesus is telling His disciples about the Holy Spirit. He is preparing them for His death and encouraging them not to worry because He will send them a helper, after He is gone. And the comforter, the Holy Spirit, the third member of the holy trinity, is the Spirit of Truth. He "dwelleth with you," because Jesus was with them and the same Spirit resided within Him. And soon that Spirit would reside within them! The unbelievers of the world could not see Him (God, Jesus, or the Holy Spirit) because they did not believe the truth about Jesus. Again, we cannot understand the truth about God or Jesus if He does not disclose Himself to us by interacting with us spiritually. This self-disclosure is the task of the Holy Spirit.

John 15:26 But when the Comforter is come, whom I will send unto you from the Father, even the Spirit of truth, which proceedeth from the Father, he shall testify of me:

Notice here all three members of the holy trinity are present. Jesus the Son, says after He ascends to God the

Father, He will send the Holy Spirit, the Spirit of Truth. And the reason is simple; In Jesus' absence The Spirit of Truth will tell you, and everyone else as long as the earth exists, the truth about Jesus. There is but One expression of truth in human form, Jesus Christ. And there is One source of truth, God the Father, and there is One dispenser of truth, the Holy Spirit.

> *Matthew 16:15 He saith unto them, But whom say ye that I am? 16 And Simon Peter answered and said, Thou art the Christ, the Son of the living God. 17 And Jesus answered and said unto him, Blessed art thou, Simon Bar-jona: for flesh and blood hath not revealed it unto thee, but my Father which is in heaven.*

Again this is pretty clear. Peter says Jesus is the One He claims to be and Jesus says only the Spirit of God could reveal it to you. Why? Because, and at the risk of appearing redundant, a person can only understand and accept this truth spiritually and then only if the Spirit of God, Who is the Spirit of Truth, reveals it. Ask yourself a question right now. What are you thinking about what you are reading? Do you believe it to be true? Or are there voices speaking to you telling you this discussion is just a bunch of religious nonsense? If there is a conflict within you right now, what is the source of that conflict?

Do you realize you listen to four voices? Yes, there are four different entities competing for your attention on this, or any, subject. The first one is your own voice. Next are the voices of people you have listened to all of your life. For instance, various voices may be those of your parents, siblings, spouses, teachers, priests, coaches, employers, etc. Then there is the voice of the Holy Spirit, the Spirit of Truth. And finally, you might hear the voices of God's enemies. Now think again for a moment. Which voice should you trust to tell you the truth?

John 16:13 Howbeit when he, the Spirit of truth, is come, he will guide you into all truth: for he shall not speak of himself; but whatsoever he shall hear, that shall he speak: and he will show you things to come.

The Spirit of Truth will always tell us the truth, just as Jesus did. Including, in this case, the things that will take place after Jesus' ascension to be with the Father. This presents another example of the trinity. The three of them are always in harmony with each other. Jesus once remarked, that he did and said only that which was pleasing to the Father (John 8:28-29).

John 17:17 Sanctify them through thy truth: thy word is truth.

The Scripture above and the one below are taken from Jesus' last prayer with His disciples just before He went out to be crucified. It was a difficult time for Him because the cross was waiting. It was a hard time for His disciples as well as He was about to leave them on their own. They would no longer be able to sit with Him at the supper table asking the difficult questions. They, like all believers now, would need to rely on the Word of God and the Spirit of Truth for their understanding. And He was concerned for them. He knew they would be vulnerable and at risk because their new found faith in Him was not popular with many of their friends and family members.

To be sanctified means to be made pure or holy. And Jesus asks God in this prayer to make the disciples pure, holy, and consequently eternally free. By exposing oneself to the Word of God, so the Spirit of Truth can teach the truth, one can live in harmony with the truth and experience a freedom that is not available through any other means. But the choice is an individual one. Many are the distractions of modern life. And we will have many critics as we follow the life and teachings of Jesus. Yet only by a lifelong study of the Word of Truth with the Spirit of Truth as our guide will we understand the Truth and enjoy the freedom, which is available only through this understanding.

John 17:19 And for their sakes I sanctify myself, that they also might be sanctified through the truth.

Jesus lived the same kind of life we live. Tempted in every way as we are. But He remained pure, sanctified. He did this by setting His will to resist temptation and by relying upon the Holy Spirit, the Spirit of Truth, to help Him. He tells us here that He did that for our sake. As He is sanctified, kept Holy, He can now expect us to receive the same help, by the Holy Spirit, to live the same way.

Romans 1:22 Professing themselves to be wise, they became fools, 23: And changed the glory of the incorruptible God into an image made like to corruptible man, and to birds, and four-footed beasts, and creeping things. 23: Wherefore God also gave them up to uncleanness through the lusts of their own hearts, to dishonor their own bodies between themselves: 25 Who changed the truth of God into a lie, and worshiped and served the creature more than the Creator, who is blessed forever. Amen.

This is from Paul's letter to the believers in Rome. He shows how mankind becomes pathetically hopeless by rejecting the truth of God. To believe anything about God that conflicts with what He said is to be foolish. In philosophy we call this a slippery slope. A small error leads to a larger error, if followed long enough. For example, if one deviates from a compass course by even the slightest degree he will indeed be lost a hundred miles down the road! God cautions man not to worship anything, not angel, bird, flower, tree, goat, cow, snake, wealth, fame, children, parents, sex, or any other so called or self- proclaiming god. In all of history there is but One who is truly worthy of worship.

1Corinthians 13:6 Rejoiceth not in iniquity, but rejoiceth in the truth.

Again from Paul's pen we have a description of true love. The 13th chapter of 1 Corinthians is called the love chapter. In it Paul presents a long list of qualities pertaining to true love. One of the most important qualities of true love is that true love rejoices in the truth. And conversely it hates lies. It is fun to read this passage of Scripture and replace the word, love, with the word, God.

Galatians 3:1 O foolish Galatians, who hath bewitched you, that ye should not obey the truth, before whose eyes Jesus Christ hath been evidently set forth, crucified among you?

Disobeying (rejecting) the truth after recognizing and acknowledging the truth is truly foolish. The passionate Paul asks, "Who has changed your mind on this very important subject?" In other words, "Who have you been listening to since I told you the truth, who has succeeded in changing your mind?"

Galatians 4:16 Am I therefore become your enemy, because I tell you the truth?

Paul shared the good news of Jesus with the Galatians on one of his missionary journeys to the region. They had become born again children of God because of his preaching the truth about Jesus. But they have fallen away from the truth and gone back to former fruitless religious practices. Now in a letter to them Paul is asking why the Galatians are mad at him, when he reminds them of the importance of following the truth. This is similar to when Jesus accused the Jews of trying to kill Him just because He told them the truth. And it's similar to you getting mad at me for reminding you to buckle your seat belt before driving away! Or for telling you the truth about Jesus.

Ephesians 1:13 In whom (Jesus) ye also trusted, after that ye heard the word of truth, the gospel of your salvation: in whom also after that ye believed,

ye were sealed with that Holy Spirit of promise.
(parentheses mine)

The Ephesians had trusted Jesus to be who Paul said He was and they received salvation, and the confirming indwelling of Holy Spirit as a sign of approval.

Ephesians 4:21 If so be that ye have heard him, and
have been taught by him, as the truth is in Jesus:

Where is the truth? In Jesus. The relative, debatable, truth? No. The absolute, undisputed, one and only eternal truth.

Colossians 1:5 For the hope which is laid up for you
in heaven, whereof ye heard before in the word of
the truth of the gospel;

Heaven awaits those who have heard and believe the truth of the good news about Jesus Christ.

2Thessalonians 2:10 And with all deceivableness of
unrighteousness in them that perish; because they
received not the love of the truth, that they might
be saved.

They could enjoy the freedom of eternal life, but they rejected the truth and therefore they will perish. Perish here means to be destroyed.

2Thessalonians 2:12 That they all might be damned
who believed not the truth, but had pleasure in
unrighteousness.

17

Paul is speaking of the unfortunate folks who find their pleasure in unrighteousness. They traded the truth for a lie and received temporary pleasure instead of eternal peace. Harsh, yes; but true nonetheless. Wouldn't you want someone to tell you the truth if what you believed to be the truth (and were relying on to protect you) would ultimately destroy you?

> *2Thessalonians 2:13 But we are bound to give thanks always to God for you, brethren beloved of the Lord, because God hath from the beginning chosen you to salvation through sanctification of the Spirit and belief of the truth.*

Paul thanks God knowing his friends are safe in Christ. Here again Paul ties believing the truth to God's Spirit of Truth and to being saved from impending destruction.

> *2Timothy 2:15 Study to show thyself approved unto God, a workman that needeth not to be ashamed, rightly dividing the word of truth.*

Paul exhorts young Timothy to study God's Word so he can understand it correctly. And so he can help others understand it.

> *1John 1:6 If we say that we have fellowship with him, and walk in darkness, we lie, and do not the truth.*

If we say we know God yet do not know Him as He declares Himself to be in the Word of Truth, the Bible, we actually do not know the truth. Believing something to be something other than what it is does not make it what we believe it to be. Christians do not have faith in what they believe. They have faith in God's truth as revealed by Him in the Bible. To have faith in faith means I am putting my trust in what I believe is the truth, even if it isn't. I am trusting the erroneous concept because I believe by trusting it, it will save me. I can believe the devil is a mythological creature that never existed and does not exist now. But that does make it true. Just as I can believe the earth has existed for billions of years and that man began as primordial ooze, which somehow miraculously evolved into intelligent life. But my belief or confidence in any concept does not make it true.

1John 2:4 He that saith, I know him, and keepeth not his commandments, is a liar, and the truth is not in him.

"Keep the commandments" is not limited to the Torah and Talmud, or the Ten Commandments. It means the total will of God for life as He designed it. And which Jesus reduced to the two greatest commandments. Love God and love others.

Matthew 6:12, Matthew 22:37-39, I Corinthians 13:13, Psalm 19 7-11.

1John 2:21 I have not written unto you because ye know not the truth, but because ye know it, and that no lie is of the truth.

John, the beloved apostle, writes to the church at large just before his own death and says he is writing to them because he knows they know the truth. That's what makes them true believers and members of God's family, and members of the church.

> *1John 3:18 My little children, let us not love in word, neither in tongue; but in deed and in truth. 19 And hereby we know that we are of the truth, and shall assure our hearts before him.*

John asks us to make our love true. Not merely in our word, or speech only, but in our actions because if we know the truth it will be verified in our loving behavior. Just as John witnessed it in Jesus.

> *1John 5:6 This is he that came by water and blood, even Jesus Christ; not by water only, but by water and blood. And it is the Spirit that beareth witness, because the Spirit is truth.*

Once again we have the Spirit of Truth being credited for bringing us the truth. Anyone who claims to know or to possess the truth, in the philosophical/theological sense, and yet does not acknowledge Jesus to be the truth, the way, and the life, does not know the Holy Spirit and thus, does not know the truth. There is but One source of absolute truth.

The final two Scriptures for our consideration offer a truly wonderful salutation for this subject.

> *John 1:3 Grace be with you, mercy, and peace, from God the Father, and from the Lord Jesus Christ, the Son of the Father, in truth and love.*

Grace, mercy and peace from our God and Savior Jesus Christ can be ours as we experience His love by embracing His truth.

1John 1:4 I have no greater joy than to hear that my children walk in truth.

Isn't it fitting that God would speak this tender hearted conclusion through John, the last of the twelve apostles to die. God our heavenly Father, has no greater joy than to know His beloved children, those from every tribe and tongue and nation who profess faith in His atoning work through Christ, are continuing to live their lives based upon the absolute truth presented by Him through The Holy Son, The Holy Spirit, and the Holy Word.

In concluding this section let us remember the single source of absolute truth. God the Father of the Lord Jesus Christ is the One and the only One who possesses absolute truth. Truth originated with Him, has been transmitted to us by Him through His Word, Jesus Christ, and the Holy Spirit, and in the end this truth will judge every man's life. The Bible is filled with warnings about believing some other person or some other truth. Perhaps Paul says it best in Galatians 1:8, "But though we, or an angel from heaven, preach any other gospel unto you than that which we have preached unto you, let him be accursed."

Dear friend, read the Bible. Find a translation you can understand and read it for yourself. Ask the Holy Spirit to guide you and to reveal the truth to you. He will.

II The Word of Truth

We have explored the Bible to discover the truth about God and His plan for mankind through Jesus Christ. But why should we believe the Bible any more than any other book? Compared to all the other books published throughout history the Bible is truly unique. Consider these interesting facts about the Bible.

The word "bible" from the Greek, *biblion*, means, roll, or scroll, or in the modern sense, book. However, by way of common and repeated use the Bible became known as the book. It is referred to as the Holy Bible, sanctified book, which distinguishes it from all other books. It is holy or sanctified because the One who inspired its writing is God. Those who read it and believe it, and act upon the truth contained within it's pages, do so because they know it contains the inspired, infallible counsel of God. Therefore the Bible is unique among books. But there are many other interesting facts that support its uniqueness.

The various books of the Bible were written by more than forty different authors over a period of more than 40 generations spanning more than 1500 years. These sacred texts were written on three different continents, Europe, Asia, and Africa, in Hebrew, Aramaic, and Greek. The various books of the Bible include, poetry, history, law, biography, personal letters, memoirs, and diaries. In addition the authors included kings, shepherds, rabbis, a military general, fishermen, a prime minister, a tax collector, and a physician. And yet the authors, many who had never met each other and who had never read what the others wrote, were in complete agreement. Certainly this alone makes the Bible unique among books.

The Bible has never been popular with all people. In AD303 the Roman Emperor Diocletian issued an edict to stop Christians from worshipping, "and to destroy their Scriptures." Twenty-five years later, the Emperor Constantine, who followed Diocletian, had 50 copies of the Scriptures transcribed at the government's expense!

The very first major book to be printed was an early bible, the Latin Vulgate, and was printed on the first printing press, Gutenberg's (1396-1468). By 1966 the Bible had been translated into more than 1,280 languages. Today millions upon millions of Bibles have been printed and it continues to be, by far, the most widely distributed book in history! Ironically, the French philosopher, Voltaire, who died in 1778, said Christianity would be extinct in 100 years. However, only 50 years after his death, the Geneva Bible Society used Voltaire's home and his press to print scores of Bibles! (And according to the author of a recent book, the number of Christians on the earth is now increasing faster than the population of the earth.)

While the Bible is certainly the most popular book of all time, it is also the most hated book of all time. Many have tried to destroy it, have criticize its portrayal of Truth, attacked it's authenticity, and yet it is still here and still growing in popularity. Of all books it continues to be the most widely owned, read, studied, and practiced book in history!

Throughout the centuries emperors, popes, kings, priests, princes, rulers, the US Supreme court, congress, presidents, humanists, evolutionists, communists, and Nazis have tried to silence it. Hindus, Muslims, Mormons, Freemasons, Satanists, have altered the truth contained in this wonderful book to fit their agenda. Yet, these ignorant critics all died, and will be judged by the One who inspired the Bible's text for their benefit. Despite these attacks the Bible lives on to inspire others to come to the Truth so "you will know the truth and the truth will set you free." Truly, if this book had not been the Word of God given by inspiration and for a divine purpose it would have been destroyed long ago!

Now lets see what the Bible says about itself.

Genesis 1:3 And God said; "Let there be light:" and there was light.

God spoke and the earth was formed. This certainly should give us an appreciation and respect for the power and majesty displayed in His will and through voice.

John 1:1 In the beginning was the Word and the Word was with God, and the Word was God.

John 1:14 And the Word was made flesh, and dwelt among us, (and we beheld his glory, the glory as of the only begotten of the Father,) full of grace and truth.

Hebrews 1:1-3 puts it this way;

God, who at various times and in various ways spoke in time past to the fathers by the prophets, has in these last days spoken to us by His Son, in whom He has appointed heir of all things, through whom also He made the worlds, who being the brightness of His glory and the express image of His person, and upholding all things by the word of His power, when He had by Himself purged our sins, sat down at the Majesty on high,

There certainly is no way to disconnect Jesus Christ from God and from the creative power of God's word, be it written or spoken or manifested in Jesus Christ. In this passage we have God speaking, Jesus manifesting on earth to testify and demonstrate the Word, and the authors inspired by God and moved on by the Holy Spirit to write it down for us to read. Wow!

2:Timothy 3:16 All Scripture is given by inspiration of God, and is profitable for doctrine, for correction, for instruction in righteousness.

Deuteronomy 8:3 man does not live by bread alone but by every word that proceeds out of the mouth of God.

Psalm 33:4 For the word of the LORD is right; and all his works are done in truth.

Psalm 33:6 By the word of the LORD were the heavens made; and all the host of them by the breath of his mouth.

Psalm 107:20 He sent his word and healed them, and delivered them from their destructions.

Psalm 119:11 Thy word have I hid in mine heart, that I might not sin against thee.

Psalm 119:89 Forever, O LORD, thy word is settled in heaven.

Psalm 119:105 Thy word is a lamp unto my feet, and a light unto my path.

Psalm 119:140 Thy word is very pure: therefore thy servant loveth it.

Psalm 119:160 Thy word is true from the beginning: and every one of thy righteous judgments endureth forever.

Psalm 119:172 My tongue shall speak of thy word for all thy commandments are righteousness.

Proverbs 13:13 Whoso despiseth the word shall be destroyed: but he that feareth the commandment shall be rewarded.

Proverbs 30:5 Every word of God is pure: he is a shield unto them that put their trust in him.

Isaiah 40:8 The grass withereth, the flower fadeth: but the word of our God shall stand forever.

John 17:17 Sanctify them through thy truth: thy word is truth.

Hebrews 4:12 For the word of God is quick, and powerful, and sharper than any two-edged sword, piercing even to the dividing asunder of soul and spirit, and of the joints and marrow, and is a discerner of the thoughts and intents of the heart.

2Peter 3:3 Knowing this first, that there shall come in the last days scoffers, walking after their own lusts, 4 And saying, Where is the promise of his coming? for since the fathers fell asleep, all things continue as they were from the beginning of the creation. 5 For this they willingly are ignorant of, that by the word of God the heavens were of old, and the earth standing out of the water and in the water:

1John 5:4 For whatsoever is born of God overcometh the world: and this is the victory that overcometh the world, even our faith. 5 Who is he that overcometh the world, but he that believeth that Jesus is the Son of God? 6 This is he that came by water and blood, even Jesus Christ; not by water only, but by water and blood. And it is the Spirit that beareth witness, because the Spirit is truth. 7 For there are three that bear record in heaven, the Father, the Word, and the Holy Ghost: and these three are one.

Rev 19:11 And I saw heaven opened and behold a white horse; and he that sat upon him was called

Faithful and True, and in righteousness he doth judge and make war. 12 His eyes were as a flame of fire, and on his head were many crowns; and he had a name written, that no man knew, but he himself. 13 And he was clothed with a vesture dipped in blood: and his name is called The Word of God.

In conclusion remember, the mind of man cannot fully grasp the plans and purposes of God. This is due to the corruption that man embraced when he rejected God's fellowship in the Garden by rejecting God's truth. Since that time mankind has tried to live well on the earth. History has sadly shown how difficult this is.

However, mankind's days on earth (yours and mine) are numbered and temporary. Soon each one must face God and see Him as He truly is. Some will be shocked and destroyed. Some will be thrilled beyond any joy possible on earth! All men will be divided into these two camps; those who know God and those who do not. God with patience and unending grace is making Himself known to all who are willing to know the truth.

I pray you, dear reader, will receive Him now and enjoy Him forever.

CHAPTER 2

God's Love

*1 John 4:10 This is love: not that we loved God,
but that he loved us and sent his Son as an atoning
sacrifice for our sins.*

There is no more pleasant subject for me to write about than the loving nature of Almighty God. He is the All Mighty Sovereign, capable of frightening displays of majesty and power. Yet, He wants to be known to us as our Father. Of all the lofty titles His power inspires, of all the various names and titles associated with Him, His favorite name is, Father. His choice of that name means He wants us to think of Him as our primary provider and protector. He has no rival in power, authority, and fearsomeness. Yet His awesome, indescribable, fear-inducing character is permeated by love. His desire is always to love, to care, to help, to heal, to build, correct, restore, and solve every problem and remove every pain. Every action of His is motivated by His love. He is the antithesis of all that man attempts to achieve by the exaggeration and marketing of his own puny power. Man is aggressive, assertive, demanding, domineering because he is flawed, corrupt, broken, shameful, insecure and guilty. But God is eternally loving and He is eternally incorruptible.

Man's Way

It is man's insatiable quest for supremacy that causes most of the pain he inflicts upon himself and his world. Be it animal, vegetable, or mineral, every form and level of life is harmed by one man's determination to rule over another man. He poisons the environment with the wrappers of his self-indulgent opulence. He pollutes the food chain with chemical additives that are designed to increase production and/or enhance flavor and appearance. And he makes the perpetuation of his specie more vulnerable by the week with the acid rain of his arrogant promotion of sexual promiscuity with its corollary exploitation of wounded women and helpless children.

It can be quite enlightening for one to step out of real life for a moment and view it as if it is a macabre theatre production. It is sadly ironic that no one appears to take the evening news seriously enough to actually change their own behavior. As millions watch the unfolding debacle of human pain and suffering daily via their television and computer screens how often do they stop and say, "that's my life!" It seems that the horror of corruption in politics, a billion dollar illegal drug industry, senseless murder, and family abuse is always happening to someone else. This safe, yet far-sighted perspective is classic "denial." Perhaps the dreaded desensitization that many feared would eventually creep into man's intellect as he tolerated more and more violence has finally arrived. The new indifference says, "it isn't too bad or too important if it isn't happening to me."

Yet even if a good man chooses to maintain a biblical "turn the other cheek" or "do unto others" mentality, there are no guarantees. His life may be interrupted by a less thoughtful rogue who practices "after me you come first," or "what's yours is mine too," situational ethics. What then? Some people would maintain that if one tries to be thoughtful of others, is kind and helpful, and yet becomes a victim of thoughtless brutality, he has a divine right and perhaps a God-given obligation to retaliate.

These are tough times on planet earth to be sure. And tough questions need to be asked by each man living in concert with other men. "How will I respond to violence?" "What do I believe about mercy and justice?" These and many other questions must be and are answered by each individual. Unfortunately, they are often addressed in the heat of the battle. It's always easier to give advice than to take it. Lets face it, there's less risk for the advice giver. It is easy to say, "I love you," to those who treat us well. But, loving those who persecute us, do us physical harm, and who consciously or accidentally maim or murder our innocent loved ones, is a difficult task.

Perhaps the answers to these questions are moot. Perhaps there are no definitive answers. And yet maybe there is a higher standard by which to judge human behavior. In fact, the Bible teaches that all behavior, and every idle word spoken, will be judged by God. The Bible further teaches that speaking disrespectfully about another person is action deserving of severe punishment. And in a more specific case Jesus said, "If you look upon" a woman (other than your wife) with sexual intentions, you deserve the same punishment as an adulterer!

The Golden Rule

When Jesus spoke the famous golden rule He said, "Whatever you want men to do to you, do also to them. This is the Law and the Prophets." A simple statement to be sure. Though to understand the significance of it requires a closer look at what he said, as well as what he did not say.

Notice first the statement He made following the golden rule. "This is the Law and the Prophets." His statement indicates that all of the Mosaic law and all of the revelation of the prophets can be summed up and demonstrated in your loving treatment of others! God gave the Law through Moses because He wanted to have a group of people represent Him on the earth. He hoped they would live their lives in a manner that would demonstrate His love to their heathen neighbors. The rules were given to help them learn the difference between right and wrong from God's perspective. He wanted there to be no guessing. Yet, their best attempts to obey the Law also pointed out to them how hard it was to consistently behave in a godly way.

From God's perspective, it was okay to occasionally, and accidentally, break one or more of the Laws. He had a plan to cover such innocent infractions. But the people were selfish, rebellious, and more often than not, unconcerned with obeying God's law. They thought the rules were too hard and that the reward was not worth the effort.

To speak to the people for Him, God also set prophets among the people for bringing encouragement, warning, or correction. He hoped if they did not always understand the written Law maybe they would gain understanding if a prophet spoke to them in person. In ancient times the most celebrated prophets were those who spoke a word of encouragement or correction or gave a warning and later it came to pass. The people were not always kind to the prophets or receptive to the messages they conveyed. In fact, many of the prophets were treated very rudely.

In Jesus' stating of the Golden Rule he simplified the whole problem. He said all that has been written in the Law and all that has been spoken through the prophets, can be demonstrated by you. If you want to prove you are following the rules of God, and that you have heard the message of the prophets, you should love people by treating them at least as well as you would like to be treated. Now, that's not too difficult to understand. And if this axiom is true then the reverse of it must be true as well. That is; if you think you are obeying the law and at the same time you are treating other people with contempt, putting yourself first, striving to get your way, etc., you are suffering from delusion. In fact, Jesus constantly butted heads with the religious leaders of his day for this very reason! They claimed to be the spiritual elite, claimed to know the Law and prophets intimately and yet they were pompous, hypocritical tyrants who strained a gnat and swallowed a camel. Jesus was so intent on clearing up this confusion that He said to the general population, "unless your righteousness (godly behavior) exceeds that of the Pharisees, you will by no means enter the Kingdom of heaven."

Do or Do Not Do?

Next, notice that Jesus said, "Do" to others, etc. He did not say, "do not do..." Yet many people will self-righteously claim, "Well, I don't steal and cheat and so no one should steal from me or cheat me." Such erroneous thinking suggests if they are not treating people badly they are living by the golden rule. However, Jesus did not admonish men to merely cease treating people poorly, "don't do..." He said, "Do..." This is a positive statement which calls for a proactive response. Jesus was showing us God's perspective. Rather than concerning ourselves with the treatment we receive from others, we should follow His example, and treat others the way we would really like to be treated. That is, treat others lovingly, even if or when, they treat us unlovingly. That is what Jesus did. He treated everyone lovingly. He gave them the benefit of the doubt. He tried to believe the best about them even when they revealed their ignorant, hateful, selfishness.

And in the end Jesus died because he believed it was better for everyone if he did not return "insult for insult" or "evil for evil." The Bible says, "for the joy set before him He endured the Cross, despising its shame." By remaining silent and refusing to hurl insults on his accusers He was fulfilling the Scripture. His selfless behavior is a demonstration of the wonderful Scripture, which I paraphrase here, "God loves each citizen of the world so much that He sent His only son to die as a punishment for their rebellion."

It was no easy thing for Jesus to willingly go to the Cross. He did not want to go. Who would? It's not unreasonable to think He had seen a crucifixion. Although hideous, it was a common form of Roman punishment. Jesus had probably seen more than a few in his 33 years of life. When He entered the Garden of Gethsemane late on that spring evening he knew he had some praying to do. He asked his pals to pray with him. But they fell asleep. Their attitude was much like the people who watch other people suffer on TV. Remember the denial response? "If it doesn't happen to me it could not be too bad or too important."

The Cross

The thought of that horrible crucifixion drove Jesus, an innocent man, who had committed no crime, to his knees on the grass of the Garden. There, in desperation he begged, he pleaded, he cried, and he sweated in anguish until blood broke through the vessels lining his tear stained face! The horror of the pain, and the humiliation of the cross, weighed down on him like the very chains of death itself. He who promised to help carry man's burdens had no one to help him carry his. There was no rest available for this One who promised to give rest to the weary. Some make light of his ordeal when they say he knew God would save him. He knew He would raise him from the dead, and that He would take all the shame and pain away. True, though it is, don't think for a moment, dear reader, that knowing the fullness of God's plan made it any easier. Think how you might feel if you were asked to endure the same treatment.

Others try to minimize the stress of that night in the garden by saying, "Well, Jesus was divine, he was God, so of course he could rise to the occasion." True again. But Jesus was both God and man. He had skin that was subject to sunburn. He had feelings that were sensitive to what people said about him and what people thought about him. He was self-conscious. He wanted to look decent in public, he wanted to be accepted and received as one of the good guys. It is not too much to suggest that he did not want to be stripped naked in public. Or that he did not want to be beaten by the painful punches of the Roman guards. He did not want his friends or family to see him treated like an evil criminal by the crowds lining the street. He did not want to be jeered at and spit upon any more than you would. He didn't want his mother to be subjected to the humiliation and scorn of the crowd.

Yes, a great injustice is done when one tries to minimize the agony Jesus endured that night in the garden. And as incredible as it might seem, it is still true. An innocent man whose compassionate heart was filled with nothing but love was brutally beaten and then executed. And for what purpose the skeptic might ask? Only this. To prove, once and for all time, and finally and forever, that God's love for His wayward child is unconditional. It has no restrictions, no favorites. None are neglected. All criminals can be pardoned. All crimes can be forgiven.

About the crucifixion Scripture records much and one passage is very pertinent to this discussion, "And he died for all, that those who live should no longer live for themselves, but for Him who died for them and was raised again." Once again, God is speaking to man and asking, "Will you live for Me? Will you be men and women dedicated to demonstrating My love for all others? When they treat you rudely, disrespectfully, hurt you, hate you, beat you, and persecute you; Will you love them for Me?"

The Majesty of God

The crucifixion of Christ is an event so hideous it is difficult to imagine. Yet the event may be the clearest demonstration of the mysterious majesty of God. Though we study about Him and pray to Him, and place our trust in His plan, and try feebly to obey Him, His true identity remains obscure beyond the capabilities of our comprehension. His majesty is literally beyond our ability to fully comprehend. For to what can we compare God? What is there about your life that can shed light on His eternity. How does one who is born to a woman, who lives for ninety or so years, and suffers all manner of lack, heartache, and loss, understand the One who was never born, will never die, and has never had a plan go bad?

It matters little how you think of the age of the universe. Is it ten thousand or ten billion years old? Either way, God existed before it! How can one understand the planets? They just keep spinning out there. How does the Sun hang forever in the great expanse of space? What fuels it's flames which burn with such ferocious intensity that it blisters the skin of a beach-goer, ninety-six million miles away? With all due respect to the numerous scientific theories regarding this phenomena, the reason the Sun has burned for all these years is because God wants it to. And when He decides it has burned enough, He will blow it out!

God's personality is perfect. Man cannot know perfection. It does not exist outside the holy character of God. God's life is eternal. Man cannot fathom eternity. How long is it? How many millions or billions or trillions or sextillions of years is eternity?

Yet as vast and incomprehensible as He is in His eternity, God's personality is really quite balanced. All of His thoughts, feelings, and behaviors are always in harmony with each other. He is all-powerful yet He is tender toward those who are vulnerable due to their lack of power. He is mistake free and yet He is tolerant of those who constantly make mistakes. His Law requires punishment for law-breakers but His mercy suspends their sentence. He is never more loving than He is judgmental. Yes, He rules the universe with a perfect harmonizing of His justice and mercy.

It is the love of God that prompted Him to create man. It was for the primary purpose of sharing His love with man that He created him. It is God's love that motivates Him to continue, for a while longer, to tolerate mankind's rebellion. And it is His love that holds man's self destructive behavior in check so that each repentant man may have time to turn from his rebellious ways and return to the Father who created him. God has nothing to gain by this. His love for man motivates Him to spare man the agony and the tragedy of eternal separation from His loving presence.

The First Man

According to the Biblical record, God created the earth for man. He then created man and placed him in the garden and gave him the authority to manage the affairs of the garden. Man was to rule over the animal kingdom and the vegetable kingdom. Man was to govern the affairs of earth as his heavenly Father managed the affairs of the remainder of the universe. That is, with discretion, grace, mercy, and ultimate decision making authority. He was to oversee the expansion of the garden/earth, to be fruitful, and to multiply. Man was to accomplish all of his tasks by working in harmony with God's will and in submission to God's authority. But, Man abandoned God's will by rejecting God's authority. Since the time man rebelled and disobeyed God, God has always looked for one who would obey. He found one in His Son, Jesus Christ. But since Jesus left the earth, no other man has obeyed so perfectly.

When God finished building the garden, he placed man in it and noticed that man was missing something important. He had the love and fellowship of the Father, the company of the animals and plants, and the view of the heavenly bodies, both day and night. But still, something was missing. God said, it was "not good for the man to be alone," and He decided to do something about it.

The Second Man

As the story goes, God caused a deep pre-surgery sleep to come upon man. While man slept God opened the side of his body and removed a rib. Closing the wound, He then fashioned the rib into the body of another one like man. But, this new one was different in one way. She was different in gender. True, her hair was in the same place as her man's. Her eyes were of the same number and sat on her face in the same position as her man's. She had elbows and knees, feet and fingers, just like his. And many other of her externals and internals were identical to those of her man's. Yet there was a difference. It was her sexual components, which were unique to her and different than man's, that made her a woman. But even though they were different, those parts were quite compatible with his.

After the surgery, God wakened man and, we can imagine, He asked, "What do you think?" And man replied, "This is bone of my bone and flesh of my flesh and she will be called woman because she was taken out of man." He was certainly correct in his description. She was just like him. And he was probably delighted with the woman God had made for him.

God then spoke again and declared, "For this reason a man shall leave his father and mother and cleave to his wife and the two shall become one flesh." In modern vernacular the term, "one flesh," doesn't mean much. However, most readers would agree that unity and harmony with one another is implied. But, not too many people really consider the deeper intentions of God when He spoke. A further study of the original language reveals the term, "one flesh," to mean, "to function as one organism." This is certainly an accurate rendering. Think about it. When God removed a bone from man, man was no longer whole, as he was originally designed. A piece was missing. He was incomplete and now that there were two pieces of man those two pieces could no longer function in unity automatically. The unity God desired for the two to share had to be experienced through desire, effort, and commitment, and loyalty.

From One to Two to One

After God's surgery, in the place of natural oneness, there was division. Yet there was a purpose to be served by the division. Since the part was removed, the two separated pieces would be forced, by circumstance, to discover an element of God's divine unity in their own duality. That is, two or more separate entities can unify to achieve a commonly pursued goal. Oneness would not be achieved unless each entity desired to have a part of it. This is love. For two to become one requires both to want oneness and both to pursue oneness. Each must put forth the effort to meet in the middle of their differences. They must realize the plan is that they become one. And each must do his or her individual part in the process of becoming one. This effort requires activating two elements of the concept. First, mutual surrender of self for the good of the other. And, second, mutual commitment to share the work in order to share the reward for the work. In doing so the two enjoy the love that is also shared by the three members of the godhead.

God is a tri-part being. He is three distinct personalities. He is at the same time, the Father, the Son, and the Spirit. Yet though the three are identical in form, they are three separate personalities. All three work in harmony to promote and to accomplish the Father's will. Both the Son and the Spirit are unshakably committed to this role. Both work at and delight in accomplishing their part in fulfilling the Father's will. They love Him.

Likewise, as the man and the woman work together under the direction of the Holy Spirit, they accomplish the Father's will and mimic the divine composition of the loving triune godhead. In the divine trinity the three are the Father, the Son, and the Spirit. Similarly there now exists on earth, the Godhead, the man, and the woman. To accomplish this oneness the man and the woman must overcome their separate desires and seek to fulfill the desires of the other. In taking on this task they act like the Son and the Spirit. Their unfailing desire is to love the Father by fulfilling the Father's will. Should they lose the desire to submit to the other, the system breaks down into all manner of dysfunction. The resulting dysfunction infects every level of human life. Why? Because the man and the woman are the source from which springs every other human life. The procreative relationship which exists between a husband and a wife mirrors the procreative power of God. Had the first man and woman lived in harmony with God's will, life as we know it, would be wonderfully different than it is.

Love is divine as it was first shared between God and His Son, and the Spirit. Next it was shared between God and man. And then the love they shared was extended to the woman. And from those three all the earth should have experienced the same love. Unfortunately, there was trouble in the garden.

Garden Conflict

In the Garden story, it was not long before the two who were divinely designed and destined to enjoy the deepest love experienced a life-threatening conflict. How did this happen? There was another citizen present in the Garden. The serpent, satan, the devil, had previously been cast out of heaven for his rebellion. And to earth he was sent. Jesus said, "I saw satan fall like lightning from heaven." Luke 10:18. This one who had previously separated himself from God committed a grievous felony against the man and his wife. The story goes like this.

The Serpent

God had planted two special trees in the garden. One was the Tree of the Knowledge of Good and Evil. The other was the Tree of Life. God instructed them to refrain from eating from either of these special trees. One day the woman was visited by the serpent. He convinced her that God was trying to keep from her something which was good for her. He talked her into eating some of the fruit from the Tree of the Knowledge of Good and Evil. She in turn gave some fruit to her husband and he ate. Scripture records, "Then the eyes of both of them were opened and they knew that they were naked; and they sewed fig leaves together and made themselves coverings." And the next time they heard God walking in the garden they hid themselves from Him. What a strange thing for loving people to do. Why would you hide from someone who loves you? They tried to hide from God because they were guilty and ashamed of their rebellious behavior. Disobedience always causes division. It is sin and as such it is the opposite of love. And if sin is allowed to continue unchecked it forces people to flee from the Loving One who possesses every solution to every problem. Through the prophet Isaiah God said, "Come let us reason. Though your sins are like scarlet, they shall be as white as snow. Though they are like crimson, they shall be as wool."

When the man and his wife disobeyed God's rules for life in the garden they broke the loving unity they shared with each other and with the Godhead. They chose to believe the serpent's false accusation that God could not be trusted. Through their rebellion they demonstrated they were untrustworthy, not God. In so doing they lost their identity with God and became identified with the rebellious untrustworthy serpent! They broke the unity they shared with God and destroyed the loving relationship they enjoyed previously.

Instead of running to the Father for help, man ran away from Him to avoid punishment.

It was not possible for him to do otherwise since his disobedience caused shame which then caused him to fear God. Disobedience always has a divisive effect. It separates loved ones from each other by causing guilt, shame, mistrust, and fear.

Rejecting God's Love

God intended man to willingly participate in the loving relationship God designed for him. Man was to learn to love by being the object of God's love. God was going to continue to show man what love was by loving man. But man rebelled against God's love. In essence, he rejected God's love when he was led by the serpent to erroneously believe God was trying to prevent man from experiencing something good. This is the same lie that has been carried down through succeeding generations of men since that time. While the lie takes on many different forms depending on each man's particular situation the basic theme goes something like this; "God can't be trusted."

By severing the unity of the Garden man created a new danger. If he and his wife ate from the other tree, the Tree of Life, they would live eternally. God knew nothing could be more terrible so, as a precaution, He sent them away from the garden to spare them the agony of living forever in their rebellious condition.

Man was forcefully removed from his beautiful garden home and sent to live in the wasteland of the earth that surrounded the garden. The wasteland was outside the provision and protection of God. Through his rebellion man had placed himself in a difficult predicament. By refusing to submit to God's plan of loving obedience he was now banished from God's presence and destined to learn about love the hard way; through trial and error. That is until God would send His Son.

The New Adam

With the birth of Jesus Christ God was among men once again. This time though they were not living together in the Garden, but in the wasteland. God had come to earth in the form of sinless man. Jesus of Nazareth, referred to as the last Adam, (I Corinthians 15:45) had one mission and one objective. His mission was to demonstrate a loving relationship between man and God while being subjected to the same temptation that had defeated the first Adam in the Garden. He would live a sinless life, remain faithful to God's love, prove His trustworthiness, and thereby present Himself as a suitable sacrifice for the sin of mankind. All of this would be accomplished in spite of the relentless attack of the serpent and his many cohorts.

Through His victory Jesus Christ reestablished man's position with God, reconciled God and man, and removed the consequences of sin. He also enabled man to see God, to encounter God's love and to embrace once again his original demon defeating authority!

God said, "If you love me you will keep my commandments." Why is it that sinful human beings do not understand the power of love? It is the most powerful instrument He has given them for serving Him by serving others. Jesus said the person who would be numbered among the most famous in the Kingdom of Heaven are those who will be humble servants.

For more understanding of the wonderful subject of God's love please review the following Scriptures.

Deuteronomy 6:5
Psalm 31:23-24
Psalm 145:20
Micah 6:7-8
Matthew 5:44-46
John 15:9-17
1 Corinthians 13 The Love Chapter
Romans 12 The Love Chapter
Ephesians 5:1-2, 15-17, 22, 25, 6:1-4
Colossians 3:1-24
1 John 4:7-5:5

Chapter 3

The Parables of The Kingdom

Mark 4:11 He told them, "The secret of the kingdom of God has been given to you. But to those on the outside everything is said in parables.

Jesus often taught the people of Judea by using a long form metaphor known as a parable. There are four different grammatical tools available to illustrate a principle or to make a point. Each is a form of analogy, which compares one object to another. The shortest of these is the simile (sim-ul-ee). "He is slow as molasses." Next; a metaphor (met-ah-for) is a word or phrase where one kind of object or action is used in place of another to suggest a likeness between them. "The ship plows the seas." A parable (pair-ah-bull) is a brief story used to explain a principle that is new or difficult to understand. The subject is illustrated by using a common example from the everyday life of the listener. The fourth tool is an allegory (al-leh-gor-ee). This is the longest analogy. An allegory is a lengthy story or fable that uses symbolic fictional figures, places, and actions to illustrate truths. J.R.R. Tolkein's "The Lord of The Rings" is a modern and excellent example of allegory.

In Matthew chapter 13 are recorded seven parables used by Jesus to illustrate the Kingdom of God.

The Parable of the Sower.
The Parable of the Wheat and Tares.
The Parable of the Mustard Seed.
The Parable of the Yeast.
The Parable of the Hidden Treasure.
The Parable of the Pearl.
The Parable of the Net.

As Jesus began the first parable, the parable of the sower, He just told the story. In all of the subsequent parables, He began by saying, "The Kingdom of Heaven is like..." According to Matthew He shared the additional parables because the disciples asked Him to help them understand the first one. He answered their questions, giving them even more understanding. Herein lies the central truth of this entire teaching. Those who have received the truth will desire more of it, will come to Him for it, and will be given more. The important question then becomes, "How much do I want?"

The Parable of the Sower is one of the most important parables regarding the Kingdom. We could say it is the one that provides a platform for the rest of them. It is upon the foundation of this one that the others rest. It is interesting to note that the parable of the sower is also the first of many recorded in Scripture.

It is helpful if we begin our study by exploring some background and terminology. Jesus uses two different phrases to name His subject. The Kingdom of God and, the Kingdom of Heaven. We needn't get too picky about the difference. Matthew's gospel uses both phrases interchangeably, whereas the rest of the gospel writers, Mark, Luke, and John, use, the Kingdom of God, exclusively. Even though Matthew's gospel is first in order of appearance in the Bible, most scholars agree Mark's was probably written first. Mark was not a Jew, like Matthew, and his gospel is the shortest and most action oriented of the four. Mark speaks about Jesus and the works He did. He doesn't dwell too much on the teaching of Jesus. On the other hand Matthew, being a Jew, explains that Jesus is the fulfillment of the Law and the Lion from the Tribe of Judah. Matthew relates many long teaching sessions conducted by Jesus such as The Sermon on the Mount, which fills three entire chapters. The parables we are discussing are presented in another one of Jesus' long discourses found between the beginning of Matthew's chapter ten and the end of chapter thirteen. Two examples of the different use of the Kingdom are as follows.

Matthew 13:11 [(1161)] *He*[3588] *answered*[611] *and said*[2036] *unto them,*[846] *Because*[3754] *it is given*[1325] *unto you*[5213] *to know*[1097] *the*[3588] *mysteries*[3466] *of the*[3588] *kingdom*[932] *of heaven,*[3772] *but*[1161] *to them*[1565] *it is not*[3756] *given.*[1325]

Mark 4:11 And[2532] *he said*[3004] *unto them,*[846] *Unto you*[5213] *it is given*[1325] *to know*[1097] *the 3588 mystery*[3466] *of the*[3588] *kingdom*[932] *of God*[2316] *but*[1161] *unto them¹⁵⁶⁵ that³⁵⁸⁸ are without,¹⁸⁵⁴ all these things³⁹⁵⁶ are done¹⁰⁹⁶ in¹⁷²² parables.³⁸⁵⁰*

The word kingdom refers to a realm of rule. In modern language, we might say a kingdom is a specific geographical area governed by a certain King. He has rules or laws to be obeyed if one desires to live in harmony with Him and the others who share His Kingdom. Of God lets us know which King is governing the Kingdom. And of heaven lets us know which specific Kingdom is being governed. Heaven refers to the unseen Kingdom located in either the ether (unseen area surrounding us) or sky (geographically speaking). Perhaps this Kingdom is a geographic place in some part of the Universe unexplored as yet by man's latest deep space probes. And maybe, as Jesus tells us, it is right here among us. Or just maybe it is both! The main thing to remember is this; we are discussing a Kingdom which most of mankind cannot see in operation most of the time. This Kingdom Jesus is referring to is the Kingdom created by and governed by the Eternal Creator of the Universe, Almighty God.

So, lets look closely at this parable and discover some of the mysteries of the Kingdom it was purposed to reveal. We'll present the Scriptures first and then follow with our comments. We are using the *King James Version* of the Bible because we can include reference numbers from Strong's Concordance. You, of course, may read from any other Bible version you prefer.

Matthew 13:1 The same¹⁵⁶⁵ day²²⁵⁰ went¹⁸³¹ Jesus²⁴²⁴ out of⁵⁷⁵ the³⁵⁸⁸ house,³⁶¹⁴ and²⁵³² sat²⁵²¹ by³⁸⁴⁴ the³⁵⁸⁸ sea side.²²⁸¹

13:2 And²⁵³² great⁴¹⁸³ multitudes³⁷⁹³ were gathered together⁴⁸⁶³ unto⁴³¹⁴ him,⁸⁴⁶ so that⁵⁶²⁰ he⁸⁴⁶ went¹⁶⁸⁴ into¹⁵¹⁹ a ship,⁴¹⁴³ and sat;²⁵²¹ and²⁵³² the³⁵⁸⁸ whole³⁹⁵⁶ multitude³⁷⁹³ stood²⁴⁷⁶ on¹⁹⁰⁹ the³⁵⁸⁸ shore.¹²³

Jesus went out to sit on the shore of the Sea of Galilee, which was near His temporary residence with Peter and his family in Capernaum. He had already had a great day of doing miracles, and confronting the Pharisees, twice. Here, perhaps He wanted to rest and enjoy the sunny afternoon at the beach. As usual, a large group of people gathered to see Him and hear Him teach. Perhaps as many as several hundred showed up. Some of them were His friends and disciples, and some were not. Some were thinking of becoming one of His disciples and some weren't sure yet. Some were hecklers and critics who stopped by to get more evidence to support their theory that He was nothing more than a vagabond or popular and controversial itinerant teacher. And mingled in the crowd that day were those that hated Him and wanted Him to be silenced. These, the Pharisees, saw Him as a threat to the current Jewish religious system, which controlled the daily lives of most of the Jewish population in the area. They were listening to hear Him say something blasphemous so they could arrest Him as a heretic. Can you imagine it? Their reaction proves people can be so deceived by their theology they actually accuse God of being demonized!

Soon the crowd that joined Him at the seaside grew so large He was forced to climb into a boat pulled up on the shore so He could be heard by more of them. Once in the boat He began to tell them the story of the Sower, who went out to plant seed. In this first parable Jesus explains what happened to the seed as the farmer sowed it. Imagine a farmer, in first century Judea, spreading seed by hand carried in a bag hanging from his shoulder. He walks slowly across his field reaching into the bag and pulling out a handful of seed and scattering it by waving his hand back and forth from left to right, in front of himself as he walks.

13:3 And[2532] *he spake*[2980] *many things*[4183] *unto them*[846] *in*[1722] *parables,*[3850] *saying,*[3004] *Behold,*[2400] *a sower*[4687] *went forth*[1831] *to sow;*[4687]

13:4 And[2532] *when he*[846] *sowed,*[4687] *some*[3739, 3303] *seeds fell*[4098] *by*[3844] *the*[3588] *way side,*[3598] *and*[2532] *the*[3588] *fowls*[4071] *came*[2064] *and*[2532] *devoured them up:*[2719]

13:5 ([1161]*) Some*[243] *fell*[4098] *upon*[1909] *stony places,*[4075] *where*[3699] *they had*[2192] *not*[3756] *much*[4183] *earth:*[1093] *and*[2532] *forthwith*[2112] *they sprung up,*[1816] *because they had*[2192] *no*[3361] *deepness*[899] *of earth:*[1093]

13:6 And[1161] *when the sun*[2246] *was up,*[393] *they were scorched;*[2739] *and*[2532] *because they had*[2192] *no*[3361] *root,*[4491] *they withered away.*[3583]

13:7 And[1161] *some*[243] *fell*[4098] *among*[1909] *thorns;*[173] *and*[2532] *the*[3588] *thorns*[173] *sprung up,*[305] *and*[2532] *choked*[638] *them:*[846]

13:8 But[1161] *other*[243] *fell*[4098] *into*[1909] *good*[2570] *ground,*[1093] *and*[2532] *brought forth*[1325] *fruit,*[2590] *some*[3739, 3303] *a hundredfold,[1540], [1161] some[3739] sixtyfold,[1835], [1161] some[3739] thirtyfold.[5144]*

So here is the story told in very clear terminology. The seed is cast on the ground and falls upon various conditions of soil. Jesus concludes His parable saying, "Listen carefully to what you have heard because it is important."

13:9 Who hath[2192] ears[3775] to hear,[191] let him hear.[191]

13:10 And[2532] the[3588] disciples[3101] came,[4334] and said[2036] unto him,[846] Why[1302] speakest[2980] thou unto them[846] in[1722] parables?[3850]

13:11 [1161] He[3588] answered[611] and said[2036] unto them,[846] Because[3754] it is given[1325] unto you[5213] to know[1097] the[3588] mysteries[3466] of the[3588] kingdom[932] of heaven,[3772] but[1161] to them[1565] it is not[3756] given.[1325]

The disciples reply, "Why do you teach them using stories?" Jesus answered their question in a peculiar way and we must be sure we understand His answer or, like many listening that day, we may miss the meaning as well. He replies, "To you it has been given to know the mysteries of the Kingdom." Essentially He is saying, "The difference between you and them is that you understand the message already and they do not. So, I teach them in simple terms they might understand more easily." In other words, the mystery of the Kingdom has not been purposely hidden from the multitude and given only to the disciples. If this were true He certainly would not teach the mystery using more simple terminology.

No. He is trying to make it clear enough to them so they will understand. He used parables to inform them, not to deceive them. He wanted to include them in the Kingdom, not exclude them from it.

So why then did they not understand the mystery even though He explained it in these simple illustrations from every day life? Simply put, the Pharisees were too proud of their own knowledge, others were too reluctant to change their life, and some were too seduced by the material pleasures of the kingdom of man. To answer the disciples' question Jesus went to great length to explain the elements used in the parable. In addition He will use three more parables, The Wheat and Tares, The Mustard Seed, and The Leaven, to explain the mystery of the Kingdom even further!

Matthew 13:12 For[1063] whosoever[3748] hath,[2192] to him[846] shall be given,[1325] and[2532] he shall have more abundance:[4052] but[1161] whosoever[3748] hath[2192] not,[3756] from[575] him[846] shall be taken away[142] even[2532] that[3739] he hath.[2192]

13:13 Therefore[1223], [5124] speak[2980] I to them[846] in[1722] parables:[3850] because[3754] they seeing[991] see[991] not,[3756] and[2532] hearing[191] they hear[191] not,[3756] neither[3761] do they understand.[4920]

Again, Jesus tells the disciples, "The majority just don't get it yet." And if they did they would want to see and hear even more, just as these disciples desired. Disciples today are no different. Everyone who understands the mystery of the Kingdom desires to know more about it. Why?

A disciple, disciplined follower, has already embraced Kingdom life. He is interested in things pertaining to the Kingdom. He is a foreigner in the kingdom of men. Though he dwells among men and the physical world, he is happy to be governed by the Eternal Invisible King of the Kingdom of God.

13:14 And[2532] in[1909] them[846] is fulfilled[378] the[3588] prophecy[4394] of Isaiah,[2268] which saith,[3004] By hearing[189] ye shall hear,[191] and[2532] shall not[3364] understand;[4920] and[2532] seeing[991] ye shall see,[991] and[2532] shall not[3364] perceive:[1492]

13:15 For[1063] this[5127] people's[2992] heart[2588] is waxed gross,[3975] and[2532] their ears[3775] are dull of hearing,[191, 917] and[2532] their[848] eyes[3788] they have closed;[2576] lest at any time[3379] they should see[1492] with their eyes,[3778] and[2532] hear[191] with their ears,[3775] and[2532] should understand[4920] with their heart,[2588] and[2532] should be converted,[1994] and[2532] I should heal[2390] them.[846]

13:16 But[1161] blessed[3107] are your[5216] eyes,[3778] for[3754] they see:[991] and[2532] your[5216] ears,[3775] for[3754] they hear.[191]

Jesus tells the disciples how truly spiritually blind and philosophically deaf these people are. Their mind, emotions, and will have been so calloused to the things of God by the kingdom of man they can no longer grasp the spiritual truth of the Kingdom of God, even when it is revealed by the King through His words and deeds! Imagine if you can, watching Jesus heal a blind and mute man and tell you He has done it because He represents

God. And you react with disbelief. It seems impossible doesn't it? Yet, it happens all the time. This supports the idea that one cannot understand the Kingdom of God intellectually. It is a spiritual concept that must be discerned spiritually.

You cannot talk someone into being a member of this Kingdom. You might win the argument with so much proof that they say, "Oh yeh, I get it." They might agree with you intellectually, but doing so will not make them members of the Kingdom of God. They might go to church for a while but unless they receive this good news in their spirit they will remain ignorant of Kingdom life. Do you know anyone that claims to be a Christian but thinks, acts, speaks and treats others, like he did before he "accepted" Jesus into His heart? One does not "accept" Jesus to become a member of God's Kingdom. That's not how it happens. That's like saying by accepting the truth about communism I become a communist. A communist is a person who puts into practice the philosophy of communism. Likewise, a man is a Christian when he spiritually understands and then acts upon the rules for Kingdom life. Jesus' came preaching, "Repent, for the Kingdom is at hand." In modern language His proclamation can be translated, "Turn away from, and forsake the ways of the kingdom of men because the Kingdom of God is being made available to you." However, the choice belongs to each individual.

One enters the Kingdom through understanding and putting into practice the Truth of the Kingdom. The first step is to hear the words of Jesus and then based on your understanding reject now and forever the rules of the kingdom of men. This repentance, turning from, implies one thinks about life from the perspective of the King, separating the temporary from the eternal, the holy from the profane, and the Spirit from the flesh. A new believer will do his best to speak to others the way the King speaks to him, kindly, softly and compassionately. And he will treat others the way the King treats him, with mercy and grace and forgiveness.

The personality of God is beyond man's ability to understand intellectually. Just like His eternal nature, His story of creation is not easily embraced by the intellect. To think He just decided one day to make the earth, the garden, and placed man in it, cannot be understood intellectually.

How difficult is it? As an example, consider for a moment the case of the theory of evolution. How many people do you know personally that believe it is true? Did you know paleontologists, archeologists, and geologists have been trying to prove Darwin's theory of evolution for 150 years, by examining the fossil record? They have desperately attempted to validate the ridiculous notion that one species evolved into another one. Their unsupported theory goes like this; Over billions of years an unexplainable muddy ooze evolved into a fish that over billions of years grew feet and stepped out of the ooze and over billions of years exchanged its gills for a nose, and grew hair on its body and began to walk upright first like a chimpanzee, and eventually like a man!

Some of the most brilliant minds in the kingdom of men actually believe that unsubstantiated theory. And yet after 150 years of research and the collecting and cataloging of more than one million fossils, from all over the earth, not one example has been found of any species in any fossil to prove Darwin was right! And yet some of these obviously brilliant men and women continue to look for evidence. Some scientists say the reason they continue to attribute the origin of the universe to the non-scientific theory of evolution is because the only other alternative is to believe the Biblical record, which is too ridiculous for them to believe! How ironic that, according to their own admission, after billions of years of evolution, Darwin's unsubstantiated theory is the best they can dream up to compete with the majesty and simplicity of God's truth.

13:17 For¹⁰⁶³ verily²⁸¹ I say³⁰⁰⁴ unto you,⁵²¹³ That³⁷⁵⁴ many⁴¹⁸³ prophets⁴³⁹⁶ and²⁵³² righteous¹³⁴² men have desired¹⁹³⁷ to see¹⁴⁹² those things which³⁷³⁹ ye see,⁹⁹¹ and²⁵³² have not³⁷⁵⁶ seen¹⁴⁹² them; and²⁵³² to hear¹⁹¹ those things which³⁷³⁹ ye hear,¹⁹¹ and²⁵³² have not³⁷⁵⁶ heard¹⁹¹ them.

13:18 Hear¹⁹¹ ye⁵²¹⁰ therefore³⁷⁶⁷ the³⁵⁸⁸ parable³⁸⁵⁰ of the³⁵⁸⁸ sower.⁴⁶⁸⁷

Jesus tells the disciples how blessed they are to have witnessed not only the miracles but also to be reckless enough to receive the most miraculous miracle; that God is with them in Galilee, the King of the Kingdom is living among them on the shore of the Lake, teaching and doing these things. The purpose of His miracles is to remove all doubts and confirm the truth about His Kingdom! He proceeds to explain the parable even further, interpreting various elements, making comparisons of various groups of people who hear the message.

13:19 *When any one[3956] heareth[191] the[3588] word[3056] of the[3588] kingdom,[932] and[2532] understandeth[4920] it not,[3361] then cometh[2064] the[3588] wicked[4190] one, and[2532] catcheth away[726] that which was sown[4687] in[1722] his[846] heart.[2588] This[3778] is[2076] he which received seed[4687] by[3844] the[3588] way side.[3598]*

13:20 *But[1161] he that received the seed[4687] into[1909] stony places,[4075] the same[3778] is[2076] he that heareth[191] the[3588] word,[3056] and[2532] anon[2117] with[3326] joy[5479] receiveth[2983] it;[846]*

13:21 *Yet[1161] hath[2192] he not[3756] root[4491] in[1722] himself,[1438] but[235] endureth for a while:[2076, 4340] for[1161] when tribulation[2347] or[2228] persecution[1375] ariseth[1096] because[1223] of the[3588] word,[3056] by and by[2117] he is offended.[4624]*

13:22 *He also that received seed[4687], [1161] among[1519] the[3588] thorns[173, (3778)] is[2076] he that heareth[191] the[3588] word,[3056] and[2532] the[3588] care[3308] of this[5127] world,[165] and[2532] the[3588] deceitfulness[539] of riches,[4149] choke[4846] the[3588] word,[3056] and[2532] he becometh[1096] unfruitful.[175]*

13:23 *But[1161] he that received seed[4687] into[1909] the[3588] good[2570] ground[1093] is[2076] he that heareth[191] the[3588] word,[3056] and[2532] understandeth[4920] it; which[3739] also[1211] beareth fruit,[2592] and[2532] bringeth forth,[4160]*

some[3588], [(3303)] *a hundredfold*[1540], [(1161)] *some*[3588]
sixty,[1835], [(1161)] *some*[3588] *thirty.*[5144]

When anyone hears the message of the Kingdom you can be sure there will be great opposition. The entire demonic host is arrayed against any man or woman who hears this life-altering truth. Jesus tells us the attack of the wicked one prevents many who hear the invitation from entering into the Kingdom. The Pharisees are representative of this group of people. These are the demonized critics and false prophets who are so deceived by demons of personal and religious pride that they are actually accusing God of being demonized!

Some others hear the message and get excited about it, for a while. But they don't take it too seriously, don't grow strong in the faith, and as soon as the going gets tough they lose touch with the joy of the kingdom and King. Soon they give up and give into their old ways of thinking and living. They complain, saying its too hard to fight the good fight of faith.

Still others hear the truth and think for a moment it might be a good idea. But they are too distracted by the party scene going on in the kingdom of men. These are the ones that claim they are "living large," have the world by the tail, and self-righteously boast, "it doesn't get any better than this!"

Then Jesus tells us about those who hear, believe, and act on the principles of the Kingdom. These are the disciples. These are the good soil which received the good seed and which will produce a good crop of fruit. These are the faithful, who turn their back on the kingdom of men because they see the futility of all the sensual pleasure and temporary reward it offers. The disciples determine in their heart to know Jesus, the King, and to serve Him all the days of their lives. He is indeed their King but He is their role model as well. They want to be like Him, talk like Him, and act like Him. They want to love Him and enjoy His love in return. These are the ones who are so excited about finally hearing the life-altering truth of the Kingdom of God, they have no regrets about anything they left behind in the kingdom of man. These are also the ones with whom Jesus shares more of the mystery.

13:24 Another[243] parable[3850] put he forth[3908] unto them,[846] saying,[3004] The[3588] kingdom[932] of heaven[3772] is likened unto[3666] a man[444] which sowed[4687] good[2570] seed[4690] in[1722] his[848] field:[68]

13:25 But[1161] while men[444] slept,[2518] his[846] enemy[2190] came[2064] and[2532] sowed[4687] tares[2215] among[303, 3319] the[3588] wheat,[4621] and[2532] went his way.[565]

13:26 But[1161] when[3753] the[3588] blade[5528] was sprung up,[985] and[2532] brought forth[4160] fruit,[2590] then[5119] appeared[5316] the[3588] tares[2215] also.[2532]
13:27 So[1161] the[3588] servants[1401] of the[3588] householder[3617] came[4334] and said[2036] unto him,[846] Sir,[2962] didst not[3780] thou sow[4687] good[2570] seed[4690] in[1722] thy[4674] field?[68] from whence[4159] then[3767] hath[2192] it tares?[2215]

13:28 (1161) He[3588] said[5346] unto them,[846] An(444) enemy[2190] hath done[4160] this.[5124] The[3588] servants[1401] said²⁰³⁶ *unto him,*⁸⁴⁶ *Wilt*²³⁰⁹ *thou then*³⁷⁶⁷ *that we go*⁵⁶⁵ *and*²⁵³² *gather them up?*⁴⁸¹⁶, ⁸⁴⁶

*13:29 But*¹¹⁶¹ *he*³⁵⁸⁸ *said,*⁵³⁴⁶ *Nay,*³⁷⁵⁶ *lest*³³⁷⁹ *while ye gather up*⁴⁸¹⁶ *the*³⁵⁸⁸ *tares,*²²¹⁵ *ye root up*¹⁶¹⁰ *also the*³⁵⁸⁸ *wheat*⁴⁶²¹ *with*²⁶⁰ *them.*⁸⁴⁶

*13:30 Let*⁸⁶³ *both*²⁹⁷ *grow together*⁴⁸⁸⁵ *until*³³⁶⁰ *the*³⁵⁸⁸ *harvest:*²³²⁶ *and*²⁵³² *in*¹⁷²² *the*³⁵⁸⁸ *time*²⁵⁴⁰ *of harvest*²³²⁶ *I will say*²⁰⁴⁶ *to the*³⁵⁸⁸ *reapers,*²³²⁷ *Gather ye together*⁴⁸¹⁶ *first*⁴⁴¹² *the*³⁵⁸⁸ *tares,*²²¹⁵ *and*²⁵³² *bind*¹²¹⁰ *them*⁸⁴⁶ *in*¹⁵¹⁹ *bundles*¹¹⁹⁷ *to burn*²⁶¹⁸ *them:*⁸⁴⁶ *but*¹¹⁶¹ *gather*⁴⁸⁶³ *the*³⁵⁸⁸ *wheat*⁴⁶²¹ *into*¹⁵¹⁹ *my*³⁴⁵⁰ *barn.*⁵⁹⁶

This parable builds on the previous one. Here Jesus declares the truth that it is difficult for men to determine who belongs to God and who does not. God knows His children. That is the most important point here. Men look alike and some can even fake their Christ-likeness in the presence of others. God looks at the heart. He knows who belongs to Him and who belongs to the enemy.

Implied in this parable is another important aspect of Kingdom life for us to consider. It is not time for the harvest. It is not time for the full manifestation of the Kingdom. Not yet. One day soon the King will return and set up His Kingdom on earth. However, only the King knows when that will be accomplished. Until such time the people of the Kingdom of God and the people of the kingdom of men live side by side. This is to allow more time for more men to hear the message of the Kingdom, give up their futile selfish pursuits and come in! This is the time for the disciples to live their Kingdom lives in such a way that they might attract more to come in (2 Peter 3:9-18).

In verse 31 Jesus introduces yet another parable of the Kingdom. A short one to be sure yet, another important aspect of the Kingdom is illustrated. By sharing it, He continues to make His point clear; "he that has some will be given more."

13:31 Another²⁴³ parable³⁸⁵⁰ put he forth³⁹⁰⁸ unto them,⁸⁴⁶ saying,³⁰⁰⁴ The³⁵⁸⁸ kingdom⁹³² of heaven³⁷⁷² is²⁰⁷⁶ like to³⁶⁶⁴ a grain²⁸⁴⁸ of mustard seed,⁴⁶¹⁵ which³⁷³⁹ a man⁴⁴⁴ took,²⁹⁸³ and²⁵³² sowed⁴⁶⁸⁷ in¹⁷²² his⁸⁴⁶ field.⁶⁸

13:32 Which³⁷³⁹ indeed³³⁰³ is²⁰⁷⁶ the least³³⁹⁸ of all³⁹⁵⁶ seeds:⁴⁶⁹⁰ but¹¹⁶¹ when³⁷⁵² it is grown,⁸³⁷ it is²⁰⁷⁶ the greatest³¹⁸⁷ among herbs,³⁰⁰¹ and²⁵³² becometh¹⁰⁹⁶ a tree,¹¹⁸⁶ so that⁵⁶²⁰ the³⁵⁸⁸ birds⁴⁰⁷¹ of the³⁵⁸⁸ air³⁷⁷² come²⁰⁶⁴ and²⁵³² lodge²⁶⁸¹ in¹⁷²² the³⁵⁸⁸ branches²⁷⁹⁸ thereof.⁸⁴⁶

The message of the Kingdom does not appear large and grand in style compared to the kingdom of men. It is not impressive in an outward way, especially in seed form. But if you give it time to germinate in your heart, if you feed it, water it, and keep the weeds away it will grow into a large and beautiful tree filled with blessings of all kinds!

And finally Jesus finishes this long session with one more and the smallest parable. The parable of the leaven.

13:33 Another[243] parable[3850] spake[2980] he unto them;[846] The[3588] kingdom[932] of heaven[3772] is[2076] like unto[3664] leaven,[2219] which[3739] a woman[1135] took,[2983] and[2532] hid[1470] in[1519] three[5140] measures[4568] of meal,[224] till[2193] the[(3739)] whole[3650] was leavened.[2220]

The leaven speaks of the subtle yet powerful influence the Kingdom of God on the kingdom of man. Currently the Kingdom of God is expanding on planet earth. More and more people are hearing the message. Unprecedented numbers of people are hearing it. More men have heard the Kingdom message in the last 50 years than in the entire history of the earth! And it is coming, growing, slowly creeping into the remotest parts of the earth, into the remotest people groups. All across the globe in every nation and tribe and tongue, in meetings, in homes and huts, in schools and in businesses, from Singapore to Sri Lanka to Saskatchewan, people of the Kingdom of God begin their day with prayer and worship. The leaven of the Kingdom is affecting the world.

The phrase, "til the whole was leavened," refers to the fulfillment of the plan and time-frame of God. The day is coming when, according to this parable, the leavening will be completed and all God desires is fulfilled. The end of the most critical era in the history of mankind is coming soon. The King is about to return for the second time.

Matthew 13:34 All[3956] these things[5023] spake[2980] Jesus[2424] unto the[3588] multitude[3793] in[1722] parables;[3850] and[2532] without[5565] a parable[3850] spake[2980] he not[3756] unto them:[846]

13:35 That⁴³⁷⁰⁴ it might be fulfilled⁴¹³⁷ which was spoken⁴⁴⁸³ by¹²²³ the³⁵⁸⁸ prophet,⁴³⁹⁶ saying,³⁰⁰⁴ I will open⁴⁵⁵ my³⁴⁵⁰ mouth⁴⁷⁵⁰ in¹⁷²² parables;³⁸⁵⁰ I will utter²⁰⁴⁴ things which have been kept secret²⁹²⁸ from⁵⁷⁵ the foundation²⁶⁰² of the world.²⁸⁸⁹

Here in verse 35 Jesus removed all doubt, if any remained, as to His motive when He quoted Psalm 78:2.

Psalm 78:2 I will open⁶⁶⁰⁵ my mouth⁶³¹⁰ in a parable:⁴⁹¹² I will utter⁵⁰⁴² dark sayings²⁴²⁰ of⁴⁴⁸⁰ old:⁶⁹²⁴

78:3 Which⁸³⁴ we have heard⁸⁰⁸⁵ and known,³⁰⁴⁵ and our fathers1 have told⁵⁶⁰⁸ us.

78:4 We will not³⁸⁰⁸ hide³⁵⁸² them from their children,⁴⁴⁸⁰, ¹¹²¹ showing⁵⁶⁰⁸ to the generation¹⁷⁵⁵ to come³¹⁴ the praises⁸⁴¹⁶ of the LORD,³⁰⁶⁸ and his strength,⁵⁸⁰⁷ and his wonderful works⁶³⁸¹ that⁸³⁴ he hath done.⁶²¹³

How clear is that? Jesus is not kidding around here. We must not take His words lightly. This is a big day in the history of the earth and of mankind. God has come to earth to speak with His children. This speech, as well as Jesus' life and ministry, introduces a dramatic directional change in earth's history! Jesus' earth life marks the dividing line of history. From this day onward the schedule of events on earth is moving toward it's conclusion. Jesus came to prepare men for the termination of the world as they know it!

"I will utter things which have been kept secret from the foundations of the world!"

"I will open my mouth in a parable. I will utter dark sayings of old."

Wow! This is the real deal! Do you think we should pay attention? Let him with ears, hear! For the first, time since Adam and Eve were expelled from the Garden, God has come to the earth personally. He stands in our presence, in our town, on our beach, and He says, "I am revealing to you the most profound mystery of all time. Never in the history of the earth have I, the One True God, come to you (the multitudes) in Person. And now that I have I want you to understand the greatest mystery ever revealed! I am the Eternal King, I rule the Eternal Kingdom, and I want to offer you the unprecedented opportunity to joyously embrace an eternal residence in it."

Can you, dear reader, take it in? Can you grasp the monumental importance of this event? I certainly hope so.

In verse 36 Jesus finished His lecture, dispersed the crowd, and went back to the house.

Matthew 13:36 Then[5119] Jesus[2424] sent the multitude away,[863, 3588, 3793] and went[2064] into[1519] the[3588] house:[3614] and[2532] his[846] disciples[3101] came[4334] unto him,[846] saying,[3004] Declare[5419] unto us[2254] the[3588] parable[3850] of the[3588] tares[2215] of the[3588] field.[68]

The disciples, probably many more than the twelve, followed Him home. They wanted more from Him. They were not satisfied as was the rest of the multitude that had gathered earlier at the shore. These came home with Him and asked Him to tell them more about one of the additional parables He had used to explain the Kingdom. Again, desiring they know as much as they wanted, He replied with a clear explanation. His detailed answer proved, once again, He wanted them to understand the eternal significance of His message. He used three more parables to further their understanding! The hidden treasure, the pearl, and the net.

I think it is clear by now Jesus wants his listeners to know how significant this message truly is. In fact all of life, eternal life, hangs in the balance. As incredible as it is to think of Him, God Incarnate, standing on the beach teaching them, remember this; just as incredible is the fact that He had Matthew write it down so you and I could read it two thousand years later, and hear the same message and be offered the same truly amazing opportunity!

Before I met Jesus I studied and practiced many different forms of religious and spiritual rituals. And in many, if not all of these, the teachings of Jesus were thought to be either myth, legend, no more important than others, or allegory. Yet if one reads the Bible text as presented it is impossible to misunderstand Jesus' central theme. "I am God and I am your advocate, your helper, your healer. And only I can reconcile you to God and grant you eternal peace with Him."

Parable Context

Now lets back up a bit to see exactly how significant this teaching truly is. This lengthy discourse, which culminates with the parables of the Kingdom, began earlier in the day, and is introduced in Matthew 12:22, with a demonstration of Jesus' Kingdom power.

Matthew 12:22 Then[5119] was brought[4374] unto him[846] one possessed with a devil,[1139] blind,[5185] and[2532] dumb:[2974] and[2532] he healed[2323] him,[846] insomuch that[5620] the[3588] blind[5185] and[2532] dumb[2974] both[2532] spake[2980] and[2532] saw.[191]

12:23 And[2532] all[3956] the[3588] people[3793] were amazed,[1839] and[2532] said,[3004] Is[2076] not[3385] this[3778] the[3588] son[5207] of David?[1138]

12:24 But[1161] when the[3588] Pharisees[5330] heard[191] it, they said,[2036] This[3778] fellow doth not[3756] cast out[1544] devils,[1140] but[1508] by[1722] Beelzebub[954] the prince[758] of the[3588] devils.[1140]

When Jesus demonstrated Kingdom power all the bystanders were amazed. Their reactions were varied. Some said among themselves, "Whoa, maybe this guy is the son of David?" They meant maybe Jesus was the messiah! And others, the religious nobility of the day, the Pharisees, scoffed and said, "This guy is an emissary of satan."

Jesus, knowing their thoughts, hearing them murmur, became very serious. He began to teach them about citizenship in various kingdoms. First, He proves the ignorance of their accusation that His power is from a source other than God.

Matthew 12:25 And[1161] Jesus[2424] knew[1492] their[846] thoughts,[1761] and said[2036] unto them,[846] Every[3956] kingdom[932] divided[3307] against[2596] itself[1438] is brought to desolation;[2049] and[2532] every[3956] city[4172] or[2228] house[3614] divided[3307] against[2596] itself[1438] shall not[3756] stand:[2476]

12:26 And[2532] if[1487] Satan[4567] cast out[1544] Satan,[4567] he is divided[3307] against[1909] himself;[1438] how[4459] shall then[3767] his[846] kingdom[932] stand?[2476]

12:27 And[2532] if[1487] I[1473] by[1722] Beelzebub[954] cast out[1544] devils,[1140] by[1722] whom[5101] do your[5216] children[5207] cast them out?[1544] therefore[1223, 5124] they[846] shall be[2071] your[5216] judges.[2923]

12:28 But[1161] if[1487] I[1473] cast out[1544] devils[1140] by[1722] the Spirit[4151] of God,[2316] then[686] the[3588] kingdom[932] of God[2316] is come[5348] unto[1909] you.[5209]

In this retort Jesus starts to introduce the mystery of the Kingdom. Essentially He says, "Every Kingdom must be discerned and assessed by each man and woman. Some who witnessed the miracle said, "its from God". Others said, "its from satan." And Jesus added,

Matthew 12:29 Or else[2228] how[4459] can[1410] one[5100] enter[1525] into[1519] a strong man's[2478] house,[3614] and[2532] spoil[1283] his[846] goods,[4632] except[3362] he first[4412] bind[1210]

the³⁵⁸⁸ strong man²⁴⁷⁸ and²⁵³² then⁵¹¹⁹ he will spoil¹²⁸³ his⁸⁴⁶ house.³⁶¹⁴

In other words, "I am stronger than the demons that were affecting the man I healed. So I bound the demons and healed the man. It could not happen any other way."

12:30 He that is⁵⁶⁰⁷ not³³⁶¹ with³³²⁶ me¹⁷⁰⁰ is²⁰⁷⁶ against²⁵⁹⁶ me;¹⁷⁰⁰ and²⁵³² he that gathereth⁴⁸⁶³ not³³⁶¹ with³³²⁶ me¹⁷⁰⁰ scattereth abroad.⁴⁶⁵⁰

And you better decide who's team I'm on and who's team you're on. Because I am on God's team and any team that opposes this team will lose.

12:31 Wherefore¹²²³, ⁵¹²⁴ I say³⁰⁰⁴ unto you,⁵²¹³ All manner³⁹⁵⁶ of sin²⁶⁶ and²⁵³² blasphemy⁹⁸⁸ shall be forgiven⁸⁶³ unto men:⁴⁴⁴ but¹¹⁶¹ the³⁵⁸⁸ blasphemy⁹⁸⁸ against the³⁵⁸⁸ Holy Ghost⁴¹⁵¹ shall not³⁷⁵⁶ be forgiven⁸⁶³ unto men.⁴⁴⁴

12:32 And²⁵³² whosoever³⁷³⁹, ³⁰² speaketh²⁰³⁶ a word³⁰⁵⁶ against²⁵⁹⁶ the³⁵⁸⁸ Son⁵²⁰⁷ of man,⁴⁴⁴ it shall be forgiven⁸⁶³ him:⁸⁴⁶ but¹¹⁶¹ whosoever³⁷³⁹, ³⁰² speaketh²⁰³⁶ against²⁵⁹⁶ the³⁵⁸⁸ Holy⁴⁰ Ghost,⁴¹⁵¹ it shall not³⁷⁵⁶ be forgiven⁸⁶³ him,⁸⁴⁶ neither³⁷⁷⁷ in¹⁷²² this⁵¹²⁹ world,¹⁶⁵ neither³⁷⁷⁷ in¹⁷²² the³⁵⁸⁸ world to come.³¹⁹⁵

Here Jesus throws down the gauntlet. You better be careful how you judge what you have just witnessed. You better take a minute to understand what's happening here because your reaction to it could place your future in extreme jeopardy! The Pharisees have proven which team they support. Essentially Jesus is saying there is no hope for them, because they have not only rejected Jesus, they have blasphemed God. He meant that the words you say, with such conviction, indicate that your heart is far from God continually. He did not say everything you utter under duress is a blasphemy against God. He is talking about the condition of your heart toward God. Not only could they not hear the truth Jesus spoke of, they were so ungodly, they attributed the work of God to demons! They were on satan's team and did not know it! How much more ignorant can a man be than to think he and God are teammates only to find he is an opponent of God? In the day of God's final judgment, these blind Pharisees would suffer the same fate as satan and his demons. How truly sad indeed?

Matthew 12:33 Either[2228] make[4160] the[3588] tree[1186] good,[2570] and[2532] his[846] fruit[2590] good;[2570] or else[2228] make[4160] the[3588] tree[1186] corrupt,[4550] and[2532] his[846] fruit[2590] corrupt:[4550] for[1063] the[3588] tree[1186] is known[1097] by[1537] his fruit.[2590]

12:34 O generation[1081] of vipers,[2191] how[4459] can[1410] ye, being[5607] evil,[4190] speak[2980] good things?[18] for[1063] out[1537] of the[3588] abundance[4051] of the[3588] heart[2588] the[3588] mouth[4750] speaketh.[2980]

12:35 A good[18] man[444] out[1537] of the[3588] good[18] treasure[2344] of the[3588] heart[2588] bringeth forth[1544] good things:[18] and[2532] an evil[4190] man[444] out of[1537] the[3588] evil[4190] treasure[2344] bringeth forth[1544] evil things.[4190]

12:36 But[1161] I say[3004] unto you,[5213] That[3754] every[3956] idle[692] word[4487] that[3739, 1437] men[444] shall speak,[2980] they shall give[591] account[3056] thereof[4012, 846] in[1722] the day[2250] of judgment.[2920]

12:37 For[1063] by[1537] thy[4675] words[3056] thou shalt be justified,[1344] and[2532] by[1537] thy[4675] words[3056] thou shalt be condemned.[2613]

Jesus assures them that thoughts and feelings and the words that support them will indicate to which kingdom you belong. Interestingly, in verse 38, the Pharisees, the most religious group of the day, challenges Him, "Prove it!"

Mathew 12:38 Then[5119] certain[5100] of the[3588] scribes[1122] and[2532] of the Pharisees[5330] answered,[611] saying,[3004] Master,[1320] we would[2309] see[1492] a sign[4592] from[575] thee.[4675]

Matthew 12:39 But[1161] he[3588] answered[611] and said[2036] unto them,[846] An evil[4190] and[2532] adulterous[3428] generation[1074] seeketh after[1934] a sign;[4592] and[2532] there shall no[3756] sign[4592] be given[1325] to it,[846] but[1508] the[3588] sign[4592] of the[3588] prophet[4396] Jonah:[2495]

12:40 For[1063] as[5618] Jonah[2495] was[2258] three[5140] days[2250] and[2532] three[5140] nights[3571] in[1722] the[3588] whale's[2785] belly;[2836] so[3779] shall the[3588] Son[5207] of man[444] be[2071] three[5140] days[2250] and[2532] three[5140] nights[3571] in[1722] the[3588] heart[2588] of the[3588] earth.[1093]

12:41 The men[435] of Nineveh[3536] shall rise[450] in[1722] judgment[2920] with[3326] this[5026] generation,[1074] and[2532] shall condemn²⁶³² it:⁸⁴⁶ because³⁷⁵⁴ they repented³³⁴⁰ at¹⁵¹⁹ the³⁵⁸⁸ preaching²⁷⁸² of Jonah;²⁴⁹⁵ and,²⁵³² behold,²⁴⁰⁰ a greater⁴¹¹⁹ than Jonah²⁴⁹⁵ is here.⁵⁶⁰²

12:42 The queen⁹³⁸ of the south³⁵⁵⁸ shall rise up¹⁴⁵³ in¹⁷²² the³⁵⁸⁸ judgment²⁹²⁰ with³³²⁶ this⁵⁰²⁶ generation,¹⁰⁷⁴ and²⁵³² shall condemn²⁶³² it:⁸⁴⁶ for³⁷⁵⁴ she came²⁰⁶⁴ from¹⁵³⁷ the³⁵⁸⁸ uttermost parts⁴⁰⁰⁹ of the³⁵⁸⁸ earth¹⁰⁹³ to hear¹⁹¹ the³⁵⁸⁸ wisdom⁴⁶⁷⁸ of Solomon;⁴⁶⁷² and,²⁵³² behold,²⁴⁰⁰ a greater⁴¹¹⁹ than Solomon⁴⁶⁷² is here.⁵⁶⁰²

12:43 When³⁷⁵² the³⁵⁸⁸ unclean¹⁶⁹ spirit⁴¹⁵¹ is gone¹⁸³¹ out of³⁷⁵ a man,⁴⁴⁴ he walketh¹³³⁰ through¹²²³ dry⁵⁰⁴ places,⁵¹¹⁷ seeking²²¹² rest,³⁷² and²⁵³² findeth²¹⁴⁷ none.³⁷⁵⁶

12:44 Then⁵¹¹⁹ he saith,³⁰⁰⁴ I will return¹⁹⁹⁴ into¹⁵¹⁹ my³⁴⁵⁰ house³⁶²⁴ from whence³⁶⁰⁶ I came out;¹⁸³¹ and²⁵³² when he is come,²⁰⁶⁴ he findeth²¹⁴⁷ it empty,⁴⁹⁸⁰ swept,⁴⁵⁶³ and²⁵³² garnished.²⁸⁸⁵

12:45 Then⁵¹¹⁹ goeth⁴¹⁹⁸ he, and²⁵³² taketh³⁸⁸⁰ with³³²⁶ himself¹⁴³⁸ seven²⁰³³ other²⁰⁸⁷ spirits⁴¹⁵¹ more wicked⁴¹⁹¹ than himself,¹⁴³⁸ and²⁵³² they enter in¹⁵²⁵ and dwell²⁷³⁰ there:¹⁵⁶³ and²⁵³² the³⁵⁸⁸ last²⁰⁷⁸ state of that¹⁵⁶⁵ man⁴⁴⁴ is¹⁰⁹⁶ worse⁵⁵⁰¹ than the³⁵⁸⁸ first.⁴⁴¹³ Even so³⁷⁷⁹ shall it be²⁰⁷¹ also²⁵³² unto this⁵⁰²⁶ wicked⁴¹⁹⁰ generation.¹⁰⁷⁴

Jesus reminds the Pharisees, and every one else standing there, that a sign has already been given. He just performed a miracle (verse 22). And in addition many other signs have been given and the people of Nineveh, and the queen of Sheba recognized them. And the greatest of all signs is standing right in front of you and you do not believe Him! Then He insults them further by comparing them to a man who had been delivered of demons by God and yet did not live any differently. So when the demons came back, as demons are inclined to do, they found their former residence swept clean but empty and resuming their former activity made the man's condition worse than before!

Who was Jesus talking about? The Pharisees! They represented all the religious nonsense and blasphemy of the stiff-necked, hard-hearted Hebrew nation. Consider how God delivered them from bondage in Egypt in truly miraculous ways. And yet they grumbled and complained, and went whoring after the gods of other nations. They squabbled for a king and got a mess of bad ones that divided their own nation, and sent them finally into exile, not once but twice! So bad was their sin before God that He actually stopped speaking to them and through them for nearly five hundred years! And yet here they were again five hundred years after the last of their prophets prophesied, with their messiah standing in their midst and they were so demonized they claimed he was in league with satan! I guess Jesus had a point. Their present condition indicated they were in worse shape than they had been in Egypt! (For more on this subject see Psalm 106).

Now Jesus begins the discourse on the Kingdom, which eventually leads us back into Matthew chapter 13.

Mathew 12:46 While[1161] he[846] yet[2089] talked[2980] to the[3588] people,[3793] behold,[2400] his mother[3384] and[2532] his[846] brethren[80] stood[2476] without,[1854] desiring[2212] to speak[2980] with him.[846]

Mathew 12:47 Then[1161] one[5100] said[2036] unto him,[846] Behold,[2400] thy[4675] mother[3384] and[2532] thy[4675] brethren[80] stand[2476] without,[1854] desiring[2212] to speak[2980] with thee.[4671]

Mathew 12:48 But[1161] he[3588] answered[611] and said[2036] unto him that told[2036] him,[846] Who[5101] is[2076] my[3450] mother?[3384] and[2532] who[5101] are[1526] my[3450] brethren?[80]

Mathew 12:49 And[2532] he stretched forth[1614] his[848] hand[5495] toward[1909] his[848] disciples,[3101] and said,[2036] Behold[2400] my[3450] mother[3384] and[2532] my[3450] brethren![80]

Mathew 12:50 For[1063] whosoever[3748] shall do[4160] the[3588] will[2307] of my[3450] Father[3962] which[3588] is in[1722] heaven,[3772] the same[846] is[2076] my[3450] brother,[80] and[2532] sister,[79] and[2532] mother.[3384]

Some members of the throng call to him that His mother and siblings are outside and want to see Him. He uses the moment to teach on the Kingdom. Basically He says, I belong to a different family than the one desiring to see me outside. And those of you who hear what I'm saying here today and believe I am speaking the truth, you are children of my father and we are siblings! What? Yes each one who believes this truth proves by your belief that you are my family. He uses the phrase, "does the will of my Father, which is in heaven," to describe those that hear the message of the Kingdom and decide to live differently. Their decision based on their understanding of Jesus and His message of the Kingdom prompts them to live differently than they did before they heard and understood the message. In other words, they heard and UNDERSTOOD, so they were willing to submit to the new rule, enter the new kingdom, and do the will of their new King, the King of the Universe! They have, in fact, embraced the life altering mystery of the Kingdom of God. (Notice there is no mention of a sinner's prayer.)

Jesus taught this eighty-verse message of the Kingdom of God one day in Galilee. It included healing a blind and mute man, a rebuke of the religious leaders of the day, the path of justification and condemnation, as well as eight parables with in-depth explanations! In closing the revelation of the mystery He asks a simple, short, and very important question.

Matthew 13:51 Jesus²⁴²⁴ saith³⁰⁰⁴ unto them,⁸⁴⁶ Have ye understood⁴⁹²⁰ all³⁹⁵⁶ these things? They⁵⁰²³ say³⁰⁰⁴ unto him,⁸⁴⁶ Yea,³⁴⁸³ Lord.²⁹⁶²

Have you, like the listener in Jesus' day, have you, the reader of this Bible passage, and you, the reader of this Bible study, have you understood? Have you comprehended this life-altering principle at a level that inspires you to change your way of life, while there is still time? All these things; have you understood every parable and every one of Jesus' explanations and interpretations of them?

A couple things are implied in this simple question. One; will your hearing translate into doing? And two; does Jesus need to try once again to explain it so you can understand it?

The answer that day long ago was simple, direct, and hopefully as sincere as the question: "Yes, Lord."

The word Lord in the Greek here is kurios, and means, owner, master, controller. We could extend the definition in modern language by saying, my Lord is "the One I acknowledge to be the Ruler I submit to. He is the One that makes rules for my life, and that I confidently trust and willfully obey." To answer "yes" is to say I have heard and understood the significance of the message. To say "yes" is to confirm I see my life needs to change; my motives, habits, plans, speech and behavior must be in harmony with the will of my King.

If you had been among the multitude on the shore of Galilee that day how would you have reacted? The Pharisees heard the word and said Jesus was demonized. They represent seed falling along the wayside, which was immediately devoured by the birds. The majority of the multitude heard the word and wandered off back into their businesses and homes, to pursue worldly pleasures. These represent the seed falling onto the stony places, and among the thorns.

But several in the crowd that day followed Him home, even though He tried to send them away. These ignored previous commitments. They probably made some people angry by missing scheduled appointments.

Maybe some even upset members of their own families by lingering behind to hear more from Jesus. Yet, they had to linger. They had more questions. They had been touched at the core of their being by something He said. They had received hope that a long buried dream might possibly be fulfilled. They felt something stir deep inside as they listened to Him speak of the Kingdom. They hadn't heard with their ears, they heard with their heart. They were not satisfied by what they heard, but made hungry for more. Though they had met Him only hours ago they felt as though they knew Him. His voice, or maybe it was His words, something about Him was familiar to them. At the same time, they knew this man was different. They didn't know how they knew He was different, they just knew He was not like all the rest they had listened to before. And they knew, from this moment forward, they were going to be different.

These few who wouldn't go home, not just yet; these were the good soil. They were about to produce a crop. Their trees were going to be full of fruit and that fruit would be full of seed! You see, since they had received the seed in good soil, they were assured they would receive even more because they were determined to produce an abundant crop.

Remember, the seed in the parable of the sower is the once mysterious message of the Kingdom. Jesus removed the shroud of mystery surrounding the message. He came to earth proclaiming, "Turn away from the kingdom of men and come into the Kingdom of God."

Matthew 4:17 From[575] that time[5119] Jesus[2424] began[756] to preach,[2784] and[2532] to say,[3004] Repent:[3340] for[1063] the[3588] kingdom[932] of heaven[3772] is at hand.[1448]

Jesus removed the Kingdom from the darkness of mystery and moved it into the light of reality so each one could hear it and decide what to do about it. He removed the majesty of the Kingdom from the shroud of religious ignorance. He uncovered it so those who hear and understand will act on it by submitting to their new King. These alone can expect to receive even further understanding. On the other hand, those who hear and do not change their lifestyles to reflect Kingdom life and primarily submission to the will of the King, will eventually lose even what little joy they experienced initially.

Conclusion

To conclude this study of the Kingdom parables lets look at another Scripture that highlights the timeliness of the message. Peter wrote the following letter after the resurrection of Jesus and after the coming of the Holy Spirit. In the early 60's AD, 30 years after Jesus' resurrection, he wrote to encourage those who were being tempted, mistreated, and rejected by the world in which they lived because of their obedience to their new King. He wrote to encourage the good seed which had fallen on good soil, but whose confidence was being challenged by the hatred of the followers of other gods.

1 Peter 1:1 Peter,⁴⁰⁷⁴ an apostle⁶⁵² of Jesus²⁴²⁴ Christ,⁵⁵⁴⁷ to the strangers³⁹²⁷ scattered throughout¹²⁹⁰ Pontus,⁴¹⁹⁵ Galatia,¹⁰⁵³ Cappadocia,²⁵⁸⁷ Asia,⁷⁷³ and²⁵³² Bithynia,⁹⁷⁸

1:2 Elect¹⁵⁸⁸ according²⁵⁹⁶ to the foreknowledge⁴²⁶⁸ of God²³¹⁶ the Father,³⁹⁶² through¹⁷²² sanctification³⁸ of the Spirit,⁴¹⁵¹ unto¹⁵¹⁹ obedience⁵²¹⁸ and²⁵³² sprinkling⁴⁴⁷³ of the blood¹²⁹ of Jesus²⁴²⁴ Christ:⁵⁵⁴⁷ Grace⁵⁴⁸⁵ unto you,⁵²¹³ and²⁵³² peace,¹⁵¹⁵ be multiplied.⁴¹²⁹

1:3 Blessed²¹²⁸ be the³⁵⁸⁸ God²³¹⁶ and²⁵³² Father³⁹⁶² of our²²⁵⁷ Lord²⁹⁶² Jesus²⁴²⁴ Christ,⁵⁵⁴⁷ which according²⁵⁹⁶ to his⁸⁴⁸ abundant⁴¹⁸³ mercy¹⁶⁵⁶ hath begotten us again³¹³, ²²⁴⁸ unto¹⁵¹⁹ a lively²¹⁹⁸ hope¹⁶⁸⁰ by¹²²³ the resurrection³⁸⁶ of Jesus²⁴²⁴ Christ⁵⁵⁴⁷ from¹⁵³⁷ the dead,³⁴⁹⁸

1:4 To¹⁵¹⁹ an inheritance²⁸¹⁷ incorruptible,⁸⁶² and²⁵³² undefiled,²⁸³ and²⁵³² that fadeth not away,²⁶³ reserved⁵⁰⁸³ in¹⁷²² heaven³⁷⁷² for¹⁵¹⁹ you,²²⁴⁸

1:5 Who are kept⁵⁴³² by¹⁷²² the power¹⁴¹¹ of God²³¹⁶ through¹²²³ faith⁴¹⁰² unto¹⁵¹⁹ salvation⁴⁹⁹¹ ready²⁰⁹² to be revealed⁶⁰¹ in¹⁷²² the last²⁰⁷⁸ time.²⁵⁴⁰

1:6 Wherein¹⁷²², ³⁷³⁹ ye greatly rejoice,²¹ though now⁷³⁷ for a season,³⁶⁴¹ if¹⁴⁸⁷ need be,¹¹⁶³, ²⁰⁷⁶ ye are in heaviness³⁰⁷⁶ through¹⁷²² manifold⁴¹⁶⁴ temptations:³⁹⁸⁶

1:7 That²⁴⁴³ the³⁵⁸⁸ trial¹³⁸³ of your⁵²¹⁶ faith,⁴¹⁰² being much⁴¹⁸³ more precious⁵⁰⁹³ than of gold⁵⁵⁵³ that perisheth,⁶²² though¹¹⁶¹ it be tried¹³⁸¹ with¹²²³ fire,⁴⁴⁴² might be found²¹⁴⁷ unto¹⁵¹⁹ praise¹⁸⁶⁸ and²⁵³² honor⁵⁰⁹² and²⁵³² glory¹³⁹¹ at¹⁷²² the appearing⁶⁰² of Jesus²⁴²⁴ Christ:⁵⁵⁴⁷

1:8 Whom³⁷³⁹ having not³⁷⁵⁶ seen,¹⁴⁹² ye love;²⁵ in¹⁵¹⁹ whom,³⁷³⁹ though now⁷³⁷ ye see³⁷⁰⁸ him not,³³⁶¹ yet¹¹⁶¹ believing,⁴¹⁰⁰ ye rejoice²¹ with joy⁵⁴⁷⁹ unspeakable⁴¹² and²⁵³² full of glory:¹³⁹²

1:9 Receiving²⁸⁶⁵ the³⁵⁸⁸ end⁵⁰⁵⁶ of your⁵²¹⁶ faith,⁴¹⁰² even the salvation⁴⁹⁹¹ of your souls.⁵⁵⁹⁰

1:10 Of⁴⁰¹² which³⁷³⁹ salvation⁴⁹⁹¹ the prophets⁴³⁹⁶ have inquired¹⁵⁶⁷ and²⁵³² searched diligently,¹⁸³⁰ who prophesied⁴³⁹⁵ of⁴⁰¹² the³⁵⁸⁸ grace⁵⁴⁸⁵ that should come unto¹⁵¹⁹ you:⁵²⁰⁹

Peter reminded them who they were. They were His disciples, thirty years after His death and resurrection. They were His siblings thirty years after the last time anyone on earth hugged Him. They were children of God thirty years after He performed His last miracle. They were His students thirty years after He spoke His last parable, and they were citizens of the Kingdom of God thirty years after He revealed the mystery of the Kingdom. These were the good seed.

Think for a moment about the people Peter was addressing thirty years after Jesus' resurrection. Many who had seen Him in person were getting old. Some had already died. And some of those who read Peter's letter had never seen Jesus perform a miracle or heard Him speak of the Kingdom. They were just like you and me! Born again believers who faithfully lived as if He was with them still. They believed the message of the Kingdom and they behaved accordingly. And they rejoiced, knowing the eventual outcome of their faith would bring not just the salvation of their souls, but their reunion with Him!

It is imperative for our continued growth and spiritual health as children of God, members of His family, and citizens of His Kingdom, to put into practice the principles of the Kingdom. For even though we are living in a world filled with godless greed, corruption, and violence, we are also living under the loving, caring, watchful eye of our Father, the King.

May He bless you with more of Himself as you pursue His love and fulfilll His will with all you heart, soul, mind, and strength.

CHAPTER 4

Strength Training For Kingdom Living

Matthew 4:17 From that time Jesus began to preach, and to say, Repent: for the kingdom of heaven is at hand.

Matthew 4:23 And Jesus went about all Galilee, teaching in their synagogues, and preaching the gospel of the kingdom, and healing all manner of sickness and all manner of disease among the people.

Jesus came preaching the message of the Kingdom. Many mistakenly believe He came preaching the good news of salvation. Yet, this is not an accurate description of His mission. His good news was much more about life here and now, and its impact on life after death. He called men to "repent," that is, to choose to live a different lifestyle than they were currently living. The salvation message is often used to teach that His mission was to save us from the fires of Hell. Yet the plan of God demonstrated through Jesus Christ was to restore men to a right relationship with Him. Escaping the fires of hell is a wonderful by-product of embracing the Kingdom of God. However, God desires so much more for us than merely to be saved from the painful agony of hell. He wants us to develop a relationship with Him. Hell is the terrible place it is because once there a human being, made in the image of God, has no hope of being restored to God ever again. It is by developing and maintaining a relationship with God that hell is avoided and eternal life is secured. In fact according to Scripture, salvation is a lifestyle that unfolds as we pursue the relationship. Scripture not only says we are saved, but that we are being saved, and eventually we will experience the fulfillment of salvation. Salvation refers to all of the following; saved by, saved from, saved to, and saved for.

We are saved by Jesus' sacrificial death and resurrection.

We are saved from destruction.

We are saved to God.

And we saved for godly works!

Matthew 10:22 And²⁵³² ye shall be²⁰⁷¹ hated³⁴⁰⁴ of⁵²⁵⁹ all³⁹⁵⁶ men for my name's sake:¹²²³, ³⁴⁵⁰, ³⁶⁸⁶ but¹¹⁶¹ he that endureth⁵²⁷⁸ to¹⁵¹⁹ the end⁵⁰⁵⁶ shall be⁽³⁷⁷⁸⁾ saved.⁴⁹⁸²

Matthew 24:13 But¹¹⁶¹ he that shall endure⁵²⁷⁸ unto¹⁵¹⁹ the end,⁵⁰⁵⁶ the same³⁷⁷⁸ shall be saved.⁴⁹⁸² 14 And²⁵³² this⁵¹²⁴ gospel²⁰⁹⁸ of the³⁵⁸⁸ kingdom⁹³² shall be preached²⁷⁸⁴ in¹⁷²² all³⁶⁵⁰ the³⁵⁸⁸ world³⁶²⁵ for¹⁵¹⁹ a witness³¹⁴² unto all³⁹⁵⁶ nations;¹⁴⁸⁴ and²⁵³² then⁵¹¹⁹ shall the³⁵⁸⁸ end⁵⁰⁵⁶ come.²²⁴⁰

Jesus' name, in the original Hebrew language is yeshua, or salvation. Therefore, He is our salvation. And the purpose of His salvation is to restore man to a right relationship with God. This is what Jesus shared with God. A relationship based upon God's terms. Jesus came to earth to demonstrate a right relationship with God. He had to. For many years a variety of God's men attempted to do this. Adam, Noah, Abraham, Moses, Jacob, Joseph, David, Solomon, and the nation of Israel as a whole, were all expected to demonstrate Kingdom living to the ungodly men of the world at large. None of them succeeded. So, God, The Eternal Word, came to earth in the form of a man.

John 1:1 In¹⁷²² the beginning⁷⁴⁶ was²²⁵⁸ the³⁵⁸⁸ Word,³⁰⁵⁶ and²⁵³² the³⁵⁸⁸ Word³⁰⁵⁶ was²²⁵⁸ with⁴³¹⁴ God,²³¹⁶ and²⁵³² the³⁵⁸⁸ Word³⁰⁵⁶ was²²⁵⁸ God.²³¹⁶

1:2 The same³⁷⁷⁸ was²²⁵⁸ in¹⁷²² the beginning⁷⁴⁶ with⁴³¹⁴ God.²³¹⁶

1:3 All things³⁹⁵⁶ were made¹⁰⁹⁶ by¹²²³ him;⁸⁴⁶ and²⁵³² without⁵⁵⁶⁵ him⁸⁴⁶ was not³⁷⁶¹ any thing¹⁵²⁰ made¹⁰⁹⁶ that³⁷³⁹ was made.¹⁰⁹⁶

1:4 In[1722] him[846] was[2258] life;[2222] and[2532] the[3588] life[2222] was[2258] the[3588] light[5457] of men.[444]

1:5 And[2532] the[3588] light[5457] shineth[5316] in[1722] darkness;[4653] and[2532] the[3588] darkness[4653] comprehended[2638] it[846] not.[3756]

John 1:14 And[2532] the[3588] Word[3056] was made[1096] flesh,[4561] and[2532] dwelt[4637] among[1722] us,[2254] (and[2532] we beheld[2300] his[846] glory,[1391] the glory[1391] as[5613] of the only begotten[3439] of[3844] the Father,)[3962] full[4134] of grace[5485] and[2532] truth.[225]

Colossians 1:13 Who[3739] hath delivered[4506] us[2248] from[1537] the[3588] power[1849] of darkness,[4655] and[2532] hath translated[3179] us into[1519] the[3588] kingdom[932] of his[848] dear[26] Son:[5207]

1:14 In[1722] whom[3739] we have[2192] redemption[629] through[1223] his[846] blood,[129] even the[3588] forgiveness[859] of sins:[266]

1:15 Who[3739] is[2076] the image[1504] of the[3588] invisible[517] God,[2316] the firstborn[4416] of every[3956] creature:[2937]

1:16 For[3754] by[1722] him[846] were all things[3956] created,[2936] that[3588] are in[1722] heaven,[3772] and[2532] that[3588] are in[1909] earth,[1093] visible[3707] and[2532] invisible,[517] whether[1535] they be thrones,[2362] or[1535] dominions,[2963] or[1535] principalities,[746] or[1535] powers:[1849] all things[3956] were created[2936] by[1223] him,[846] and[2532] for[1519] him:[846] 1:17 And[2532] he[846] is[2076] before[4253] all things,[3956] and[2532] by[1722] him[846] all things[3956] consist.[4921]

1:18 And²⁵³² he⁸⁴⁶ is²⁰⁷⁶ the³⁵⁸⁸ head²⁷⁷⁶ of the³⁵⁸⁸ body,⁴⁹⁸³ the³⁵⁸⁸ church:¹⁵⁷⁷ who³⁷³⁹ is²⁰⁷⁶ the beginning,⁷⁴⁶ the firstborn⁴⁴¹⁶ from¹⁵³⁷ the³⁵⁸⁸ dead;³⁴⁹⁸ that²⁴⁴³ in¹⁷²² all³⁹⁵⁶ things he⁸⁴⁶ might have¹⁰⁹⁶ the preeminence.⁴⁴⁰⁹

1:19 For³⁷⁵⁴ it pleased²¹⁰⁶ the Father that in¹⁷²² him⁸⁴⁶ should all³⁹⁵⁶ fullness⁴¹³⁸ dwell;²⁷³⁰

Jesus' mission was meant to accomplish several things simultaneously. These include but are not limited to the following.

1. To reveal the truth of God's Kingdom through teaching.
2. To demonstrate Kingdom Living through living His life among men.
3. To make a path for all men into the Kingdom by His death and resurrection.

All men are to look to Him as their role model for Kingdom living. But remember Kingdom living begins, continues, and is fulfilled through developing a right relationship with God, on His terms. This is what Jesus lived out before the men of His day. We modern men must not make the mistake that so many in the past have made. We must not hold onto an outward form of religion and ignore God's desire to have fellowship with us. We must never think we are right with God because we prayed a prayer at some point in our lives. If we are not involved in building a personal relationship with God, we are in danger of losing everything in the end.

Matthew 23:27 Woe[3759] unto you,[5213] scribes[1122] and[2532] Pharisees,[5330] hypocrites![5273] for[3754] ye are like unto[3945] whited[2867] sepulchers,[5028] which[3748] indeed[3303] appear[5316] beautiful[5611] outward,[1855] but[1161] are within full[1073, 2081] of dead mens' bones and[2532] of all[3956] uncleanness.[167]

2Timothy 3:1 This[5124] know[1097] also,[1161] that[3754] in[1722] the last[2078] days[2250] perilous[5467] times[2540] shall come.[1764]

3:2 For[1063] men[444] shall be[2071] lovers of their own selves,[5367] covetous,[5366] boasters,[213] proud,[5244] blasphemers,[989] disobedient[545] to parents,[1118] unthankful,[884] unholy,[462]

3:3 Without natural affection,[794] trucebreakers,[786] false accusers,[1228] incontinent,[193] fierce,[434] despisers of those that are good,[865]

3:4 Traitors,[4273] heady,[4312] highminded,[5187] lovers of pleasures[5369] more[3123] than[2228] lovers of God;[5377]

3:5 Having[2192] a form[3446] of godliness,[2150] but[1161] denying[720] the[3588] power[1411] thereof:[846] from such turn away.[665, 5128]

Therefore, we should make it our life's most important goal, to learn to live like He lived, and first of all, to live in constant awareness of God's destiny for our lives, as men created in His image and likeness. For we are men who have been reconciled to Him through the sacrificial death and glorious resurrection of Jesus Christ.

So, how do we do that? We are surrounded on every side by a corrupt, morally diseased society of men and women who appear to want nothing more from life than the next new thrill or toy. They lie, cheat, deceive, lust after, and blindly follow any man or woman who promises a more exciting life. Make more money, lose more weight, tighten those abs, run faster, love longer. They scream at us, "I did it and you can too!" There is nothing evil about wanting firm abs or more money. But to pursue those things as if they will make our life more meaningful or more secure is the height of ignorance.

Luke 12:19 And²⁵³² I will say²⁰⁴⁶ to my³⁴⁵⁰ soul,⁵⁵⁹⁰ Soul,⁵⁵⁹⁰ thou hast²¹⁹² much⁴¹⁸³ goods¹⁸ laid up²⁷⁴⁹ for¹⁵¹⁹ many⁴¹⁸³ years;²⁰⁹⁴ take thine ease,³⁷³ eat,⁵³¹⁵ drink,⁴⁰⁹⁵ and be merry.²¹⁶⁵

12:20 But¹¹⁶¹ God²³¹⁶ said²⁰³⁶ unto him,⁸⁴⁶ Thou fool,⁸⁷⁸ this⁵⁰²⁶ night³⁵⁷¹ thy⁴⁶⁷⁵ soul⁵⁵⁹⁰ shall be required⁵²³ of⁵⁷⁵ thee:⁴⁶⁷⁵ then¹¹⁶¹ whose⁵¹⁰¹ shall those things³⁷³⁹ be,²⁰⁷¹ which thou hast provided?²⁰⁹⁰

12:21 So³⁷⁷⁹ is he³⁵⁸⁸ that layeth up treasure²³⁴³ for himself,¹⁴³⁸ and²⁵³² is not rich⁴¹⁴⁷, ³³⁶¹ toward¹⁵¹⁹ God.²³¹⁶

Building Spiritual Strength

To experience God's Kingdom, while living here on earth we must develop our spiritual awareness. Our spiritual strength. To develop this strength we must follow a training regimen, and train diligently. We must become strong swimmers if we are to make progress against the surging current of the secular world.

Below I offer a routine that helped Michele and me grow strong very rapidly many years ago during our early days of Kingdom life. First I will list the four elements of our training routine and then in the following pages I will discuss each one briefly. These are the four main ingredients in the victorious Kingdom life.

1. Word Study
2. Prayer
3. Worship
4. Spiritual Warfare

Word Study

It is impossible to know God without knowing His Word. No matter what you know about God, no matter who has taught you, including me, if you have not learned the value of studying the Word of God on your own you are vulnerable and at risk. God has disclosed Himself to you in the Word. The Bible is undeniably the most reliable source of information about God. You may or may not have been deceived by well-meaning but misinformed teachers, preachers and pastors. But you will never know for sure if you have not read the Word for yourself. But you say, "But I'm no student, I can't understand the Bible."

The Holy Spirit was given to you for the purpose of educating you in the issues of life concerning God's

Kingdom. The first step in the learning process is to know what God and Jesus have said about themselves and the world as a whole. God had people write His story so you and I could read it. This is one of the most profound mysteries known to man. God inspired forty different men to write His word over a period of 1500 years. Other men were inspired to collect and collate it and place it in a Book so you and I could read it and learn directly from Him. As we read, His Spirit, the Holy Spirit, illuminates passages of Scripture that act like food to our spirit. Remember Jesus was Immanuel, God with us. He was the Word who had become flesh, as a man. And now He is gone from earth and He no longer teaches us by the shores of Galilee or on the hills of Judea. He teaches every one of His disciples on an individual basis, through the indwelling presence of the Holy Spirit.

John 14:12 Verily,[281] verily,[281] I say[3004] unto you,[5213] He that believeth[4100] on[1519] me,[1691] the[3588] works[2041] that[3739] I[1473] do[4160] shall he do also;[2548, 4160] and[2532] greater[3187] works than these[5130] shall he do;[4160] because[3754] I[1473] go[4198] unto[4314] my[3450] Father.[3962]

14:15 If[1437] ye love[25] me,[3165] keep[5083] my[1699] commandments.[1785]

14:16 And[2532] I[1473] will pray[2065] the[3588] Father,[3962] and[2532] he shall give[1325] you[5213] another[243] Comforter,[3875] that[2443] he may abide[3306] with[3326] you[5216] forever;[1519, 165]

14:17 Even the[3588] Spirit[4151] of truth;[225] whom[3739] the[3588] world[2889] cannot[1410, 3756] receive,[2983] because[3754] it seeth²³³⁴ him⁸⁴⁶ not,³⁷⁵⁶ neither³⁷⁶¹ knoweth¹⁰⁹⁷ him:⁸⁴⁶ but¹¹⁶¹ ye⁵²¹⁰ know¹⁰⁹⁷ him;⁸⁴⁶ for³⁷⁵⁴ he dwelleth³³⁰⁶ with³⁸⁴⁴ you,⁵²¹³ and²⁵³² shall be²⁰⁷¹ in¹⁷²² you.⁵²¹³

14:26 But¹¹⁶¹ the³⁵⁸⁸ Comforter,³⁸⁷⁵ which is the³⁵⁸⁸ Holy⁴⁰ Ghost,⁴¹⁵¹ whom³⁷³⁹ the³⁵⁸⁸ Father³⁹⁶² will send³⁹⁹² in¹⁷²² my³⁴⁵⁰ name,³⁶⁸⁶ he¹⁵⁶⁵ shall teach¹³²¹ you⁵²⁰⁹ all things,³⁹⁵⁶ and²⁵³² bring all things to your remembrance,⁵²⁷⁹, ³⁹⁵⁶, ⁵²⁰⁹ whatsoever³⁷³⁹ I have said²⁰³⁶ unto you.⁵²¹³

When we read the Word, the Holy Spirit teaches us. How can we learn if we do not read? One way is to listen to other men expound on their knowledge of the Word. This is not a bad idea. But it is not the best idea. Why? God speaks to Bible scholars about their life through the word, and he wants to speak to you about your life with Him as well. The best scholars are those who know they do not have the final interpretation of a particular passage. But even good ones are biased by their denominational background and training. How else can men arrive at such ridiculous and blasphemous notions that God condones homosexuality, or that He encourages the murder of anyone opposed to your religious views? Sure these are extreme examples that no God-fearing Christian would accept. But how about the sacraments of water baptism and communion? Is full body immersion the right way? Or is sprinkling just as good. Does infant baptism guarantee eternal life? Can one miss eternity because he was never baptized in water? And what about communion? Weekly, monthly, or daily? Does the bread become the flesh of Jesus? Or does it just represent the communion He shared with the men at the last supper? Does it matter? Who says? Who told you what to believe about the sacraments? Why do you believe the way you do? Do you really care which way is the truth?

So, we read to learn and to feed our spirit so we can become more interested and appreciative of the work God has done for us, in us, and the work He desires to do through us. If you read the Word it won't take you long to discover how often Jesus referred to it. This proves two things: He knew the Word, and He believed it was important for us to know it as well. Again He is both our teacher and the role model for our relationship with God.

I remember one of the first times I discerned God speaking to me. I was a baby Christian and was sitting on the couch praying after reading the Word. He said, "You can have as much of me as you want, but you will never have more of me than that." As I have studied the Word for the past twenty-plus years I have found that to be true. I feel I have so much more knowledge of God's word now, and yet I have a hunger to know God's word more now than I did twenty years ago!

To become strong in faith plan to study the Word on a daily basis. The longest journey begins with the first step. The sooner we get started the sooner we get there. When we begin our journey we never know what adventures the road will bring us as we make our way along it. Studying the Word is a delightfully fulfilling and rewarding journey. Another word the Holy Spirit spoke to me as I was just starting out was, "There are no shortcuts on the highway of holiness. Get on and stay on."

A good plan to start with is to read every day from several sections of the Bible. Read a Psalm and a Proverb in the morning. Read a chapter or two from the Gospels before drifting off to sleep. That way you begin and end your day with an adventure in God's Word. For example you might begin your study by reading Psalm 1 and Proverbs 1 in the morning and Matthew 1 and John 1 in the evening. Then every day continue in order until you get through the gospels and the Psalms and Proverbs. In a month you will be amazed by how you feel about God, Jesus, the Holy Spirit, and your life! (Of course this means you must spend less time in front of the TV and computer.)

Prayer

In addition to reading the Word, prayer is another way we can build our spiritual strength. Prayer is more than simply speaking to God and listening to Him. In prayer we can also do spiritual warfare for ourselves and for others. We can ask for things from God, we can thank Him for His gifts, we can intercede for others, and we can battle the forces of evil in the spirit realm. In addition we can ask for His plan, in general and specifically, to be revealed to us. But remember, effective prayer is the natural result of our relationship with God. We desire to know God more intimately so we develop a consistent prayer schedule. We are not trying to earn points with Him or impress Him with our righteousness, we are pulling up a chair and having a discussion with the Wisest One who happens to love us more than we can imagine!

John 14:23 Jesus²⁴²⁴ answered⁶¹¹ and²⁵³² said²⁰³⁶ unto him,⁸⁴⁶ If¹⁴³⁷ a man⁵¹⁰⁰ love²⁵ me,³¹⁶⁵ he will keep⁵⁰⁸³ my³⁴⁵⁰ words:³⁰⁵⁶ and²⁵³² my³⁴⁵⁰ Father³⁹⁶² will love²⁵ him,⁸⁴⁶ and²⁵³² we will come²⁰⁶⁴ unto⁴³¹⁴ him,⁸⁴⁶ and²⁵³² make⁴¹⁶⁰ our abode³⁴³⁸ with³⁸⁴⁴ him.⁸⁴⁶

14:24 He that loveth²⁵ me³¹⁶⁵ not³³⁶¹ keepeth⁵⁰⁸³ not³⁷⁵⁶ my³⁴⁵⁰ sayings:³⁰⁵⁶ and²⁵³² the³⁵⁸⁸ word³⁰⁵⁶ which³⁷³⁹ ye hear¹⁹¹ is²⁰⁷⁶ not³⁷⁵⁶ mine,¹⁶⁹⁹ but²³⁵ the Father's³⁹⁶² which sent³⁹⁹² me.³¹⁶⁵

14:25 These things⁵⁰²³ have I spoken²⁹⁸⁰ unto you,⁵²¹³ being yet present³³⁰⁶ with³⁸⁴⁴ you.⁵²¹³

14:26 But¹¹⁶¹ the³⁵⁸⁸ Comforter,³⁸⁷⁵ which is the³⁵⁸⁸ Holy⁴⁰ Ghost,⁴¹⁵¹ whom³⁷³⁹ the³⁵⁸⁸ Father³⁹⁶² will send³⁹⁹² in¹⁷²² my³⁴⁵⁰ name,³⁶⁸⁶ he¹⁵⁶⁵ shall teach¹³²¹ you⁵²⁰⁹ all things,³⁹⁵⁶ and²⁵³² bring all things to your remembrance,⁵²⁷⁹, ³⁹⁵⁶, ⁵²⁰⁹ whatsoever³⁷³⁹ I have said²⁰³⁶ unto you.⁵²¹³

John 15:7 If¹⁴³⁷ ye abide³³⁰⁶ in¹⁷²² me,¹⁶⁹⁸ and²⁵³² my³⁴⁵⁰ words⁴⁴⁸⁷ abide³³⁰⁶ in¹⁷²² you,⁵²¹³ ye shall ask¹⁵⁴ what3⁷³⁹, ¹⁴³⁷ ye will,²³⁰⁹ and²⁵³² it shall be done¹⁰⁹⁶ unto you.⁵²¹³

15:8 Herein¹⁷²², ⁵¹²⁹ is my³⁴⁵⁰ Father³⁹⁶² glorified,¹³⁹² that²⁴⁴³ ye bear⁵³⁴² much⁴¹⁸³ fruit;²⁵⁹⁰ so²⁵³² shall ye be¹⁰⁹⁶ my¹⁶⁹⁸ disciples.³¹⁰¹

Men and women who think they know God but do not have a relationship with Him pray fruitlessly. They become frustrated because they feel their prayers are seldom heard or if heard they are not rewarded. Yet Jesus said fruitful prayer was founded upon a right relationship with God. His prayers recorded in Scripture are good examples of this.

Prayer can be divided into two groups. Those we pray with our understanding through our native language, English for example. And the praying we do in an unknown language as the Holy Spirit prays through us.

Ephesians 6:18 Praying⁴³³⁶ always¹²²³, ³⁹⁵⁶, ²⁵⁴⁰ with¹⁷²² all³⁹⁵⁶ prayer⁴³³⁵ and²⁵³² supplication¹¹⁶² in¹⁷²² the Spirit,⁴¹⁵¹ and²⁵³² watching⁶⁹ thereunto¹⁵¹⁹, ⁸⁴⁶, ⁵¹²⁴ with¹⁷²² all³⁹⁵⁶ perseverance⁴³⁴³ and²⁵³² supplication¹¹⁶² for⁴⁰¹² all³⁹⁵⁶ saints;⁴⁰

Mark 16:17 And¹¹⁶¹ these⁵⁰²³ signs⁴⁵⁹² shall follow³⁸⁷⁷ them³⁵⁸⁸ that believe;⁴¹⁰⁰ In¹⁷²² my³⁴⁵⁰ name³⁶⁸⁶ shall they cast out¹⁵⁴⁴ devils;¹¹⁴⁰ they shall speak²⁹⁸⁰ with new²⁵³⁷ tongues;¹¹⁰⁰

Jude 1:20 But¹¹⁶¹ ye,⁵²¹⁰ beloved,²⁷ building up²⁰²⁶ yourselves¹⁴³⁸ on your⁵²¹⁶ most holy⁴⁰ faith,⁴¹⁰² praying⁴³³⁶ in¹⁷²² the Holy⁴⁰ Ghost,⁴¹⁵¹

Romans 8:26 ⁽¹¹⁶¹⁾ Likewise⁵⁶¹⁵ the³⁵⁸⁸ Spirit⁴¹⁵¹ also²⁵³² helpeth⁴⁸⁷⁸ our²²⁵⁷ infirmities:⁷⁶⁹ for¹⁰⁶³ we know¹⁴⁹² not³⁷⁵⁶ what⁵¹⁰¹ we should pray for⁴³³⁶ as²⁵²⁶ we ought:¹¹⁶³ but²³⁵ the³⁵⁸⁸ Spirit⁴¹⁵¹ itself⁸⁴⁸ maketh intercession[5241] for[5228] us[2257] with groanings[4726] which cannot be uttered.[215]

When learning to develop a consistent prayer life it is good to have an outline to follow so you don't just ramble on. In 1Thessolonians 5:17 Paul encourages us to, "Pray[4336] without ceasing."[89] By the statement Paul does not mean to pray without a plan or direction, just "blethering" away, as my Scottish friends say. He means to stress the importance of praying consistently, daily. When I was first learning to pray consistently I found the following outline helpful.

1. Worship
2. Thanksgiving
3. Intercession
4. Petition
5. Thanksgiving
6. Tongues

1. Worship God by praising and declaring His virtues. Mention His love, majesty power, authority, His divine plan for you and for the Universe, etc.

2. Thank God for His wonderful grace that allowed you to know Him. And then thank Him for everything you can think of. Make a list and be real. We all have so much to thank God for.

3. Ask God to bless family members, friends, your government, etc. Ask Him to extend His grace to the lost, to bring salvation to them, and to the hopeless individuals that do not know Him.

4. Ask Him for those things you need to live a better, happier, healtier, more godly life.

5. Thank Him again for hearing your requests and thank Him for answering your prayers.

6. Now sit back and pray quietly in your prayer language. Tongues is the unknown language that you received when you asked Him to baptize you with the Holy Spirit.

To be strengthened spiritually to experience God's Kingdom on earth we need to learn to pray confidently and consistently.

Worship

Worship is reciting all the great and good things about God. Worship can be done by speaking or by singing. Since we already discussed worship in prayer I will address singing here. The Word encourages us to sing to the Lord.

1Corinthians 14:15 What[5101] is[2076] it then?[3767] I will pray[4336] with the[3588] spirit,[4151] and[1161] I will pray[4336] with the[3588] understanding[3563] also:[2532] I will sing[5567] with the[3588] spirit,[4151] and[1161] I will sing[5567] with the[3588] understanding[3563] also.[2532]

James 5:13 Is any among you afflicted?[2553, 5100, 1722, 5213] let him pray.[4336] Is any merry?[2114, 5100] let him sing psalms.[5567]

Psalm 30:4 Sing²¹⁶⁷ unto the LORD,³⁰⁶⁸ O ye saints²⁶²³ of his, and give thanks³⁰³⁴ at the remembrance²¹⁴³ of his holiness.⁶⁹⁴⁴

Psalm 13:6 I will sing⁷⁸⁹¹ unto the LORD,³⁰⁶⁸ because³⁵⁸⁸ he hath dealt bountifully¹⁵⁸⁰ with⁵⁹²¹ me.

Psalm 9:2 I will be glad⁸⁰⁵⁵ and rejoice⁵⁹⁷⁰ in thee: I will sing praise²¹⁶⁷ to thy name,⁸⁰³⁴ O thou most High.⁵⁹⁴⁵

Psalm 33:3 Sing⁷⁸⁹¹ unto him a new²³¹⁹ song;⁷⁸⁹² play⁵⁰⁵⁹ skilfully³¹⁹⁰ with a loud noise.⁸⁶⁴³

Certainly we are encouraged to sing to the Lord. We sing to Him, for Him, about Him. He loves to hear us sing. Music and singing is referred to as the international language. Everyone needs to sing. Singing lifts your spirit and can pull you out of discouragement and sadness. It can put a smile on your face and a sparkle in your eye. Christians should sing more than anyone else because they have so much to sing about. The goodness of God is certainly worth singing about!

In this day and time music is everywhere. In malls, shops, restaurants, offices, stores, hospitals, even elevators. If you listen you will realize you can hardly get through a day without hearing someone singing about something! Even though you don't ask for it you are constantly listening to someone's song. Quite often the song isn't one you want to sing and the subject matter is obnoxious. But you hear it anyway. What can you do? Sing your own song of course!

You may think you can't sing but sing anyway. And sing about God. Sing about His goodness and His grace. Sing Him a love song; make it up as you go along. Its fun. Get silly, loosen up and sing! Before you know it you will be worshipping God just like the Scripture encourages you to. And you will discover why so many people love to do it. Listening to the latest worship CD is great. But try singing along with it. Its even better.

Spiritual Warfare

Spiritual warfare should be a normal part of the daily activity of Christians. It was for Jesus, and again, He is our role model for Kingdom living. Why would it be any different for you and me? It is a necessary part of the total training regimen for every Christian. One thing is for certain, if you study the Word of God very long you will discover God's enemy, the Christian's adversary, is alive and active! I say, "the sooner you learn about him the better off you will be." The key to victory in any contest is to know your opponent. To deal swiftly with him you must know his tactics, his strengths, and his weaknesses. And you must know and use the authority given to you by Jesus Christ.

Exodus 23:22 But[3588] if[518] thou shalt indeed obey[8085, 8085] his voice,[6963] and do[6213] all[3605] that[834] I speak;[1696] then I will be an enemy[340 (853)] unto thine enemies,[341] and an adversary[6696 (853)] unto thine adversaries.[6887]

1Peter 5:8 Be sober,[3525] be vigilant;[1127] because[3754] your[5216] adversary[476] the devil,[1228] as[5613] a roaring[5612] lion,³⁰²³ walketh about,⁴⁰⁴³ seeking²²¹² whom⁵¹⁰¹ he may devour:²⁶⁶⁶

To defeat our adversary we must know who he is, what he does, and how he does it. And we must know how to fight and win.

2Corinthians 10:4 (For¹⁰⁶³ the³⁵⁸⁸ weapons³⁶⁹⁶ of our²²⁵⁷ warfare⁴⁷⁵² are not³⁷⁵⁶ carnal,⁴⁵⁵⁹ but²³⁵ mighty¹⁴¹⁵ through God²³¹⁶ to⁴³¹⁴ the pulling down²⁵⁰⁶ of strongholds;)³⁷⁹⁴

10:5 Casting down²⁵⁰⁷ imaginations,³⁰⁵³ and²⁵³² every³⁹⁵⁶ high thing⁵³¹³ that exalteth itself¹⁸⁶⁹ against²⁵⁹⁶ the³⁵⁸⁸ knowledge¹¹⁰⁸ of God,²³¹⁶ and²⁵³² bringing into captivity¹⁶³ every³⁹⁵⁶ thought³⁵⁴⁰ to¹⁵¹⁹ the³⁵⁸⁸ obedience⁵²¹⁸ of Christ;⁵⁵⁴⁷

Epheshians 6:12 For³⁷⁵⁴ we²²⁵⁴ wrestle²⁰⁷⁶, ³⁸²³ not³⁷⁵⁶ against⁴³¹⁴ flesh⁴⁵⁶¹ and²⁵³² blood,¹²⁹ but²³⁵ against⁴³¹⁴ principalities,⁷⁴⁶ against⁴³¹⁴ powers,¹⁸⁴⁹ against⁴³¹⁴ the³⁵⁸⁸ rulers²⁸⁸⁸ of the³⁵⁸⁸ darkness⁴⁶⁵⁵ of this⁵¹²⁷ world,¹⁶⁵ against⁴³¹⁴ spiritual⁴¹⁵² wickedness⁴¹⁸⁹ in¹⁷²² high²⁰³² places.

Luke 10:19 Behold,²⁴⁰⁰ I give¹³²⁵ unto you⁵²¹³ power¹⁸⁴⁹ to tread³⁹⁶¹ on¹⁸⁸³ serpents³⁷⁸⁹ and²⁵³² scorpions,⁴⁶⁵¹ and²⁵³² over¹⁹⁰⁹ all³⁹⁵⁶ the³⁵⁸⁸ power¹⁴¹¹ of the³⁵⁸⁸ enemy:²¹⁹⁰ and²⁵³² nothing³⁷⁶² shall by any means³³⁶⁴ hurt⁹¹ you.⁵²⁰⁹

Matthew 18:18 Verily²⁸¹ I say³⁰⁰⁴ unto you,⁵²¹³ Whatsoever³⁷⁴⁵, ¹⁴³⁷ ye shall bind¹²¹⁰ on¹⁹⁰⁹ earth¹⁰⁹³ shall be²⁰⁷¹ bound¹²¹⁰ in¹⁷²² heaven:³⁷⁷² and²⁵³² whatsoever³⁷⁴⁵, ¹⁴³⁷ ye shall loose³⁰⁸⁹ on¹⁹⁰⁹ earth¹⁰⁹³ shall be²⁰⁷¹ loosed³⁰⁸⁹ in¹⁷²² heaven.³⁷⁷²

18:19 Again³⁸²⁵ I say³⁰⁰⁴ unto you,⁵²¹³ That³⁷⁵⁴ if¹⁴³⁷ two¹⁴¹⁷ of you⁵²¹⁶ shall agree⁴⁸⁵⁶ on¹⁹⁰⁹ earth¹⁰⁹³ as touching⁴⁰¹² any³⁹⁵⁶ thing⁴²²⁹ that³⁷³⁹, ¹⁴³⁷ they shall ask,¹⁵⁴ it shall be done¹⁰⁹⁶ for them⁸⁴⁶ of³⁸⁴⁴ my³⁴⁵⁰ Father³⁹⁶² which³⁵⁸⁸ is in¹⁷²² heaven.³⁷⁷²

18:20 For¹⁰⁶³ where³⁷⁵⁷ two¹⁴¹⁷ or²²²⁸ three⁵¹⁴⁰ are¹⁵²⁶ gathered together⁴⁸⁶³ in¹⁵¹⁹ my¹⁶⁹⁹ name,³⁶⁸⁶ there¹⁵⁶³ am¹⁵¹⁰ I in¹⁷²² the midst³³¹⁹ of them.⁸⁴⁶

We defeat our enemy the adversary, the devil, demons, evil spirits, by using our authority as believers. We use our voice to address them and we bind them. To bind something in the biblical sense means to refuse or forbid it to act. Think of wrapping it up in rope or chain or handcuffs, or whatever. That is the concept. We have been given the authority of Jesus to do the work He did when He was on earth. We are His representatives. We act in His behalf in His absence. We have been given both His authority and the power associated with it. To have authority and no power is like being the mailman. He just delivers the message. As God's ambassadors on earth we are expected to do more than that. We represent Him by delivering the message in a way that manifests His power to change lives! That means regardless of what the situation requires, we have the solution. New birth, physical healing, hope, encouragement, truth, deliverance, whatever. The power of God is resident within us because His Spirit is resident within us. You may not feel very powerful. But if you develop your knowledge of His Word and spend time in prayer and worship, believe me, His power will be manifested through you.

> *Luke 17:20 And[1161] when he was demanded[1905] of[5259] the[3588] Pharisees,[5330] when[4219] the[3588] kingdom[932] of God[2316] should come,[2064] he answered[611] them[846] and[2532] said,[2036] The[3588] kingdom[932] of God[2316] cometh[2064] not[3756] with[3326] observation:[3907]*

> *17:21 Neither[3761] shall they say,[2046] Lo[2400] here![5602] or,[2228] lo[2400] there![1563] for,[1063] behold,[2400] the[3588] kingdom[932] of God[2316] is[2076] within[1787] you.[5216]*

"Kingdom" as Jesus used the word means; the ruling authority of the royal family. The Pharisees' question meant to spark a theological debate. They wanted to know if Jesus knew at what time in history the Kingdom of God would be manifested on earth. His answer showed them that they were looking outside themselves for something that they were expected to demonstrate. He said the Kingdom is not found by using your eyes to see geographically. The Kingdom is recognized in Jesus and experienced by you and me through our faith in His sacrifice. We, who enter the Kingdom through Jesus, are expected to experience Kingdom power personally, to possess it spiritually/inwardly, and then to demonstrate it outwardly.

Jesus' main complaint against the Pharisees was that they turned the message of Kingdom living into a worthless, useless, powerless religious routine! He came to earth to change that, once and for all! He spoke the truth, He demonstrated the truth, and He defeated death, hell, and the grave, to empower you and I with the power of God's Spirit to do the same.

Matthew 28:18 And²⁵³² Jesus²⁴²⁴ came⁴³³⁴ and spake²⁹⁸⁰ unto them,⁸⁴⁶ saying,³⁰⁰⁴ All³⁹⁵⁶ power¹⁸⁴⁹ is given¹³²⁵ unto me³⁴²⁷ in¹⁷²² heaven³⁷⁷² and²⁵³² in¹⁹⁰⁹ earth.¹⁰⁹³

28:19 Go⁴¹⁹⁸ ye therefore,³⁷⁶⁷ and teach³¹⁰⁰ all³⁹⁵⁶ nations,¹⁴⁸⁴ baptizing⁹⁰⁷ them⁸⁴⁶ in¹⁵¹⁹ the³⁵⁸⁸ name³⁶⁸⁶ of the³⁵⁸⁸ Father,³⁹⁶² and²⁵³² of the³⁵⁸⁸ Son,⁵²⁰⁷ and²⁵³² of the³⁵⁸⁸ Holy⁴⁰ Ghost:⁴¹⁵¹

Acts 1:4 And,²⁵³² being assembled together with⁴⁸⁷¹ them, commanded³⁸⁵³ them⁸⁴⁶ that they should not³³⁶¹ depart⁵⁵⁶³ from⁵⁷⁵ Jerusalem,²⁴¹⁴ but²³⁵ wait for⁴⁰³⁷ the³⁵⁸⁸ promise¹⁸⁶⁰ of the³⁵⁸⁸ Father,³⁹⁶² which,³⁷³⁹ saith he, ye have heard¹⁹¹ of me.³⁴⁵⁰

1:5 For³⁷⁵⁴ John²⁴⁹¹ truly³³⁰³ baptized⁹⁰⁷ with water;⁵²⁰⁴ but¹¹⁶¹ ye⁵²¹⁰ shall be baptized⁹⁰⁷ with¹⁷²² the Holy⁴⁰ Ghost⁴¹⁵¹ not³⁷⁵⁶ many⁴¹⁸³ days²²⁵⁰ hence.⁵⁰²⁵

Luke 24:49 And,²⁵³² behold,²⁴⁰⁰ I¹⁴⁷³ send⁶⁴⁹ the³⁵⁸⁸ promise¹⁸⁶⁰ of my³⁴⁵⁰ Father³⁹⁶² upon¹⁹⁰⁹ you:⁵²⁰⁹ but¹¹⁶¹ tarry²⁵²³ ye⁵²¹⁰ in¹⁷²² the³⁵⁸⁸ city⁴¹⁷² of Jerusalem,²⁴¹⁹ until²¹⁹³, ³⁷⁵⁷ ye be endued¹⁷⁴⁶ with power¹⁴¹¹ from¹⁵³⁷ on high.⁵³¹¹

Revelation 5:9 And²⁵³² they sung¹⁰³ a new²⁵³⁷ song,⁵⁶⁰³ saying,³⁰⁰⁴ Thou art¹⁴⁸⁸ worthy⁵¹⁴ to take²⁹⁸³ the³⁵⁸⁸ book,⁹⁷⁵ and²⁵³² to open⁴⁵⁵ the³⁵⁸⁸ seals⁴⁹⁷³ thereof:[848] *for*[3754] *thou wast slain,*[4969] *and*[2532] *hast redeemed*[59] *us*[2248] *to God*[2316] *by*[1722] *thy*[4675] *blood*[129] *out of*[1537] *every*[3956] *kindred,*[5443] *and*[2532] *tongue,*[1100] *and*[2532] *people,*[2992] *and*[2532] *nation;*[1484]

5:10 And[2532] *hast made*[4160] *us*[2248] *unto our*[2257] *God*[2316] *kings*[935] *and*[2532] *priests:*[2409] *and*[2532] *we shall reign*[936] *on*[1909] *the*[3588] *earth.*[1093]

Christians must learn to see life through Kingdom spectacles. Life is not a game. It is very serious business. There is much at stake. And the enemy does not want us to know about it. He wants us to blindly trip through life having fun, making money, going on vacations, and building vain worthless legacies to our intelligence, strength, and effort. Too many people come to the end of their lives and see the horrible mistake they have made by ignoring God's plan. But its too late. We must be very careful not to fall for satan's tactics or his deception.

Spiritual warfare includes binding the enemy's tactics whenever we see, hear, or think of doing something that is offensive to God and harmful to ourselves or others. Our beliefs, attitudes, speech and behavior must be monitored daily moment by moment. Whenever it is necessary we must continue to submit to God and resist the enemy in order to watch him flee!

James 4:7 Submit[5293] *yourselves therefore*[3767] *to God.*[2316] *Resist*[436] *the*[3588] *devil,*[1228] *and*[2532] *he will flee*[5343] *from*[575] *you.*[5216]

4:8 Draw nigh[1448] to God,[2316] and[2532] he will draw nigh[1448] to you.[5213]

You can start now, or start later. But if you plan to live life as God desires, you will eventually actively engage in spiritual warfare. When you discern the intrusion of demons into your thoughts or activity, bind them by saying something like, "I bind you spirits of discouragement in the name of Jesus and with His authority. You shut up and back off! God is my joy and my strength! He is my Father and my protector and my provider, so take a hike demon!" And then quietly go on about your business. Use some discretion here, especially in public places! Continue speaking to them until you feel relief. It may take a minute or an hour depending on the situation and the level of your maturity and faith. You are not expected to scream or make a scene; demons are not deaf. And they do like to make things worse, especially when you expose them. So, do not give them a stage on which to perform. To bind them is to refuse them to do what they want. Their main mission is to disrupt your work of making them submit to God's authority in you. You might look or sound a little silly from time to time as you deal with demons throughout your day. However, do not be discouraged if this concept of spiritual warfare is new to you. Remember, everything in life that you do well you have been doing a long time. Spiritual warfare is no different.

If you feel you must get help, then by all means, get help. Find a Christian who knows about warfare and learn from them. Ah, which Christian, though? How do I know who is doing it well or right? Find one whose lifestyle you admire for their spiritual maturity. Do they demonstrate the fruit of the Spirit? Are they, loving, joyful, patient, kind, etc.? Do they live a balanced Kingdom lifestyle in which their walk is consistent with their talk? Or, are they like the Pharisees of Jesus' day? They talk about God and at the same time put all kinds of restrictive rules, religious regulations and loveless limitations on the indwelling power of His Spirit?

Again, Jesus died and was resurrected to set you free of the attitudes, beliefs, and behaviors that restrict your understanding and your expression of the Kingdom of God. He died to remove the limitations of sin and the resulting curses associated with it. For the most part these act as open doors and invitations which demons use to keep you bound in ignorance. Make sure your religious practices are not, in fact, just more of the same!

Summary

When you read the Word, pray in your native language and in tongues as well, and worship God consistently day in and day out, you can expect to feel the presence of His power and authority. His presence will feel closer to you than ever before. As you realize His power is yours, provided for you by Jesus Himself, through His death and resurrection, and the Holy Spirit's presence, you will begin to see life on earth more accurately. You will then take charge, no longer allowing the enemy of God, your adversary, the devil and his demons push you around! As you spend time with God building your understanding of His will for you and growing in your relationship with

Him, you will begin to see yourself accurately as well. You will come to realize you are His child, that He loves you unconditionally and eternally, you have been given His authority, and are empowered by His Spirit to live in the Kingdom of God, right here on terra firma.

Personal Testimony

When Michele and I were baby Christians we were impressed by God and others around us that our lives were in peril. So we took our new birth and life with God very seriously. We knew if we were to grow strong we had to eat. So we decided to "pig out" on the Word. We decided to believe God's Word was true and if something else conflicted with it or interfered with our study of it, well, we just didn't need it! We have never looked back.

In our early days our evening routine went something like this. We would sit on the couch after supper with the TV off! (it was rarely on!) We would read our Bibles. At times we would read the same passages out loud to each other, taking turns. Sometimes we would read independently. Usually we would read for an hour or so. We would use our Strong's concordance to look up words and meanings of words and we would compare different translations. We both had NASBs at the time, and a Dake's KJV which we thoroughly enjoyed. We also read from the Living Bible and later added an NIV. Eventually we got a copy of The Book, put out by the 700 Club. We loved discovering new stuff in God's word! (For the past 14 years I have enjoyed the Spirit- Filled Life Bible.)

After reading for a while we would sit and pray quietly in tongues. Sometimes for 30 minutes or so. We did this very regularly for several months beginning shortly after we met Jesus. Eventually people who needed help started dropping by the house. We would pray for them and read the Word together. We did this every night of the week as long as people showed up and as long as we did not have anything else to do for God.

In addition to our Bible reading we read other books about spirit-filled Kingdom living. We especially liked biographies of people all over the world who developed strong relationships with God. We read about missionaries, evangelists, revivalists, and businessmen and women. All of them were inspiring stories that moved us to be like them. Dennis and Rita Bennett, Demos Shakarian, Bruce Olsen, George Whitfield, Hudson Taylor, George Mueller, William Gurnall, Martin Luther, St Augustine, Thomas A Kempis, Brother Lawrence, Reese Howells, and many, many others.

In retrospect I believe all of this explains why we grew so rapidly in our knowledge of His word. We also talked with anyone that seemed more spiritually mature than us or anyone that appeared to love the Lord and the Word as much as we did. We asked all kinds of questions of them. But for the most part we studied on our own, prayed a lot, both together and individually, and shared with others what we had learned.

Not surprisingly after a year or so of this study we had a house full of people on Saturday nights. Those were wonderful nights of praise and study and word and prayer. God did miracles often. People were healed and met Jesus, entered the Kingdom, and many grew in their own knowledge and experience with God.

We have been living in the Kingdom now since 1984! It seems a lot longer than that but then time flies when you're having fun! I truly cannot remember what life was like before I met Jesus. I don't want to know. I am not happy with who I was back then. I am embarrassed about much of my past. I certainly do not want to revisit it or to glorify those years by making them seem better than they were. I am glad they are over. I'm glad to know I know God and that I know He has a plan for my life that I am following to the best of my ability. I am not perfect; far from it! I make mistakes every day. Mistakes in judgment of others, criticizing my efforts and failures, and at times just being lazy in my pursuit of God. But I can honestly say I am doing my best to know God and submit my will to His will for me. And life is much better now than it was twenty years ago!

And yet I am still hungry for more understanding of God and His Word! I just cannot get enough. I have studied His Word for over twenty years, and in college for six of those years. Michele and I have taught in churches and various schools, presented at seminars and conferences. We have ministered God's healing power to hundreds of folks from all over the world, and have published three books, with several more currently in the writing process.

For the past fourteen years we have ministered to hundreds of God's children using Restoring The Foundations Ministry method. We use RTFM because it applies the healing power of God's word to the specific details of an individual's life. Yes, they need healing, but more importantly, this healing removes emotional, intellectual, spiritual and even physical impairment that often block the expanding revelation God knows they need to live a more enjoyable and productive Kingdom life.

Still, at this moment, I feel like a little child who is in awe of his daddy's love and strength. At this point in my life, what is most precious to me is the fact that I am still hungry for more understanding of God and of my role in His Kingdom on earth.

Michele and I hope you will find encouragement in our writing to pursue God diligently. We know if you do, you will never regret your decision or your effort. Living with God is so much better than living without Him! Why wait until you see Him face to face? You can interact with Him now. And He desires that you will. Our prayer for you is that you will find and follow God's wonderful will for your life, and most of all that you will delight in knowing Him on a personal basis. Like any athletic endeavor, if you train to win, your chances of winning are greater. Strength training for Kingdom Living is not any different. If you diligently do the work on a daily basis you will enjoy the results.

May His richest blessings be yours in abundance.

CHAPTER 5

Holy Spirit Contact

John 14:15-17 "If you love me, you will obey what I command. And I will ask the Father, and he will give you another Counselor to be with you forever—the Spirit of truth. The world cannot accept him, because it neither sees him nor knows him. But you know him, for he lives with you and will be in you."

1 Corinthians 2:6-15 (NIV)
6 We do, however, speak a message of wisdom among the mature, but not the wisdom of this age or of the rulers of this age, who are coming to nothing. 7 No, we speak of God's secret wisdom, a wisdom that has been hidden and that God destined for our glory before time began. 8 None of the rulers of this age understood it, for if they had, they would not have crucified the Lord of glory. 9 However, as it is written: "No eye has seen, no ear

has heard, no mind has conceived what God has prepared for those who love him" 10 but God has revealed it to us by his Spirit.

The Spirit searches all things, even the deep things of God. 11 For who among men knows the thoughts of a man except the man's spirit within him? In the same way no one knows the thoughts of God except the Spirit of God. 12 We have not received the spirit of the world but the Spirit who is from God, that we may understand what God has freely given us. 13 This is what we speak, not in words taught us by human wisdom but in words taught by the Spirit, expressing spiritual truths in spiritual words. 14 The man without the Spirit does not accept the things that come from the Spirit of God, for they are foolishness to him, and he cannot understand them, because they are spiritually discerned. 15 The spiritual man makes judgments about all things, but he himself is not subject to any man's judgment.

The more dependent we are on the indwelling presence, Christ-centered instruction, and declared divine comfort of the Spirit of God, the more we will know both the Father and the Son; the more blessed we will be by seeing their glory, and hearing the words of the Jesus; and the more useful we will become in promoting His truth and proliferating His Kingdom.

Who is The Spirit of God?

Genesis 1:1 In the beginning God created the heaven and the earth. 1:2 And the earth was without form, *and void; and darkness was upon the face of the deep. And the Spirit^{7307} of God^{430} moved^{7363} upon the face of the waters. 1:3 And God said, Let there be light: and there was^{1961} light.*

Genesis 41:37 And the thing was good in the eyes of Pharaoh, and in the eyes of all his servants. 41:38 And Pharaoh said unto his servants, Can we find such a one as this is, a man in whom the Spirit of God is? 41:39 And Pharaoh said unto Joseph, Forasmuch as God hath showed thee all this, there is none so discreet and wise as thou art:

1Samuel 10:10 And when they came thither to the hill, behold, a company of prophets met him; and the Spirit of God came upon him, and he prophesied among them.

Matthew 3:16 And Jesus, when he was baptized, went up straightway out of the water: and, lo, the heavens were opened unto him, and he (John the baptizer) saw the Spirit^{4151} of God^{2316} descending^{2597} like a dove, and lighting upon him (Jesus).

Why is Contact with Him Desirable?

John 15:26 But when the Comforter^{3875} is come, whom I will send unto you from the Father, even the Spirit (vital element of life) of truth, which proceedeth from the Father, he shall testify of me:

15:27 And ye also shall bear witness, because ye have been with me from the beginning.

John 16:7 Nevertheless I tell you the truth; It is expedient for you that I go away: for if I go not away, the Comforter will not come unto you; but if I depart, I will send him unto you.

John 16:13 Howbeit when he, the Spirit⁴¹⁵¹ (vital element of life) of truth,²²⁵ is come, he will guide you into all truth: for he shall not speak of himself; but whatsoever he shall hear, that shall he speak: and he will show you things to come.

16:14 He shall glorify me: for he shall receive of mine, and shall show it unto you.

16:15 All things that the Father hath are mine: therefore said I, that he shall take of mine, and shall show it unto you.

What Is to Be Gained by Contacting Him?

Romans 8:9 But ye are not in the flesh, but in the Spirit, if so be that the Spirit of God dwell in you. Now if any man have not the Spirit of Christ, he is none of his.

What do you want to rely upon for guidance? Upon the unpredictably treacherous seas of life? The comfort, wisdom, and empowerment of your ungodly flesh? Or the presence of His Spirit?

John 3:6 That which is born[1080] of the flesh is flesh;[4561] and that which is born[1080] of the Spirit[4151] is spirit.[4151]

John 6:63 It is the spirit[4151] that quickeneth;[2227] (zoopoieo: make alive) the flesh[4561 (3756)] profiteth[5623] (opheleo: benefits) nothing:[3762] (oudeis: not one thing) the words that I speak unto you, they are spirit,[4151] and they are life.[2222]

Matthew 26:41 Watch and pray, that ye enter not into temptation: the spirit indeed is willing, but the flesh is weak.

Acts 2:17 And it shall come to pass in the last days, saith God, I will pour out of my Spirit[4151] (the vital element of His life) upon all flesh: and your sons and your daughters shall prophesy, and your young men shall see visions, and your old men shall dream dreams:

Romans 8:1 There is therefore now no condemnation to them which are in Christ Jesus, who walk not after the flesh,[4561] but after the Spirit.[4151]

Romans 8:13 For if ye live after the flesh ye shall die: but if ye through the Spirit[4151] do mortify the deeds of the body,[4983] ye shall live.[2198]

Galatians 3:3 Are ye so foolish? having begun in the Spirit,[4151] are ye now made perfect by the flesh?[4561]

Galatians 5:16 This I say then, Walk⁴⁰⁴³ in the Spirit,⁴¹⁵¹ and ye shall not fulfill⁵⁰⁵⁵ the lust¹⁹³⁹ of the flesh.⁴⁵⁶¹

Fruit of the Spirit

Galatians 5:19 Now the works of the flesh are manifest, which are these; adultery, fornication, uncleanness, lewdness,

5:20 Idolatry, witchcraft, hatred, contentions, jealousy, outbursts of wrath, selfish ambitions, dissensions, heresies,

5:21 Envy, murders, drunkenness, revelries, and the like: of the which I tell you before, as I have also told you in time past, that they which do such things shall not inherit the kingdom of God.

5:22 But the fruit of the Spirit is love, joy, peace, patience, kindness, goodness, faithfulness,

5:23 gentleness, self-control: against such there is no law.

5:24 And they that are Christ's have crucified the flesh with the affections and lusts.

5:25 If we live (truly eternally exist) in the Spirit (as a result of the indwelling power of God's life force), let us also walk in (demonstrate outwardly harmony with) the Spirit.

Gifts of the Spirit

1 Corinthians 12:1-31 (NIV)
*1Now about spiritual gifts, brothers, I do not want
you to be ignorant.*

*2You know that when you were pagans, somehow
or other you were influenced and led astray to
mute idols.*

*3Therefore I tell you that no one who is speaking
by the Spirit of God says, "Jesus be cursed," and
no one can say, "Jesus is Lord," except by the Holy
Spirit.*

*4There are different kinds of gifts, but the same
Spirit. 5There are different kinds of service, but the
same Lord. 6There are different kinds of working,
but the same God works all of them in all men.*

*7Now to each one the manifestation of the Spirit is
given for the common good.*

*8To one there is given through the Spirit the message
of wisdom, to another the message of knowledge
by means of the same Spirit,*

*9to another faith by the same Spirit, to another
gifts of healing by that one Spirit,*

*10to another miraculous powers, to another
prophecy, to another distinguishing between spirits,*

to another speaking in different kinds of tongues, and to still another the interpretation of tongues.

11All these are the work of one and the same Spirit, and he gives them to each one, just as he determines.

12The body is a unit, though it is made up of many parts; and though all its parts are many, they form one body. So it is with Christ. 13For we were all baptized by one Spirit into one body—whether Jews or Greeks, slave or free—and we were all given the one Spirit to drink.

14Now the body is not made up of one part but of many.

15If the foot should say, "Because I am not a hand, I do not belong to the body," it would not for that reason cease to be part of the body.

16And if the ear should say, "Because I am not an eye, I do not belong to the body," it would not for that reason cease to be part of the body.

17If the whole body were an eye, where would the sense of hearing be? If the whole body were an ear, where would the sense of smell be?

18But in fact God has arranged the parts in the body, every one of them, just as he wanted them to be.

19If they were all one part, where would the body be?

20As it is, there are many parts, but one body.

21The eye cannot say to the hand, "I don't need you!" And the head cannot say to the feet, "I don't need you!"

22On the contrary, those parts of the body that seem to be weaker are indispensable,

23and the parts that we think are less honorable we treat with special honor. And the parts that are unpresentable are treated with special modesty,

24while our presentable parts need no special treatment. But God has combined the members of the body and has given greater honor to the parts that lacked it,

25so that there should be no division in the body, but that its parts should have equal concern for each other.

26If one part suffers, every part suffers with it; if one part is honored, every part rejoices with it.

27Now you are the body of Christ, and each one of you is a part of it.

28And in the church God has appointed first of all apostles, second prophets, third teachers, then *workers of miracles, also those having gifts of healing, those able to help others, those with gifts of administration, and those speaking in different kinds of tongues.*

29Are all apostles? Are all prophets? Are all teachers? Do all work miracles?

30Do all have gifts of healing? Do all speak in tongues? Do all interpret?

31But eagerly desire the greater gifts. And now I will show you the most excellent way.

The Holy Spirit is constantly available within every born again human. But the flesh, the ungodly unredeemed carnality of man, opposes the Spirit and the things of God. Only those who will pursue Him and be determined to develop a relationship with Him will demonstrate His presence outwardly. This is not a guarantee of bliss-filled life. It is a guarantee that whether life's path traverses the high road or low He will go along. And in the end the disciple will be rewarded with treasures beyond comprehension!

When to Make contact?

The Spirit was sent to empower, educate and comfort the disciple as he faithfully follows Christ upon the mountain tops and through the valleys of life. As incredible as it may seem, it is true, the Holy Spirit is the life force of God dwelling in man. He guides, directs, corrects, and instructs man in the ways of God. He is willing to interact with us just as He did with Jesus. His counsel is to be sought in every decision from the minor to the major. Wisdom will increase as He becomes more familiar to us.

On the other hand, if He is invited in only as pressing needs demand, His availability is limited to an emergency capacity. Yet He desires and is destined by God to be our constant and closest companion, our comforter and instructor. He is so much more than our rescuer invited in when we are lonely, weary, frightened, or in pain.

The disciple that has embraced His love and warm fellowship finds confidence growing and wisdom increasing. And fellowship becomes more satisfying than the benefits of His friendship. The disciple is motivated by desire to "be with" Him. Warmed by love for Him a transformation slowly takes place. The disciple finds himself becoming more like Jesus and less like his former unredeemed self.

This transformation is the very thing God intended to occur as a result of redemption.

Romans 8:29 ...to be conformed to the image of his Son, that he might be the firstborn among many brethren.

Romans 12:2 And be not conformed to this (carnal ungodly) world: but be ye transformed by the renewing of your mind, that ye may prove what is that good, and acceptable, and perfect, will of God.

2Corinthians 7:1 Having therefore these promises, dearly beloved, let us cleanse ourselves from all filthiness of the flesh and spirit, perfecting holiness in the fear of God.

Yet, too often the man redeemed, while thankful for escaping the eternal fires of hell, rejects the joy and peace available in daily fellowship with the Holy Spirit. Thus, though filled with the Spirit of God he continues to live, to think, and act and react to life, as a man of the world. The fruit and gifts of the Spirit are then kept in reserve, as in a closet, available but unused. And though the self-conscious Christian might attempt from time to time to "be more like Jesus" desiring to demonstrate both the gifts and fruit of the Spirit, if he has not developed the discipline of sitting with the Spirit to literally be transformed, his demonstration of the gifts and fruit of the Spirit will be undertaken by his former unchanged carnal self. This is why so many twenty-first century believers are "carnal Christians." They profess a form of godliness but cannot demonstrate His power.

Aware of His Presence

Too many disciples relegate contact with the Holy Spirit to church meetings or special functions. Whether this practice is by way of instruction or ignorance matters little. If this is your case you should correct it. If Bill Gates gave you a signed blank check, would you fill it out for $100.00? God gave you an invitation to an audience with Him. Could there be any appointment more thrilling?

The Holy Spirit's presence predates every religious system and form of worship. He was with God in the unknown past and is the agent by which God works His miracles. He is the ever-present power of God's life that indwelt Jesus Christ and empowered Him to remain sinless even though He was tempted, as we are today. This same power was available to Adam and Eve, yet they rejected it. Many believers do the same today. They try hard to maintain an awareness of God's plan and to live in harmony with that plan. But they fail to embrace the power to do so. Even if they have encounters with Him in meetings, seminars, or conferences they soon forget He is with them as they make their way through the exit doors. What a sad testimony. But such is the stuff of religious practices, to maintain an appearance of godliness yet ignore the presence of His Spirit, Who makes life with God possible.

The Holy Spirit is the same Spirit, who raised Christ from the dead, and He is granted access to the disciple during regeneration. He is available everywhere all the time and He dwells within the heart and mind of the disciple. One does not need to go anywhere to visit with Him. Contact with Him can be had on a daily basis and is entered into much the same way that one enters and maintains any other valuable relationship, frequently and happily. We may find His voice a bit difficult to hear at first. But with persistent practice and patience we find we can walk and talk with Him as easily as we do with anyone. If we learn to listen we will learn to distinguish His voice from all the others clamoring for our attention. He will improve our ability to understand the Word of

God and He will affirm our most minor efforts to be more like Jesus.

How is Contact Achieved?

Man divides his time among many interests. The more important ones get the most focused attention and the most time. We may not like our job but it is important. And it certainly is possible to go there begrudgingly every day out of a combined sense of obligation and need. However, most men do not feel obligated to go fishing, surfing, or to invest money, or dedicate time in pursuit of higher education. We do all of these things because we value them. Our pursuit continues as long as the thing we pursue gives us a valuable return on our investment, whether the investmentit is time, energy, or money.

The Holy Spirit is intended by God to be man's friend, teacher, comforter, and strength. The benefits of time with Him cannot be accurately assessed in terms of fulfillment, money, or success. Why then would one need to be commanded to enjoy His presence? Isn't He the One that rescued you from your former self-destructive lifestyle? Isn't He the One that loves you unconditionally and more intensely than you can imagine?

The disciple should not feel obligated to spend time with Him. Not only is that insulting, it will not bring about the emancipating transformation He desires for you. He is real, not a theological anomaly. He possesses real power to transform. He brings healing to broken minds and bodies. He works miracles. He calms every raging sea. Quiets every screaming voice. But He will not pursue you any more than you pursue Him. He awaits your response to His invitation. He allows the disciple to make the decision to meet. Like time spent with any other person, hobby, or interest, limited time with Him will result in limited benefits.

The disciple would benefit more quickly by pursuing conversation with Him often. A regular time of Word study and prayer is the prescription for personal growth in Christ-likeness. It is during intimate contact that the Holy Spirit will disclose to the disciple the majesty and mysteries of Christ and God. The invitation is to come expecting, come devotionally, and come often.

The Holy Spirit will even help the disciple pray. There are many things we do not know about God and His ways of overseeing this planet. His ways are way beyond our ways of finding out. But the Holy Spirit can assist the disciple in speaking with God. By shutting out the intellect and allowing the Holy Spirit to pray through us using our voice we can move beyond intellectual need-driven prayer. There is a place found by contacting Him regularly that is not available in short, quick, infrequent visits. Consistent, peaceful, devotional contact is very beneficial to the disciple's growth in Christ-likeness.

Praying in tongues, or using one's prayer language, need not bring fear of unconscious ecstasy in which we dance wildly about the room, or lose control of ourselves. The Holy Spirit can be trusted to do all things in an orderly manner. Yet in times past, and even currently, there are folks who feel the Holy Spirit moves them to demonstrate action and make sounds that can be quite entertaining. Some of the more odd manifestations bring ridicule and judgment from critics. However, while one may assess he should resist the urge to prematurely judge another man's experience with the Holy Spirit.

> *Mark 16:17 And these signs shall follow them that believe; In my name shall they cast out devils; they shall speak with new tongues;*[1100]

> *Act 2:4 And*[2532] *they were all*[537] *filled*[4130] *with the Holy*[40] *Ghost,*[4151] *and*[2532] *began*[756] *to speak*[2980] *with other tongues,*[1100] *as*[2531] *the*[3588] *Spirit*[4151] *gave*[1325] *them*[846] *utterance.*[669]

> *Acts 10:46 For they heard them speak with tongues, and magnify God.*

> *1Corinthians 14:39 Wherefore, brethren, covet to prophesy, and forbid not to speak with tongues.*

> *Ephesians 6:18 Praying always with all prayer and supplication in the Spirit, and watching thereunto with all perseverance and supplication for all saints;*

> *Jude 1:20 But ye, beloved, building up yourselves on your most holy faith, praying*[4336] *in*[1722] *the Holy*[40] *Ghost,*[4151]

For more on this subject we offer the following text by Rodman Williams. Dr. Williams was Professor of Theology at Regent University, author of Renewal

Theology, and for more than thirty years a recognized authority on the subject of the Charismatic Renewal.

Speaking In Tongues

(From a Rodman Williams, Ph. D. text. included here with permission of the author)

Finally, let me summarize a number of values of speaking in tongues. First, whatever others (in the world or church!) may think, when people speak in tongues, they begin to experience in a fresh way the reality of God. They may start with only a few syllables or words, or with the whole new language, but there is a growing sense of awe that God is present, speaking in them and through them. This new language, which is known not to have been made up or conjured up, is an audible reminder, whenever spoken, of the miraculous activity of God.

Second, speaking in tongues as it moves into singing in tongues or singing in the Spirit (where both words and melody are given by the Holy Spirit) becomes a joyful expression of praise when people are gathered together for worship. Where people not only sing psalms and hymns but also are able to sing "spiritual songs,"[3] there is the zenith of the worship of God.

Third, speaking in tongues has great benefit in the life of prayer. The apostle Paul enjoins us to "pray at all times in the Spirit" (Eph. 6:18), for such prayer is essentially that which the Holy Spirit utters in us. Many persons find themselves, like Paul, praying with the Spirit (which is praying in tongues) and praying with the mind also (cf. 1 Cor. 14:14-15), and discover in the alternation between the two an increasing enrichment of the spiritual life. It is hard to overestimate the value of tongues in the daily experience of prayer. Many begin their prayer time with praying in the Spirit and find these prayers of the Holy Spirit a rich background and force for the prayers of the mind that follow. Often people move back and forth between the two: and their life of prayer becomes all the richer and fuller. Thus it is that praying in tongues does much to build persons up in their faith. The words of Paul are indeed true: "He who speaks in a tongue edifies himself" (1 Cor. 14:4); and the words of Jude are a continuing challenge: "beloved, build yourselves up on your most holy faith; pray in the Holy Spirit" (Jude 20).

Fourth, speaking in tongues often proves to be the doorway into a deeper experience of the other gifts of the Spirit. Since tongues are such an extraordinary avenue of prayer and praise, many persons soon find themselves moving more freely in the realm of other spiritual gifts, or manifestations, of the Holy Spirit. It is not at all unusual to experience prophecy, healings, miracles and other gifts of the Spirit (see 1 Cor. 12:8-10) after having begun to speak in tongues. Tongues often are the key turning the lock of the door into the whole realm of God's extraordinary workings.

Fifth, and finally, speaking in tongues wherein the Holy Spirit communicates through us to the Father and glorifies the Son is that kind of praise which is very near to the glory of the world to come. Since the Holy Spirit provides the language, it is a pure and holy language—

whatever the imperfection of the one who speaks. Thus it is the noblest language this side of heaven.

Assessing Your Holy Spirit Contact

As Dr. Williams indicated above, building a relationship with the Holy Spirit is the fastest way to grow in the character of Christ. As His Spirit is given more and more of our time and energy we will begin to hear His voice more clearly and follow His guidance more faithfully. His love for us will draw us to spend more time with Him. Our heart will easily connect with His and our steps will confidently follow His as we traverse God's path, together.

Making contact with the Holy Spirit should become a proactive discipline for the disciple rather than a reactive rescue effort. As your spirit makes this connection with Him your flesh will slowly lose its appeal and it's command of you. His ever-present availability will invite your contact daily. No longer will your ever-changing emotional mood and attitude drive you away or force your contact. You will simply be overcome by His love and quite innocently you will desire more. Religious practice will never satisfy the disciple who is hungry for more of God. Love is the motivator to knowing God. Fulfilling a legal obligation can never satisfy a passionate desire to know God. His love for you will draw you to Him daily where you will sit relaxed and find refreshment.

Do you live your life by the power of your flesh or the presence of His Spirit? Are you motivated to visit with Him by your condition or by His availability? Is your contact with Him the result of a religious posture or a desire for relationship? When you contact Him is it to fulfill a legal obligation or to express your heartfelt devotion? Is your contact with Him reactive or proactive? Reactive contact is better than no contact. However, proactive contact is more beneficial and far more satisfying. And after developing this essential Christian discipline, the determined disciple will sigh, the words of the psalmist, "Oh taste and see, the Lord is good."

Footnotes

1   These quotations from St. Augustine and St. Thomas Aquinas are taken from Eddie Ensley's book Sounds of Wonder, 8, 53. Ensley, in this valuable book, later says, "Indications are that jubilation is a continuation of the glossolalia of the New Testament," and that "plainsong and the musical parts of the liturgy emerged from the early practice of glossolalia" (pp. 115, 117). In any event the connection between speaking in tongues and the praise of God is unmistakable.

2   By "ecstatic" reference is commonly made to speech uncontrolled by the conscious mind, which is an expression of the non-rational depths. Such expression, in which the subconscious breaks through, may have tremendous spiritual vigor and drive. However, such ecstatic utterance, in which strong emotion may dominate, often passes into irrationality, frenzy, even madness. Speaking in tongues is not ecstasy; for there is continuing control under the direction of the Holy Spirit. There is joy, elevation-but no irrationality, no lack of conscious control.

3   Paul speaks in both Ephesians and Colossians about "psalms, hymns, and spiritual songs" (Eph. 5:19; Col. 3:16). Psalms and hymns doubtless signify known and frequently used musical expressions (as is true in the church today), but "spiritual songs" (or songs inspired by the Spirit) probably refers to songs where words and melodies are spontaneously given by the Holy Spirit. In the Jerusalem Bible a footnote to Colossians 3:16 speaks of these spiritual songs as "charismatic improvisations" (!).

CHAPTER 6

Priorities

But seek first his kingdom and his righteousness, and all these things will be given to you as well. Therefore do not worry about tomorrow, for tomorrow will worry about itself. Each day has enough trouble of its own. Matthew 6:33-34

Now a word regarding this issue of prioritizing our lives as we endeavor to embrace Kingdom life. It is well to think of the Christian life as a new adventure. The Christian adventure is actually a journey which takes us from one place to another. Born-again Christians have stepped upon a new path. This new path is intended to lead to the ultimate fulfillment of God's will. We are expected to view this adventurous journey as extremely important and one requiring our undivided attention, fervent dedication, and constant effort. Jesus says, "The Kingdom of God suffers violence and the violent take it by force."(NAS) In the NIV it reads, "The kingdom of heaven has been forcefully advancing, and forceful men lay hold of it." Luke 16:16 reads, "The Law and the Prophets were proclaimed until John; since that time the gospel of the kingdom of God has been preached, and everyone is forcing his way into it."

To view it from another perspective, think of conversion as the beginning of an arduous process intended to separate us from a lifestyle of self-focus. Our new life is built upon a desire to know God, and to make Him known. This witness is accomplished as we develop a new (godly) perspective of life, and as a result of that, a new (Kingdom) lifestyle. The one godly quality, among many, that reveals to the world around us that we are Christians is the desire and willingness to serve others. Jesus tells us, "The greatest in the Kingdom is a servant of all." In other words, if we claim to know and love God we will love others with self-sacrificing love.

Therefore, to progress swiftly along on the path of our new adventure in the Kingdom of God, we must re-order our priorities. So, lets discuss priorities and the value of setting things in godly order.

Putting priorities in order is essential to the continued unhindered growth of Christ-likeness. To be successful we must get them in order and keep them in order.

This is true for several reasons. Scripture teaches us;
1. "Seek first the Kingdom of God and His righteousness …

2. "And all these things will be added unto you."

3. Our enemy, "… prowls around like a roaring lion, seeking whom he may devour."

4. "The eyes of God search the earth to strongly support those whose hearts are His."

5. "Do for others what you would like them to do for you."

When our priorities are not in order, we are not like Him, we are like them, the ones we are to be witnesses to. And we cannot be witnesses if we are not like Him. Our witness is our lifestyle. It is the practical, every day, way we conduct our affairs, interacting with others. Jesus said ,"Out of the abundance of the heart, the mouth speaks." He also said if we were to fulfill God's will we would, "Love your neighbor as yourself." And we would, "Treat others the way you would like to be treated."

Christian Witness

Some believers mistakenly continue to demonstrate their secular life-style while living in the Kingdom of God. They believe they can witness effectively for His Kingdom without re-ordering their priorities. They reason, "If it worked out there why not use it in here?"

Are you a take-charge kind of person? Do you rush around in a flurry of activity driven by the secret need to look busy, successful, or important? Do you confuse busy-ness with Kingdom life? Do you place more emphasis, more time, energy, and money "witnessing" to those outside of your immediate family? If the answer is "yes." You may have your priorities confused. Is witnessing a chore, a job, a career choice, or Holy Spirit directed lifestyle? Who are you trying to impress with your over-stuffed schedule; God, or man?

Christianity is not a religious construct. It is not a, "work related" endeavor focusing on appointments, obligations, tasks, etc. It is a spiritual mission that should impact others on an emotional and spiritual level via our interaction with them in their material world. For the Christian the fruit of the Spirit is the benchmark of all human inter-action. Love, joy, peace, patience, kindness, gentleness, goodness, faithfulness and self-control are the hallmarks of Christian behavior. Getting any job done is important. But the attitude with which we do it is even more important.

For example, if we serve with disciplined determination and forfeit love, our Christian world-view does not benefit anyone any more than that of any hard working unbeliever. If we work hard but are disrespectful, insensitive, and self-serving, we have missed the point. The Christian's perspective is to be like Christ. It focuses on how we witness as well as who we witness to. To be a witness of God's Kingdom on earth requires us to think, speak, and act and react like Jesus would.

Does your interaction with others in your home, on your job, or at church, reveal the love the Holy Spirit has deposited within you? Regardless of the nature of the encounter; whether its family, business, or church, do people leave your presence feeling His tender touch?

Walking away from that encounter with you, do they feel heard, helped, healed? To be a witness for God means to testify or share the details of a personal encounter in a way that impacts others positively. Does your behavior leave the impression that you have had a recent encounter with the Prince of Peace, the Mighty God, the Wonderful Counselor? People who saw the car accident can give verbal testimony of the details of the crash. But did they drive more carefully after witnessing the crash? I assure you, the one driving the car will change his driving habits!

If our witness of the Kingdom of God is just a verbal presentation of the facts it can always be disputed. But behavior, our treatment of others, cannot be disputed. If our witness is to have spiritual power it must be demonstrated in our interaction with other people in positive and compassionate ways. What we think and say about life should not only line up with Jesus' teaching but it should be demonstrated by behavior that is like His was as He interacted with others. Anything less is religious and hypocritical.

Living for Jesus

The word, hypocrite, refers to one who acts like someone other than who he is. It is a Greek word, which originally referred to actors on the stage. In that case it isn't a negative. But if it is applicable to one who claims to know God, it means there is contradiction between who he declares himself to be and what he says and does. Confusion is the result if you are declaring the Kingdom has come, but you are not demonstrating tender, compassionate behavior that reflects the heart of your King. It means you are not a believable witness. You are claiming to possess a lifestyle you are not actually living. You can pedal your bicycle hard and fast and make the sound of a motorcycle with your voice. But doing so won't convince anyone you are riding a motorcycle! They will know you are pretending or acting.

The problem with hypocrisy is two fold. One, you think no one can tell the difference between what you preach and what you practice. Two, they do know the difference because they hear you proclaim first, and then watch you perform.

When a Christian does not have his priorities in order he sends the message, "Following Jesus is not as important or as beneficial as I say it is." Or, "Following Jesus is too hard so don't expect to do it very well, because I can't and I have been trying longer than you."

Yet living for Jesus is fairly simple. Hear and do. The true Christian lifestyle is the result of 1) listening, 2) hearing, 3) understanding, and 4) putting into practice all that you hear and understand. Living like Jesus can only be done, will only be done, as we invite and allow the Holy Spirit to empower us to change our hearts and then to empower us to change our behavior. The Christian lifestyle is the result of a firm resolve to hear from Him and to do it. It is a spiritual endeavor, not simply an emotional or purely intellectual one. Success is only available through a connection with the Holy Spirit.

I believe many Christians do not live a more godly life for two reasons. 1) They are afraid doing so will cause them to miss out on something good. They want to live an outward rather than an inward life. 2) They think resting, sitting quietly with God, meditating on Scripture, is a waste of their precious time. And yet only as we learn to let God lead do we learn to work smarter, not harder. His presence and wisdom will also help us eliminate costly errors and time consuming mistakes.

Family Priority

Carnal Christians have difficulty making time with their spouses and children in their own home a priority. They waste their time "out there" in order to look busy, feel good, or pretend to be godly. Rather than balancing work and ministry, with family life, they run after the next blessing on the path to Jesus' promise of success and prosperity. "I'm doing all of this for God." Sounds nice, but are you really? Has God asked you to do it at the expense of your relationship witness and "witness" to your family? Maybe it is easier to love unconditionally people you have a casual relationship with? It certainly is easier to pretend to be godly with people you see casually.

God is the Father from whom every family on earth derives its name. He is the Father who put the solitary in families. He is the Father of the human race who said, "It is not good for man to be alone." He is the Father that taught religious people to pray saying; "Father in heaven ..." I believe the happiest people on the planet are people who know Jesus, have experienced the life changing power of His love for them personally, first through an encounter with the Cross, and then through the indwelling presence of His Spirit. These happy people demonstrate His love inside the four walls of their home with their spouses and children. They know their first ministry is to their family. They know their first mission field is their home.

Jesus has called us to a life of humility and service. "The greatest in the Kingdom is a servant of all." I find it amazing that so many Christians are so driven to fulfill their "ministry mandate" while ignoring the emotional and spiritual needs of their own family.

How can we who were conceived and birthed in the corruption of flesh become like Him who was conceived in the pure and holy eternal nature of God? Only by surrendering to the gentle yet awesome presence and sanctifying work of the same Spirit.

Just Doing It

For many years I have tried hard to keep my priorities straight. I begin my day by thanking Jesus for His sacrifice on my behalf and by asking the Holy Spirit to help me be more like Jesus today. I want to be the humble servant of my wife first, then of everyone else I encounter during my day. I look for opportunities to give rather than take from her, to promote her rather than promote myself, to encourage, to forgive, to extend grace and mercy to her in her time of need. I take advantage of opportunities to compliment her for her work, her talents, her time and energy in my service. I make sure to thank her regularly for her service to me. I look into her beautiful brown eyes, and speak words of love to her.

After that I go out and do the same in grocery stores, Wal-mart, the tire store, the restaurant, and the bank. I go through my day expecting to hear from the Holy Spirit, expecting to see His will and encounter His blessings. I give Him my frustration, quickly ask for His forgiveness for my mistakes, and look for His power and grace to accomplish all I have to do. And at night as I drift off to sleep I thank Him for this wonderful woman lying next to me, for my darling daughter, my wonderful son, ministry opportunities, my success, my peace, and most of all for His presence in my life.

I seek His will in situations that I am not sure about. I do not act on my impulsivity; I refuse to give in to temptations to think badly about someone or some situation, I reject the pressure to adopt a doom and gloom attitude even though I believe we are in the last days on earth. I try to remember to pray for everyone on my prayer list, which is growing quite large. I intercede for them, asking for God's blessings of grace and mercy and financial blessing and divine radiant health to be seen in abundance.

Believe me, when I say, I am not boasting. I am not suggesting I do not struggle to be more like Him or that I do not fail in my attempts. I share honestly only to encourage you to imitate me only as I imitate Him.

You want to be happy? God has given you His power to be happy. You want peace and joy in your home? God says the power to create it is within you. You want to be an effective witness? The power to live a happy life is as close as your own heart. He is the Holy Spirit. And He is inside you waiting to be granted permission to change your life. He is the accelerator and all we have to do is press down. We don't need to be smarter, richer, stronger, or healthier. Just persistent. Jesus said the "kingdom is within you." He also said He, the helper, the Holy Spirit was with the disciples but later He would be in them. Is He inside you? If so, you should take advantage of Him.

Priority in Place

Where were we? Oh yes, lets see, we were discussing priorities. If you are married, make your spouse your first priority. Speak verbal blessings in his or her hearing. Look for opportunities every day and many times a day to speak words of life, to compliment, and to thank him or her for all he or she does for you. Refuse to see her as a useless woman who is a burden, who lacks, and is weak, and isn't what you want or need. Doing so only prevents her from becoming the woman God desires her to be and the woman He is right this very minute working with. Refuse to see your husband as independent and quite capable of making it without you. Reject the notion that he is so strong that he needs nothing from you.

If you are not married, choose your spouse wisely, while you still have time. And know Jesus will expect you to treat them well, serving them sacrificially.

I cannot withhold compliments and praise for my wife, or my children, or my friends, until they become what I want, need, or think they ought to be. I have been given a mandate by Jesus to love God and to love others. I should refrain from telling them to get it together or pick up the pace or work harder or do it differently. I should resist the urge to judge them or criticize them or scold them. Above all I must refuse to share with them insights "from the Lord" about their bad behavior, ungodly attitude or ungodly desires. Doing so will only frustrate them, discourage them, wear them out, or make them afraid of me or of God. And it might even drive them away from God. The Scripture says it is "the goodness of God that draws men to repentance."

To put my priorities in order I begin by putting time with God at the top of my list. To be a true blessing to others I must experience joy in my relationship with Him first. From there I then share my joy with them. My number one priority is spending time with Him. This experience fills me with everything I need to be a blessing to others. My wife and children, are the first to get my time. My friends, pals, co-workers, disciples, extended family members, all must share what's left of my time and energy when I am through serving my family. Priorities? God first, family second, and everybody else after that. Period.

My home is first, my prayer closet, and my refuge from the pressure of the world and from the pressure of ministry. My home is my castle, my fortress, and my Garden of Eden. It is the place where I find peace and refreshment, love and affection. It is where I recharge my batteries and enjoy my most favorite and cherished roles; Husband and Father. I roll around on the floor with my kids and roll around between the sheets with my wife. We play with each other, have fun, laugh, and share meals and books and the bible and prayer time. When my daughter was younger, we would color in coloring books together. I listened to her and took an interest in the details of her day. I ask my wife and daughter about their day, their trials, their joys, and their plans and their pains. And I pray for them, lay hands on them, hug them, speak words of love to them. They are my first mission field. I treat them as well as I want to be treated whether they treat that well or not. I follow Jesus' example because He, not them, is my role model.

What Now?

If you claim to be a Christian, what is it that makes that true? Is it the result of a prayer you prayed long ago? Is it the result of reluctantly taking Sunday mornings off to visit a church service? You might think its because you give a portion of your paycheck to a ministry. But if you are a Christian it is because you are Christ-like in your thoughts, attitudes, speech, and behavior. You have seen the error of living for the good life. And you have found the joy of living God's life. You are a witness of

His Kingdom on earth because, and only if, the King has taken up residence within you. If He has, let Him out.

Is it time to re-order your priorities? You can do it, dear one. I know you can. Why? Because even though I cannot be with you right now, He is by virtue of the indwelling presence of His Holy Spirit. Right now. He's waiting. And He will meet with you and fill you up with His love, joy, and peace. He will, day after day, until you are so full it will be impossible to keep Him inside.

Michele and I love you and thank God for allowing us to walk His path together with you.

CHAPTER 7

Surrender

Matthew 10:37-39 "Anyone who loves his father or mother more than me is not worthy of me; anyone who loves his son or daughter more than me is not worthy of me; and anyone who does not take his cross and follow me is not worthy of me. Whoever finds his life will lose it, and whoever loses his life for my sake will find it.

Michele and I are often encouraging people to resist the urge to make life with God more difficult than it needs to be. Jesus has been my role model in this for more than 20 years now, my how time flies! I truly believe many Christians are stressed because they are confused about the subject of surrender.

Jesus said, give it up, lay it down, parents, children, houses etc. He meant that we should get our priorities in order. His Kingdom business comes first, then life on earth. Our first priority in Kingdom business is developing our relationship with Him. It is from this new platform that we can address all the issues of life on earth more successfully.

When this "first things first" perspective is in place He can use us in truly wonderfully miraculous and personally fulfilling ways to conduct Kingdom business on the earth. At the same time He promised to give us so much more to offer those other people and things we have surrendered to Him.

But balance must be maintained here. Jesus means to surrender (forsake) those things if they are causing you to neglect or compromise the Kingdom life-style. If they are competing against God's will for your life. If they threaten to displace God in your life.

"Seek first the Kingdom of God and His righteousness and all these things will be added to you."

Kingdom surrender begins when we recognize the value of living in harmony with God. Kingdom business should be first regardless of the impact that lifestyle has on those who would demand we continue to live with them as they demand. Selfish insensitivity or toxic co-dependency is the theme of life unless we know God personally through the indwelling of His Spirit. The benefits of life with God are realized increasingly as we reject anything that interferes with it.

I believe many Christians live well below God's expectations for them because they never learn, or simply refuse, to surrender pre-redemption secular mindsets in favor of the sacred. Typically this error is made if new believers do not grow in their relationship with Him through reading His Word. Since they never learn the value and joy of reading the Scripture they are forced, by default, to rely on others to interpret it for them. Perhaps this is why there is so much confusion and conflict within the body of Christ.

However, the call to Christ-like surrender does not propose that born-again spirit-filled husbands and fathers are commissioned to neglect wives and children for the purposes of fulfilling God's call to ministry! Nothing could be further from the character of God our Father.

Those who are confused on the subject of surrender are because they have not spent enough personal time with God. So, mistakenly thinking they know Him intimately, they run out to do His will in the earth while neglecting to do His will in their home! Perhaps, and to give them the benefit of the doubt, they have confused God's role with their own. They somehow think they must be "out there" doing His work for Him, that He cannot run the world without their help. They may think it is a godly attribute to neglect their family for the purpose of ministry. It is such a secular mind-set which positions man, instead of God, as the central figure of the Universe!

A husband told me recently, "I just want to fulfill God's will for my life." He was speaking of his ministry gifting, but he was implying that to do so meant his wife and children might feel neglected because of the demands of the ministry. I disagree. In fact, according to Scripture each man is called to love and serve God by loving and serving his wife sacrificially. Each man is cautioned to avoid causing his children to be frustrated by his insensitive, impatient treatment of them. The truth might be, he feels more valued by his work in the outside world than he does inside his home. Ministry to others (which is casual, not intimate) is easier, more gratifying, more appreciated, etc. Many of those called to five-fold ministry make this mistake.

I wonder how many men reading this were neglected or mistreated by their fathers? And how many of those neglected sons now neglect their wives, sons and daughters, because they are too busy giving their time and energy to other people and things that demand their attention? We certainly expect this from people who would not claim to know God. The secular corporate world is built upon this foundation! Sacrifice all for the good of the "Company."

I wonder how many Christians are actually fearful of surrendering their lives, plans, careers and hence their futures, to God's plan for them? And I wonder how much better the world would be if more humans, made in the image and likeness of God, did so? Why do we settle for so little, when God has provided so much?

The spiritual world we see so little of is the more important world because the spirit world has such tremendous impact on the physical world. My experience with the Word and with the hundreds we have counseled has taught me that too many Christians have no understanding of this concept. Perhaps this is because it is only as we focus our attention on Him over an extended period of time that we discover this reality.

True Christ-likeness is more concerned with the spirit realm, interacting there, in personal lifestyle and ministry intent, because only the Holy Spirit can provide an accurate and balanced perspective of the difference between the two. Jesus claimed to do only what He saw the Father do, and to say, only what He heard the Father say. We would agree He was in touch with God.

Religious minded people think they appear to be Christians to the outside world. But if they do not spend time interacting with The Spirit of God, and the Word of God, to be empowered to be effective witnesses, they probably are not. How much time do you spend reading the Word? How much time do you spend in prayer? Your understanding of God and His plan for the family of man is perhaps the most basic of all Christian disciplines

The confusion of surrender might be because Christians are taught to get saved and be witnesses. However, Jesus said, "… wait until the Holy Spirit comes upon you to be my witnesses." And, "If you continue in My Word you'll be my disciples indeed and you will know the Truth and the truth will set you free." The coming of the Holy Spirit was not a one time historical event that somehow affected every believer since. It is an event that each believer must experience just as those present in Jerusalem in 33AD did. Each believer has been given access to the Holy Spirit.

155

The Holy Spirit is available now for each one. But we cannot assume because He is available everywhere all the time that each believer has surrendered to inner working of His indwelling presence. To think this is to assume everyone who prays the "sinner's prayer" is submitted to the Lordship of Jesus Lord. Oh, that it was true!

I find many immature Christians try to portray themselves to be something they are not. And the world (physical and spiritual) ridicules them. Unknowingly, by lack of interaction with the Holy Spirit, they profess a "form of godliness but deny its power," Just as Paul said they would. They may call Jesus Lord and Savior but do not know His Word, do not engage in prayer, and do not possess true faith. They may feed the hungry, cloth the naked, and care for widows or orphans. But their marriages fail due to lack of Christ likeness. Their children and spouses feel unloved, neglected, and unwanted. Their dedication to the "ministry" may be the source of their identity and yet the world might rightly ask them, "Who do you think you are?"

To love and serve God in a balanced way men must spend time with God, allowing the Holy Spirit to build Christ-like character into them. According to the apostle Paul, they must be transformed by the renewing of their minds, so they can present their bodies as living sacrifices, which is their reasonable service to God. How can anyone expect to surrender to God's will if that person does not know God's will. And how can a man who spends the majority of his time estranged from God, due to the stressful demands of career, secular or sacred, believe he knows God? Could this be a case of having the cart in front of the horse? And could this be the reason his life is so stressful? And could these be the ones Jesus referred to in Matthew chapter 7?

Be encouraged dear one, the Holy Spirit is with you and in you. He is your teacher. He is the One Jesus said would "take the things of mine and disclose them to you." He patiently awaits your visit, and your surrender. Will you come? Today? We pray for you, that His love for you will draw you in again.

CHAPTER 8

Obedience

If you obey my commands, you will remain in my love, just as I have obeyed my Father's commands and remain in his love. John 15:10

The primary goal of the born-again child of God is to learn to love God. No other pursuit can bring the child closer to his Father. And no other action will bring the child more joy. It was out of His great love for His wayward children that He reconciled them to Himself. Even though they did not love Him, He loved them so much that He came to Earth and suffered the penalty of death so they could be reunited with Him.

The secondary purpose of learning to love God is to demonstrate that love to others. The primary way we love God and others is by serving them. Jesus said, "The greatest in the kingdom is a servant of all."

However, as beneficial as loving God is, it is not something people do well. Too often the child of God tries to obey the rules God has given for holy living with the hope that doing so will bring blessings into his life. He mistakenly thinks by doing so he will receive smiles from God, and accolades from others. Yet how easily frustrated one becomes when this attempt to please God through obedience does not produce a higher quality of life. The higher life is realized only as we draw nearer to God and are touched by His affirming presence on a regular basis.

The truth is, attempting to obey God out of a sense of obligation or mere duty will never satisfy the child. Neither does it satisfy God. For God loves a cheerful giver. God has called His child to a life much more rewarding than conscientious performance can bring. He has called His child to a life of loving fellowship with Him.

Fellowship is always God's goal for you. Throughout Scripture, from Genesis through the Revelation, God calls men to enter into the fellowship with Him made available to them by His love. This is the true relationship He seeks with His highest and best creation.

Man is the only entity in the Universe made in God's image and after His likeness. There can be no created thing more significant than that which is made in His image. And it is this very one, man, whom God desires to know Him through intimate relationship. Jesus Christ walked this earth as a man of flesh and bones. And His life was a demonstration of right relationship with God. When a man comes to God through His Son's sacrifice, he becomes God's child, just as Jesus is. The new man is not a servant in His house, he is not His slave, His grandchild, or His step-child. A born again Christian is God's son or daughter, and a joint heir with Jesus Christ. Not a slave in His stable but a child at His table.

If as a child of God you miss this point, that above all else, God desires to enjoy a loving relationship with His child, you will become a frustrated drone, a tired worker in the vineyard, an unknown laborer in the King's garden. This is so far away from His desire for you. Your Heavenly Father, the King of the Universe, desires that you, His child, would take your place at His table, in the dining hall. He has a chair there, with your name inscribed in gold leaf. That chair is reserved for you. No one sits there but you. If you are not there, the chair is empty. When He surveys the great hall He sees all of His children gathered around the table. They number in the millions. They have come from every culture on earth and from every century since the dawn of time. Yet, if you are not there, He misses you.

Will you come in today? Will you put away all the other commitments you have made? Will you postpone all those appointments that seemed so important when you made them? Will you sit with Him in that quiet room where He waits? What is it that could be more important today than meeting with God? If you come in today He will meet with you. Don't be afraid. He is not like all the others who promise and then forget. He loves you more than you can imagine. You will never truly experience His love unless you learn to sit with Him, rest in Him, and love Him.

When you come to Him, He will welcome you. Sit quietly and He will comfort you and love you like no other one can. His tenderness will heal your aching heart. His gentleness will soothe the tension. His peace will quiet your restless mind. His compassion will calm you. His affirming touch will empower you. You will taste and see how good being with Him truly is. And you will leave feeling you are known by Him, and loved by Him.

Take Me, Lord
Mike Green 1993

Take me, Lord,
into the peace of your presence.
Away from the busy-ness
of life that engulfs me.
Renew me, Lord,
with the love of your kind heart,
as I seek you in the quiet,
there your Spirit will console me.

Take comfort, O my troubled soul
in this sheltered resting place,
where God most holy meets
with man, so rude and vile.
Unshackle these chains of futile acts
that restrict your thoughts and speech,
these bonds that seek the praise of men
and ignore the love of God.

Take me, Lord,
for I long to feel your love
sift from me my hopelessness,
the pride of vain accomplishments.

Take me, Lord,
for so often would I stray.
Be still rebellious heart of flesh
and hear the voice of God.

CHAPTER 9

Forgiveness And Healing

But so that you may know that the Son of Man has authority on earth to forgive sins...." Then he said to the paralytic, "Get up, take your mat and go home." Matthew 9:6

Forgiveness is one of the most powerful healing forces in the universe. As a Christian attempting to overcome the sins of his ancestors, ungodly beliefs, soul hurts, and demonic intrusion it is important to understand the role forgiveness plays in the healing process.

There are two sides to the forgiveness coin. Side one is when I forgive you. Side two is when I ask you to forgive me. Both sides are essential to the process of defeating demons. Remember, forgiveness originated with God. It is a natural part of His flawless character. And it is the rooted in the depth of His love. As you will soon see, from man's perspective, forgiveness is the greatest of all gifts.

The word forgive is made up of two syllables. Both syllables are words which can stand alone; for and give. In the English language for is a common prefix meaning to precede in a line of events or to occur before something else can occur. The second syllable, give, means to transfer, present, or grant.

So what does forgive mean? It means to give something before it is earned, deserved or desired. God, by His grace and mercy, gave us something before we earned, deserved, or desired it. What was it? He gave us a pardon. Therefore, from God's perspective, to be forgiven is to be pardoned. But what does pardon mean? Quite simply it means to remain free of punishment even though punishment is required. Yes, the verdict is in, you are guilty as charged, and yet the highest court has decided you will not be punished for your crimes.

God said, "Your crimes against me are so hideous you must be punished. My holiness requires it and My justice demands it. If I do not punish you I will appear to be imperfect and capricious, like sinful man. And I cannot be less than perfect. I am God. I cannot be other than Who I am or I am not God. Therefore, even though I love you unconditionally, and I do not want you to suffer in any way, I must punish you."

But, I hope you realize, dear one, He did not punish us. He did not give us the punishment our crimes deserved. Instead He pardoned us. He chose to forgive us. He said, "Even though you are guilty I refuse to inflict pain upon you."

So, how did God refuse to do something His holiness and justice demanded and still remain true to Who He is? He did something only He could do. He did the unthinkable! He punished Himself!

Dear friends we cannot begin to understand the magnitude of such an unprecedented event. The truest love which life can offer us will pale in comparison to the incomparable love displayed in this incredible event! God punished Himself for our crimes against Him, so we would not suffer punishment for those crimes! That is why He could pardon us. He went to the cross as our punishment so He could give us a pardon we did not deserve. We err greatly if we believe our crimes against God went unpunished. Salvation is not free! We are not innocent, we are guilty, and we deserve to be punished for our crimes against God. Yet, we have been pardoned because He received the punishment we deserved. The next time one of your children disobeys you, go stand in the corner, put yourself on restriction, or deny yourself some of your adult privileges. If you are innocent and know your wayward child is guilty, choose to punish yourself instead of punishing them, and you may begin to understand the reality of God's incredible love for you!

Side One of the Forgiveness Coin

It is in light of this tremendous truth that God commands us to forgive those who have harmed us

(Matthew 6:12). Forgiving our debtors, or those who trespass against us, is often much easier to say than it is to do. So often we who know we should forgive others, do so without really understanding the full impact of what we are saying. From God's perspective, to forgive someone is to acknowledge their crimes against us and to surrender our desire for them to be punished for those crimes. Therefore, side one of the forgiveness coin states:

"I forgive you by telling you, and God, even though you have hurt me, I do not want you to be punished for hurting me."

And, according to God's definition of forgiveness, by forgiving you I am also declaring my intention to "never again mention your crimes against me to you or to anyone else." Believe me, dear reader, the demons oppressing you know the importance of forgiveness. They know it is critical to the quality of your life with God (Matthew 6:14-15). And the last thing they want you to do is to forgive those who have hurt you.

But, you may ask, "What's in it for me? Why should I forgive someone who has caused me so much pain?" Good question. Yet, healing is what's in it for you. What? Yes, forgiveness empowers you to access the healing power of God. As long as you hold onto anger, resentment, and un-forgiveness, you will hold onto the pain they caused you. Quite often, in Christian circles we are told we must forgive those who offend us. But no one tells us what to do with the hurt we have suffered. However, as we embrace the forgiveness process we also enter the healing process.

The healing God offers us will often remain distant until we sincerely enter the forgiveness process. Why? Because as long as we hang onto anger and resentment toward our offender, demons will continue to remind us of the offenses, hurts, and wounds others have brought upon us. Those hurts may be stored in our soul or spirit, in our heart or our mind. Yes, that mysterious unseen part of you is the storehouse for those hurts as long as you refuse to forgive. And demons will continue to remind you of the offense and pain, over and over again.

Side Two of the Forgiveness Coin

Side two of this valuable coin is the side where I ask you to forgive me. This must also be considered soberly to benefit us as God intends. When I ask you to forgive me I am confessing that I know I have offended you. I know I am guilty of crimes against you and I know I am deserving of punishment. But I do not want to be punished for my crimes. Therefore, I come to you humbly and ask you to grant me a pardon. This is the same thing I should have done to receive God's pardon.

God granted the pardon before I was born. Jesus was the sacrificial lamb slain for my sins, "from the foundation of the world." (Isaiah 53:7, John 1:29, Revelation 13:8). God had forgiven me but I had to appropriate His forgiveness for it to do me any good. Jesus died once for all (Romans 6:10) so no man needs to die unpardoned for his crimes and share the punishment reserved for demons. But each man must confess his sins before God and ask God to forgive him. However, there is an important element of this side of the coin that must be considered here as well. When we ask God or anyone to pardon us for our crimes, we are also declaring our intention to discontinue the offensive behavior. That is why we can ask for the pardon.

God said we must repent to partake of the blessings of Kingdom living (Matthew 3:2). Repentance is not merely feeling bad about doing wrong, it is the deep heart-level desire to do things differently. To ask for a pardon knowing that you are going to continue the offensive behavior is deception and will not benefit you in any way. Why? Because deception is an indication of rebellion, and demonstrates you are still thinking and acting like demons, not like Christ. Demons are deceivers and liars and satan is known in Scripture as the father of lies (John 8:44). God is the source of truth. A person who is deceived usually does not know it. If he knew it he wouldn't be deceived (James 1:26). But deceivers cannot fool God (Psalm 69:5, 1 Corinthians 1:20, Galatians 6:7). And they do not fool, for long, people from whom they are seeking forgiveness.

Currently, in criminal law, a pardon is granted those who have proved by their changed behavior, they have been rehabilitated and that they are no longer a threat to others. In God's Kingdom it is no different. Demons however, would like you to think otherwise.

Summary

In summary remember, before kicking out the demons that are ruining your life you must be ready to forgive those who have or will hurt you, perhaps over and over. When Peter asked Jesus how many times we should forgive, Jesus replied, "Seventy times seven." (Matthew 18:22). This should be a reminder that forgiveness is very important!

From the cross Jesus with His last breath moaned, "Father, forgive them for they do not know what they are doing." This was after they beat him nearly to death, spit on Him, pulled out his hair and beard, crammed a crown of thorns on His head, stripped Him naked and paraded Him through the streets! Additionally He spoke those words after they pounded nails into His wrists and feet and hung Him up like a carcass of butchered meat in the open market. He knew the importance of forgiveness very well indeed. He was born without sin and had resisted the temptation to sin for thirty-three years. To remain sinless even during His last moments of life, on the cross, He had to forgive them for this final injustice! I cannot even imagine such humility!

The pain others have caused you, however, may have been so terrible that you cannot even begin to consider forgiving them. God understands. He really does, and He can handle it. Each case is different because we're all individuals and each of us must heal at our own pace. If you are unable to or are not ready to forgive your offenders, tell God. He can help you. He will even empower you to do so. Maybe today. Maybe tomorrow.

Maybe next week, or next year. But there will come a time in your healing journey, sooner or later, when you will be ready to forgive them. That is the day you will finally slam the door on the demons associating with that particular pain. And you will experience a new refreshing depth of healing. That will be a day of celebration to be sure. Until then pray, asking God to help you move on in your Christian life. Ask Him to empower you to forgive and release others from the payment you believe they owe you. And then thank Him for hearing your prayer and for responding to it. Remember, He is faithful. He can and will help you.

Forgiveness Prayers

If you are ready to do some forgiving you may find the following prayers helpful. Pray them word for word if you like or use your own words.

Forgiving Others: Father, you have made it clear that I must forgive others so I can be forgiven and healed. You require that I forgive so I can receive your forgiveness. I choose now to forgive everyone who has set me up to enter into sin and all who have hurt me in any way. I release them, I let go of all judgments and punishments that I have thought about; I turn all of this and them over to you. Holy Spirit, I thank you for working forgiveness into my life, for granting me the grace I need to help me forgive, and for continuing to enable me to forgive. Thank you, that I now have the basis to receive your forgiveness.

Receiving God's Forgiveness: Father, I have made a decision to forgive all others. I come to you through the shed blood of Jesus and the power of His Cross asking you to forgive me of all of my sins. I acknowledge my sin and I take responsibility for each and every time I have violated your commandments. I ask you to forgive me for the sinful thoughts and plans that have been and are in my heart. Holy Spirit, I thank you for working forgiveness into my life, for healing me, and for cleansing me from all unrighteousness. Thank you Father for restoring me to fellowship with you.

Forgiving Self: Father, because You have forgiven me, I choose to forgive myself now and to release myself from all accusations, judgments, hatred, slander, mistakes, stupidity, and falling short of the mark. I choose to accept myself just as I am, because I know you accept me, and because I know You love me. I expect to begin to like myself. Holy Spirit, I give you permission, and I expect You to do your work of sanctification in me. I embrace fully, and look forward to, your work of transforming me into the image of Christ.

CHAPTER 10

Faith

*"His master replied, 'Well done, good and faithful
servant! You have been faithful with a few things;
I will put you in charge of many things. Come and
share your master's happiness!' Matthew 25:23*

God has given humans a full range of emotions. From
time to time all of us feel sad, mad, bad, and glad.
While what we feel is important, valid, and relevant, our
feelings are not always representative of the Truth. Our
feelings are emotional reactions to our interaction with life.
Our thoughts are intellectual reactions to life. Therefore,
our thoughts and feelings are very often connected. So,
bad or uncomfortable feelings like, failure, frustration,
shame and unworthiness can produce similar thoughts.
And though we should not deny either our feelings or
thoughts, we should pay close attention to the effect
they can have on our faith. Bad, sad, or mad, feelings and
thoughts are very powerful engines of behavior. If we

let bad sad or mad feelings manifest without intellectual control we may make matters worse. If we don't take destructive thoughts captive to the obedience of the Spirit of Christ within us, they will influence our attitude, speech, and behavior. And consequently, our behavior may be incongruous to our witness of life with God. So how do we balance feelings, thoughts, and subsequent behavior with our love of and work for God.

Our walk with God is literally a walk of faith. We cannot see God. We do not hear Him very well either. And when we claim to hear, we all hear something different! And even less often do we sense His tangible presence with us. Yet, through the indwelling presence of the Holy Spirit, He is here. Personal faith is the bridge that enables us to connect with His presence within us. As we begin to hear and feel Him through repeated experience, we grow stronger in the ability to do so. Our faith in God grows as it becomes strengthened by this experience with Him.

Those who desire to know God more than casually, must read His Word and pray. As we read His Word He grants us revelation. Not information, anyone can give us that. But only the Holy Spirit can give us revelation. Revelation is knowledge of God which is made real to us on a very personal level by the Holy Spirit, Spirit to spirit. Revelation is a marvelous thing; it actually transcends our intellect. We cannot know God intellectually. He is beyond our mind's limited ability to comprehend. But as we faithfully seek God's presence in fellowship, the Holy Spirit connects us to the reality of His presence, His love, His wisdom, His power, and His peace.

Therein we discover that wonderfully liberating truth that the joy of the Lord or more accurately, the joyous revelation of our Lord, is the strength we need to live in this confusing, frustrating, violent world. It is this joy we find in His revelation that sustains us when our feelings, our emotional reaction to the physical world, turn sour.

How do we respond then when we experience negative, unproductive, self-destructive, thoughts or feelings? In prayer we must prostrate ourselves before His self-revelation. We humble ourselves, empty ourselves, and speak openly and honestly with Him, just as if He was a friend sitting in the room with us. For truly, whether we discern Him or not, He is not only in the room, He is in us! Whoa! Yes, its true. In His presence, we pour out our complaint (if that is what the situation calls for), and beg Him to help us in our time of need. We do this just as if we were speaking with one another. As we "pray" (speak to and listen to God) He gives us revelation. But the revelation comes as we, "by faith," talk to Him. He reminds us He is Who He said He is. His word teaches us, "Without faith it is impossible to please God, for to come to God we must come believing He is Who He says He is." And, He says He is a rewarder of those who persistently come to Him in, by, or through, faith. The only way they can come.

So then, what is faith? Faith is the conviction in our hearts and minds that reminds us that God is who He says He is, and that He will do what He says He will do, REGARDLESS of circumstances to the contrary. Simply put, to live with this understanding is to live in the Kingdom of God. This is it. Period. We progress in our knowledge of Him and awareness of Him by faith. We experience warm times of fellowship with Him by faith, we receive ALL He has provided for us, by FAITH. That is, by believing He has provided it, and responding with gratitude.

A wise man once remarked, "Faith is nurtured in solitude, strengthened in conflict, and proven in hopelessness." That means we must develop faith in God by rehearsing His truths, found in His Word, in our quiet times of reading and prayer. Then we leave our prayer cell and go out into the world, knowing our faith will be tested time and time again. And as our faith is tested and remains firm, it grows stronger. And when the truly hopeless situation confronts us, (think Shadrach and the boys) our Faith triumphs. For we say "Even if they burn me at the stake, I will continue to believe all God said to be true about Himself, about my place with Him, my future with Him, and this hideous world that surrounds me and threatens to drown me. Everything He said is in fact still true and always will be true."

A Chinese proverb says, "The best revenge is to live a good life." I don't think the philosopher had our walk with God in mind when he said it. But I do see when I am confronted by feelings and thoughts of fear, inadequacy, doubt, confusion, and unworthiness, that the best response is to rehearse the Word of God and go on about my business of loving Him and loving others. My faith in God's self-revealed truth is the fuel that drives my determination. And His reward for my faith is additional revelation.

Confidence is another word for faith. The Scripture teaches us to "come confidently before the throne of grace to receive mercy and obtain grace in our time of need." We come confidently because we know He loves us and He desires to help us. And He has the power to help us. We have faith in Him and in His self-disclosed love.

Therefore, our response to bad, mad, or sad feelings must be twofold. First, we must continue to believe (and declare) that the promised blessings made by God will be fulfilled regardless of the unhappy events which caused the unwanted feelings. Second, and because of number one, we must take action by responding in whatever way He shows us. By responding to our negative thoughts and feelings in this way we will prevent the production of reactions to life that are unhealthy, ungodly, and counter-productive to the highest quality of life in general and especially to the quality of our life with God. And remember the quality of your life is not based on what happens, but how you respond to what happens. And it is also true that the quality of your life is a direct reflection of the quality of your relationship with God.

A faithful Christian is the man or woman who responds to the harsh trials and painful surprises of life confidently, knowing God is the Only trustworthy and Eternal source of truth, peace, and joy. But a faithful Christian is also a work in progress. He is one who has learned from experience and now reacts to life with faith in God. The faithful Christian is a human no longer driven by negative emotions and thoughts. The one filled with faith is one carried over the perilous potholes of life on earth by the wings of love. This is one who has found peace with God. Faith has replaced fear and confidence has displaced doubt. Faith trusts God to be and do all He promised.

So, knowing all of this, what changes are you going to make to the way you respond to life when it does not go as you had planned?

We pray our God and Father will continue to reveal Himself to you as you continue to seek His presence in times of prayer. We pray His love for you will strengthen your faith.

CHAPTER 11

Baptism and Christian Experience

Matthew 3:11 "I baptize you with water for repentance. But after me will come one who is more powerful than I, whose sandals I am not fit to carry. He will baptize you with the Holy Spirit and with fire."

Overview

Another controversial subject among the Christian family is the subject of Baptism. Every denomination, (or is it schism?) in the family seems to have a different view and different application of this "sacrament." And each one believes their view is the right one. Perhaps if we look directly to Scripture for clarity, and without any religious bias, we can understand baptism as our Savior did.

First a definition of the Greek word, baptiso. It means to be immersed in water, as is a newly constructed

181

wooden ship when it slides down the planks and into the water for the first time. But the word is used in a wide variety of applications in Old and New Testament Scripture.

John's (the Baptist) baptism was one of "repentance." (Matthew 3:1-5) People came to him to be baptized as they felt a need, through John's preaching, that they must "get right" with God. John was the for-runner of Jesus. He was preparing the people of the region for the coming of the Messiah. He knew the King was coming, and that many people were not prepared to meet Him. After all, it had been nearly 500 years since God had spoken through the Hebrew prophets, and this time He was going to speak in person!

Jesus was baptized by John in the Jordan River as He was about to begin His ministry years. Did this "save" Him or make Him "right with God?" No. John was opposed to the idea since he knew Jesus was the Messiah! Then what did it accomplish or why did He do it? He did it because as Jesus told John, "Lets do what Dad tells us to do." (Matthew 3:13-15).

In this act we see Jesus making a public show of His determination to consecrate His life to God's ultimate destiny. This then is what baptism originally meant to all Christians who came into God's family during Jesus' time on earth. Baptism was a public demonstration of their heart-felt determination to turn away from an ungodly lifestyle and ungodly thinking, and turn to God. Baptism was an outward display that followed their inward "born again" experience. Nowhere is Scripture does baptism precede or lead to repentance.

Mark 16:16 He who believes and is baptized will be saved; but he who does not believe will be condemned.

Notice in Mark's gospel that baptized follows believes. And that it is not he that is not baptized, that is condemned, but he that does not believe.

Matthew 28:19 Go therefore and make disciples of all the nations, baptizing them in the name of the Father and of the Son and of the Holy Spirit...

Here again we are commissioned to make disciples of people from every nation. If they believe then we baptize them in the unified name off the godhead and teach them to observe (put into practice) everything else that Jesus taught.

Baptism then was a public display of a desire to live with God. Going under the water symbolized, but did not accomplish, the death of our old life, before we met Jesus. And coming up from the water symbolized being, as He was, raised from the dead into a new life.

Romans 6:4 Therefore we were buried with Him through baptism into death, that just as Christ was raised from the dead by the glory of the Father, even so we also should walk in newness of life.

Baptism is a symbol of a changed life. Jesus was resurrected from the dead after the death on the cross. He lives a "glorified" life now, never to return to physical life with all of its limitations. In our baptism we are declaring our intentions to live a life of consecration while on earth. This consecrated life is pursued even though we are immersed in a culture that constantly tempts us to reject the ways of God. Just like the circumcision made without hands was a symbol of the Jewish tradition of actual circumcision, testifying of their connection with God, baptism is a symbol of separation from non-believers. Both declare the believer's decision to be consecrated to God, and to live the "new" life.

Colossians 2:11 In Him you were also circumcised with the circumcision made without hands, by putting off the body of the sins of the flesh, by the circumcision of Christ, 12 buried with Him in baptism, in which you also were raised with Him through faith in the working of God, who raised Him from the dead. 13 And you, being dead in your trespasses and the uncircumcision of your flesh, He has made alive together with Him, having forgiven you all trespasses,

"by putting off the body of sins of the flesh..." You did this, not God. Being convicted by the Holy Spirit's revealed truth of Christ and the cross, you made a decision to put off or put down, or leave behind, your former ungodly, selfish, temporal worldview with its mind-set, attitude, and behavior. This is repentance.

Lets Look at an Example from Scripture.

Acts 18:24 Now a certain Jew named Apollos, born at Alexandria, an eloquent man and mighty in the Scriptures, came to Ephesus. 25 This man had been instructed in the way of the Lord; and being fervent in spirit, he spoke and taught accurately the things of the Lord, though he knew only the baptism of John. 26 So he began to speak boldly in the synagogue. When Aquila and Priscilla heard him, they took him aside and explained to him the way of God more accurately.

Apollos, by name a Greek, having grown up in the modern Egyptian city of Alexandria, had repented, had been baptized, had received some instruction, but needed more. Even though he was zealous to help others repent and consecrate themselves to God, he was a new believer. So Aquila and his wife Priscilla, mature believers from Rome, took him under their wing, and instructed him further. "Though he knew only" the baptism of John, implies there was a lot more for him to know, if he was going to become an effective spokesman for God. He had some accuracy, but he needed more. In other words, his baptism did not automatically accomplish anything supernatural.

Now consider the next section of Scripture. The Hebrews letter was written before the destruction of the temple in Jerusalem in 70AD, but at least 30 years after the resurrection of Christ. Scholars agree it's too difficult to say for sure who wrote it. Most indicate one of Paul's disciples, maybe Apollos or Barnabas, but no one says for sure. There is not enough inherent evidence.

Hebrews 6:1 Therefore, leaving the discussion of the elementary principles of Christ, let us go on to perfection, not laying again the foundation of repentance from dead works and of faith toward God,

2 of the doctrine of baptisms, of laying on of hands, of resurrection of the dead, and of eternal judgment.

The author of this important letter specifically addressed it to Jewish Christians. He was concerned they were considering turning back to Judaism because of the increasing Roman persecution of Christians. They were beginning to doubt the truth that Christ was Messiah.

In this passage the author connects baptism with elementary principles and doctrines. He pleads with his readers to understand the significance of all Christ accomplished for them. In verse 9 he writes, Christ, having been perfected through His sacrifice, "became the author of eternal salvation to all who obey Him."

Christ is the author (or source) of our salvation, not baptism. Our trust must be in Him and His sacrifice, not in our response to it. Salvation is through conviction, repentance, and faith, that is; confidence, in His death and resurrection. I believe He died on the cross for my sins and rose again from the grave, and now sits at the right hand of God making intercession for all of us who come to God through the gateway which is His sacrifice.

In verse 12 the author of Hebrews writes to admonish them, though by this time you ought to be teachers, you need someone to teach you the first principals of the oracles of God; and you have come to need milk and not solid food. 13 For everyone who partakes only of milk is unskilled in the word of righteousness, for he is a babe.

The six elementary (or basic) doctrines mentioned in verse are; 1) repentance, 2) faith, 3) baptism, 4) laying on of hands, 5) resurrection of the dead, and 6) eternal judgment. The author indicates that these should "no-brainers" by now. In effect he is asking, "We don't need to continue to exhort you confidence in these, do we?"

The apostle Peter says it a little differently. But the message is still clear. Baptism though directly linked to repentance and salvation, does not cleanse us but testifies of our good conscience toward God. Baptism is undertaken because God "saved" us, not so He will save us, through the atoning work of Christ on the cross.

1 Peter 3: 21 There is also an antitype which now saves us —baptism (not the removal of the filth of the flesh, but the answer of a good conscience toward God), through the resurrection of Jesus Christ, 22 who has gone into heaven and is at the right hand of God, angels and authorities and powers having been made subject to Him.

Infant Baptism

Nowhere in Scripture are children or infants baptized. Do they need to be? Can their parents come into faith, and into the church, and into the family of God, and leave them out? I doubt it. Is Christ's grace sufficient? I think so. Will they want to be baptized one day? I hope so. Why? For the reasons stated in this discussion; that when they are able to understand the importance of living in God's Kingdom on earth, they will reject the ungodly worldview of their unbelieving peers, and consecrate their lives to knowing God and making Him known.

Jesus warned the people of His day against hindering the children who would come to Him. He did not treat children, under the age of responsibility, as lesser beings. In fact, He used them to illustrate the simplicity of life with God. He saw them as innocent, trusting, and unconcerned by the pressures of the adult world. They were fed, they slept, and they played. They were excited about life and learning and exploring. And they saw Jesus clearly as the One who loved them unconditionally. Perhaps their parents could have learned from Him how to interact with them.

Infant baptism in the modern church is a public demonstration by the parents to the congregation that they will raise their children to know God. They are, not will become, children of God by virtue of their relationship with their parents. As believers these children should be taught God's rules for Kingdom life. It is as adults during the "years of responsibility" that they will ultimately choose to know God further and continue the Christian tradition in their own homes.

Methods of Baptism

No where in Scripture, old or new testament, is it possible to understand (by reading the text) whether one being baptized was totally immersed in or sprinkled with water. Did Jesus lie down in the Jordan River? Did He kneel? How deep was the water? Did John cup some water in His hands? Does it matter? I think not. Why? Because it is the public profession of faith of the one being baptized that is the focus of the event. And if it was really important to God, He would have given us clear instructions, not left us to figure it out or argue which was the right way! God doesn't hide from us. He discloses Himself to us!

What about those who come to faith in desert areas, where there is no water? Are they "saved" if they cannot be baptized? Or in frozen areas? What about the quadriplegic, the leper, the highly contagious, death-bed conversions? Are these to be excluded from eternity with God because they can't be immersed in the church pool, a river, lake, or ocean? And what about the thief on the cross? To him Jesus said, "Today you will be with Me in paradise."

In baptism, as in the Lord's supper, we do this as a memorial to Him. You may be taught to think otherwise. And that's okay. What you believe does not change the truth. Why, not how, you observe the sacrament is the point. By faith, believing you are following Jesus' example, your action is acceptable to God. Immersion, or sprinkling, once a week once a month, or every day; none of that means a thing. It is why, not how, that is important to God. And it is why and not how which should be important to you. Why be baptized? Because you love Jesus, are grateful for Him taking the punishment you deserved, and because you now plan to live your life as He lived His.

Summary

So then, what can we learn about baptism from this discussion? For one, lets not be too critical of those who do it differently. Try to avoid hair-splitting arguments which separate us from His humility and from each other. There are millions who have not heard of Him. Maybe we should focus on them. I believe we should trust that He will take care of everything in the end.

Romans 14:1 Accept him whose faith is weak, without passing judgment on disputable matters.

2 One man's faith allows him to eat everything, but another man, whose faith is weak, eats only vegetables.
3 The man who eats everything must not look down on him who does not, and the man who does not eat everything must not condemn the man who does, for God has accepted him.

1 Timothy 6:3 If anyone teaches otherwise and does not consent to wholesome words, even the words of our Lord Jesus Christ, and to the doctrine which accords with godliness,

4 he is proud, knowing nothing, but is obsessed with disputes and arguments over words, from which come envy, strife, reviling, evil suspicions, 5 useless wranglings of men of corrupt minds and destitute of the truth, who suppose that godliness is a means of gain. From such withdraw yourself.

2 Timothy 2:22 Flee also youthful lusts; but pursue righteousness, faith, love, peace with those who call on the Lord out of a pure heart.

23 But avoid foolish and ignorant disputes, knowing that they generate strife.

24 And a servant of the Lord must not quarrel but be gentle to all, able to teach, patient,

25 in humility correcting those who are in opposition, if God perhaps will grant them repentance, so that they may know the truth,

26 and that they may come to their senses and escape the snare of the devil, having been taken captive by him to do his will.

2 Timothy 3:1 But know this, that in the last days perilous times will come:

2 For men will be lovers of themselves, lovers of money, boasters, proud, blasphemers, disobedient to parents, unthankful, unholy,

3 unloving, unforgiving, slanderers, without self-control, brutal, despisers of good,

4 traitors, headstrong, haughty, lovers of pleasure rather than lovers of God,

5 having a form of godliness but denying its power. And from such people turn away!

6 For of this sort are those who creep into households and make captives of gullible women loaded down with sins, led away by various lusts,

7 always learning and never able to come to the knowledge of the truth.

God is a big powerful Father. He is the best Father ever. And He is the role model for all fathers everywhere. He can and He will take care of everything in the end. Do you find such thoughts of Him reassuring? Or does His power make you fearful? Can you see His mercy and grace, even in the light of His powerful majesty? Can you hear His tender voice calling you to be still, to come close, and to relax and enjoy His wonderful presence? I do hope you can. Remember it is the goodness of God that draws men to repentance. He went to a lot of trouble and endured a lot of pain to reconcile you to Himself. Do you really think He will expel you from His presence if you do something wrong in your effort to worship Him?

I doubt it. Jesus reminded us, "Fear not little flock, it is your Father's good pleasure to give you the Kingdom."

May God, our gracious eternal loving Father, give you wisdom and peace as you continue to pursue His presence, discover His will, and enjoy His love.

CHAPTER 12

The Church Conflict

John 1:11-13 He came to that which was his own, but his own did not receive him. Yet to all who received him, to those who believed in his name, he gave the right to become children of God— children born not of natural descent, nor of human decision or a husband's will, but born of God.

We who name Jesus Christ as Savior and Lord are identified by several different titles. We are at once, children of God, saints, believers, disciples, and members of His body, the Church, of which He is the head. Having received this truth, we are expected to live differently than we did before meeting Him. By virtue of our incredibly amazing "born again" experience we now, and forever will (or should), live with and for the One who died and rose again in our behalf. (2 Corinthians 5:15)

From the first day of creation God the Father has always desired to have a family on earth who manifest His uncompromised truth, His unconditional love, and His absolute authority. Even though Adam's rebellion in the Garden made this very difficult God still has a plan to fulfill His desire for a family. Since Adam's sin God has been concerned for the many born of the rebellious seed and who are in great peril as a result of their ignorance. The primary role of those reconciled to God through Jesus Christ is to share with others the same incomparable love He has revealed to them through the brutal death and glorious resurrection of Christ. We who live safely with God are expected to do so just as Jesus did; empowered by His indwelling Holy Spirit, exercising His authority and demonstrating His wisdom. Pretty simple, isn't it? Therefore, the church is a family of living witnesses, His sons and daughters, who testify by their lifestyle of the unconditional and eternal love of God.

Knowing the above to be true, why is the church experience for so many of His children, so frequently the source of confusion, competition, neglect, abuse, and frustration?

The Body of Christ

There is great debate and conflict among God's children regarding the identity of the "true" or "real" church. Yet simply put, according to Jesus, His church is made up of those whose worthless lives have been rescued by the Spirit disclosed revelation that states, "You are Christ, Son of the Living God," and who, as a result, are surrendered to the Lordship of Christ. (Matthew 16:16-17). Each confessing individual is a unique part of His body by virtue of a connection to the head, Jesus Christ. (Colossians 1:18). Paul chose the metaphor of body and it's various members wisely. Lets look at this metaphorical body in more detail.

The arm is an important part of the body, no more and no less important than the leg or foot or nose or kidney. (1 Corinthians 12:12). It is always an arm, and only an arm. It can't do what the foot does. And the arm is no good at all if it is disconnected from the body. We could go so far as to say the arm is only an arm when it functions as an arm. It cannot function as an arm if it is removed from the body. Paul may have had this idea in mind when he chose the metaphor in the first place. Please note that just as the human body is made of many different parts, each having a designed function, the body of Christ, the church, is made up of many members, each with a unique function. In the human body or the body of Christ each member is distinctly different, yet by working together they comprise the whole, the body. And each body is most healthy when all of it's divergent parts function at their highest capacity in their designed task. And each part is most healthy when it is called upon, and answers the call, to do its part.

So why does Scripture use this body/member concept to our relationship with Christ and the other members of the body of Christ?

This body metaphor implies a functional connection with Christ, the Head. The arm is an arm throughout the twenty-four hour day, seven days a week. That is unless it is removed from the body by accident or surgery. Then it looks like an arm but it does not function in its designed capacity. Wherever the head directs the body, the feet carry it and the arm does its job. In like manner, daily interaction with the Spirit of Christ, who has taken up residence within him, confirms the church member's connection to the head. This connection is a result of the conversion experience which was completed when the individual "repented" of/from his former lifestyle of self-rule, and consequently declared his or her intention to, "no longer live for themselves, but for the One who died and rose again on their behalf," Jesus Christ as Savior, Lord, God, and King. Just as the brain/head directs the movement of the individual members of the human body and the body as a result, so the Holy Spirit of Christ directs the movement of the individual members of His body. Collectively then, these functioning members unified in mission and power, become known as either the church or the body of Christ.

Jesus Christ, as God in human form, came to earth for three reasons. 1. As a penalty for mankind's sins, 2. To teach man about the Kingdom in word and deed, and 3. to empower converted, redeemed, born-again men, His disciples, His children, His church, to teach others the same. Pretty simple. Only as His children consciously, faithfully, and consistently engage in their mission are they recognized as the church.

The Fake Church

A Bible study of the subject of the "church" can be quite fascinating. By doing so, one can discover the truth according to God's word, which is often quite different from the denominational or cultural bias from which many Christians suffer. Have you ever wondered why there are thousands of denominations, all claiming to be the true or genuine church? Have you ever wondered which one is right? Is it possible they are all wrong? And which one does God acknowledge as His family?

Why or how do those who claim to know God get so crazy as to hear from demons and call it hearing from God? Yet, as bizarre as it sounds, isn't this the very thing that happened in the Garden of Eden? How do those who claim to know God believe women are inferior, wealth and health is a sign of righteousness, worship can only be done on Saturday, or Sunday, or without instruments, or piano only? Why do some say baptism is to be done only in the name of Jesus, not in the name of the Father, Son, and the Holy Spirit, or you must be immersed, not sprinkled, you're not born again if you do not get baptized, the communion elements are the actual blood and body of Christ, you must take communion or celebrate the mass every time you get together? And what about the more controversial subjects like biblical prophecy, eschatology, the rapture, millennium, Armageddon, the devil, and so many other teachings, some of which are clearly blasphemous, and that far too many Christians have been taught to believe are essential to salvation? Unfortunately, many Christians believe and suffer with guilt, shame, and condemnation because of these conflicting and at times crazy ideas. Personally, I know many who, trying to submit the kooky doctrine taught by a particular denomination, have actually abandoned their faith in God as a result of the chaos, conflict, or double-standard they encountered as members of Christ's church!

Interestingly, Adam did not attend church, he was not a member of the church, and he was not baptized. Neither was Noah, Abraham, David. Neither was the thief on the cross to whom Jesus said, "Today you will be with Me in paradise." (Luke 23:43). All of those mentioned lived and died and were judged based on their relationship with their Heavenly Father. A relationship which, by the way, was not sinless, but which was founded upon and continued on God's revelation of Himself, and their fearfully reverent reaction to and life-changing respect for His Holy Majesty. Having embraced the graciously given and gloriously liberating truth of the Kingdom why is it that having so many Christians live in constant fear of failure, guilt, and condemnation?

The organized church for the most part, embraced long ago a secular corporate model. From the Edict of Constantine (313AD) onward to the present time this "religious" structure has repeatedly manipulated, controlled and abused members, and non-members, of the body of Christ. Unfortunately, time and again for two thousand years, many of those wounded by it have rejected it, only to later resurrect it. Why can we not see, if the model is wrong once it will be wrong again later? This is as futile as painting a fifteen-year-old car driven 200,000 miles. No matter how brightly it shines with its new paint, it remains an old worn-out car and it should not be trusted! It may run fine, but we should not be surprised if it lets us down when we need it most. Attractive though it may appear, it is unreliable and possibly harmful.

Power and Control

History has proven religious men continually attempt to control other men, religious and non-religious, in the name of the loving kindness of God's mercy and grace. Why?

There are two main reasons for this. The first reason; man is dominated by the fear of experiencing personal pain. Life has taught him, "If I lose control of the situation something bad will happen to me." This fear drives him to protect himself by controlling his interaction with his natural environment, animals and people, to guarantee his personal safety. This control can be passive, by withdrawal and isolation. Think of the shy "wall-flower" individual. But control can be aggressive as well. We all know people who covertly manipulate or overtly direct the behavior of anyone or thing they feel is threatening their comfort.

John Chrysostom, Bishop of Constantinople, circa 400AD, a tender-hearted pastor, was so popular with the people that the officials of the eastern church took him by force and made him Bishop. Talk about control! He caused them to regret their decision however, after he sold the precious art and jewels of the church to feed the widows and orphans! John was quoted as saying, "The desire to control others is the mother of all heresy."

The second reason man controls others is more logical. Large groups of people require control. Even though they may be similar, all people are individuals and hence, since they are driven by fear of personal pain, they are primarily self-centered. Interaction with society teaches us to always be "looking out for #1." Or, "After me, you come first." That's why all societies, all communities, all systems, made up of more than one component have a governing body which enacts laws to guarantee each one is safe from the selfish or destructive behavior others.

The Contrast

According to the bible, a local church gathering was not intended to require a corporate structure or charter. First century believers met in homes. This was the model Jesus demonstrated. I call it the original paradigm. It was the same form of church God demonstrated with Adam. One on one, personal, intimate, and loving. The contrasting model was that of the Jewish "church" system. Remember the scene in the temple, Jesus called what they had produced a …"den of thieves!" (John 2:14).

Jesus began His ministry in the synagogue. The synagogue, this misguided group of religious people claiming to follow God, rejected His claims of oneness with God. He then left that religious form of worship and went into the streets, fields, and homes of His friends, and resurrected the original paradigm. This style of church was certainly different than the former one. And for three years the religious people, the government of the Jewish nation, looked for a way to control Him in order to silence Him. On several occasions these pious religious authorities actually made plans to murder Him for impersonating God!

Crowd Control

Any time large crowds gather for any function order will become an issue. Even in the meeting of the church, if there are too many people gathered to maintain a Christ-centered, and benevolent focus, order must be maintained. Try having more than twenty or so people from divergent social, economic, educational, and ethnic backgrounds show up at your house for a Bible study and watch the chaos that ensues. Most people attending will want to know, "Who's in charge?"

The corporate model is fine for organizing and administrating a large group of individuals. This model places a Founder, President, or CEO as the head of a board of directors who then oversee a board of lesser directors who oversee the working class, who in turn get all the work done. As the organization grows it requires more directors and workers and a bigger budget. But with this model warm personal interaction is not a priority. The message of the leadership is, "We want you as long as you do your job well and with as little personal interaction as possible. But if you rock the boat or are high maintenance, "you're outa here." This "we need your skill, not you," attitude is an important part of the corporate model. The costs and efficiency of the system depends on it. But should it be adopted by the church?

In the case of modern church structure, the administrator, typically known as "shepherd" or "pastor" is obligated to make sure the programs of the church run smoothly so the various needs of the individuals "attending" the church are met. Yet this model can create a fake church. People get lost in the shuffle as the institution grows. It's the system that needs and must get all the attention. The building, the plumbing, the parking lot, the sound system, the nursery, the audio visual system, the bus program, the singles, young married, and retirees, etc. etc. etc. Consequently, the mission of the fake church becomes taking care of the needs of the institution, instead of "feeding my sheep" (John 21:17). This type of system stresses faithful compliance with "our system of church."

The fake church can also give it's members a new identity. In some denominations this is taught outright. In others it is merely implied. This new identity can quickly become a replacement for one's true identity as a disciple of Christ. Loyalty and affection, which should be reserved for Him and for each other, are given instead to the corporate church and its self-indulgent system. In addition, members then identify the church as both the source of their instruction and the demanding recipient of their time, energy, and money. Their commitment to the fake church separates them from other members of the genuine church. How often have we heard, "I'm a Presbyterian." "He's Catholic." "Oh you know those wild Pentecostals!"

Various fake churches produces long illustrious histories filled with stories of faithful founders who walked and talked with God. In most cases there is a cadre of ancestral champions supporting the doctrine. All of this is intended to lend credibility to their history and ensure the righteousness of their doctrine and the loyalty of their members. Unfortunately, this doctrine of self-aggrandizement creates elitism, sectarianism, and religious pride.

Early Church History

It did not take long for the genuine church to become dysfunctional. Just thirty years after Christ's resurrection Paul wrote all of his letters to either correct bad theology or to bring discipline to wayward members of the church. It's interesting to note that even though he was a church member, his time and energy, directed by the Holy Spirit, was given to missionary evangelism. His letters, however, were not written for evangelizing unbelievers, but for instructing and correcting members of the church. And many of them were people he had evangelized earlier!

Lets review some interesting facts regarding the early church. It will shed some much-needed light on the original concept.

While Luke published Acts in about 62 AD, he was writing about events that had occurred 30 years previously. In Acts 2:42, twenty years before Paul's corrective correspondence the believers met thus; "And they continued in the apostles' doctrine, and fellowship, in the breaking of bread, and in prayer." And later, Acts15:22-29, as Paul and Barnabas were being sent to a group of believers, a new church, in Antioch, they took a letter of introduction and instruction from the church leaders in Jerusalem. The instruction? "we should not trouble those from among the gentiles (unbelievers) who are turning to God, (note the phrase unbelievers who are TURNING TO GOD) but write to them to 1. abstain from things polluted by idols, 2. from sexual immorality, 3. from things strangled, 4. and from blood." And the result? "you will do well."

Why such simple instructions? Quite simply the new believers in Antioch, like those in Jerusalem, and like you and me, had experienced an encounter with God. This personal encounter produced in them a deeply felt healthy respect for Him. They had heard and responded to the truth about Jesus, and they desired to live as Jesus lived, as He intended them to do, and as the Holy Spirit (who had empowered Him) empowered them to do. All of this was as the apostles encouraged them to do. Pretty simple, yes? But this concept of life with God far surpasses the concept that Christianity is a religion. Religious people killed Jesus! People who have a personal encounter with the love of God as demonstrated through the cross will desire to live a higher life.

Do you see how incredible your conversion experience truly is? One does not pray a "sinner's prayer" to get right with God. There is no "sinner's prayer" in the Bible. One finds salvation, righteousness, and eternal peace with God by entering into a personal relationship with God by responding to Holy Spirit's revelation of the truth of Jesus Christ. The result is a desire to know and love God, to please God, and to be empowered by His Spirit to demonstrate to others His love in you. There's no formula, like a twelve-step program, a multi-level marketing plan, or a denominational system, that brings or guarantees eternal harmony with God. There is only a life renewed by the indwelling presence of the Holy Spirit of God. The new life of each child of God, each member of the church, is lived for God's glory through a harmonious relationship with Him.

The Apostles

Now for a defining note about the apostles. The first apostles, (Greek; ap/os/tol/os, co-missioners of), were eyewitnesses of Jesus. And while they were indeed blessed among men to have known Him personally, other than that, they were just like you and me. They had a relationship with a real man who walked among them, ate with them, slept with them, partied with them, prayed with them, and taught them the Truth about the King of the Universe, and about life in His Kingdom. These men were referred to as apostles because they were co-missioned by Him to co-mission with Him, teaching others all He had taught them about the King, and the Kingdom. The elders, the next generation of apostles (co-missioners), were (and continue to be) those within the church whose lifestyles evidence mature Christ-like character and responsibility. Elders were the ones that demonstrated they "got it," and hence, they were appointed by the original apostles to help share the good news and help new believers grow in their "relationship with HIM." Again, the idea was a fairly simple one. And the model, as well as the method, was and continues to be effective.

The twelve original apostles were no different than you or me. They were men, made in God's image, who ate, slept, loved, argued, worked, and played. They did not see themselves as more worthy or superior than other men. Their experience with Him made them want to know Him better, love Him more, and tell others about Him. Yet, church history has venerated eleven of these men, making them appear bigger than life, and leading many to believe they were more holy or righteous, more noble or wise than you and me. However, a simple reading of Scripture tells us a different story. In fact one of the twelve was so human he betrayed his savior. Then realizing the horrible thing he had done, he committed suicide!

So, who first capitalized the A in apostle? God or man? That's a good question. Yet, I would imagine it was not God. For it is man, not God, that needs to feel good about his leaders, in order to feel good about himself. Titles are very important to man. Remember, man is fearful of personal pain, therefore, man needs safety and security. For many this means knowing he is following the right guy. That he is going to the right church. That he is hearing the right revelation. And what better way to know these things than to sit under the authority of the right man, the right church, denomination, conference, or fellowship? Yet none of those things alone can give you a relationship with God or build your relationship with God. In fact, many people report the pain they have experienced and the heartache they have suffered when the right man or denomination or church turns on them, betrays their faith and trust, or robs them of their finances. In my twenty-plus years of faithful attendance it has been my experience that modern American church "services" while often entertaining can also be painfully counter-productive to my relationship with God. Members of the church have not been called to find security in knowing the pastor, preacher, priest, bishop, deacon or elder. We have been called to find security in knowing Jesus Christ through a daily interaction with His Holy Spirit. Anything less is religious. And in the end honoring a religious dogma rather than pursuing a relationship with God may prove to have been a waste of time, energy, and money.

The Genuine Church

The fake church meets in ornate, elaborate, costly and boastful buildings. However, Jesus met with His followers in homes, on beaches, hillsides, and in wide-open fields. His message was simple. First, He called all men to repent because the kingdom of God is "at hand," meaning it was available. And second, He told those who were truly repentant to actively and privately love God and quietly and tangibly love others "as you love yourself." (Matthew 6:1-6). The apostles taught everything Jesus taught. Jesus said His disciples (disciplined followers) would be known "to all men" as they demonstrated His kind of compassionate, sacrificial, love for each other.

Jesus used the word, church, two times in the gospel record. Only two. Of the church Jesus had this to say. "Upon this rock I will build my church and the gates of hell will not prevail against it." (Matthew 16:18) Peter was not being identified as the rock or foundation of the church. The solid, rock-like, unshakable foundation upon which JESUS builds and maintains HIS church was Peter's statement that Jesus is "the Christ, the son of the living God." Jesus told Peter he was blessed because he had received the revelation of Jesus' true identity. Peter had received this revelation through the only means by which this revelation is available. That is, by God-ordained revelation. You may have prayed the "sinner's prayer," and still are not living a Christ-centered life. Yet, if you have you received the revelation of the Cross, that revelation has altered your condition, and granted you membership in the church.

The word church comes from the Greek, ekklesia, which means calling out. The word is used to refer to a meeting or gathering of those who are called together by a specific source, and for a specific purpose. So, the church, at least as Jesus understood it and intended it to be known, was a grouping together of people who declared Jesus Christ to be the Son of the Living God. Once again we have here a simple concept, the definition of which needs very little discussion to be understood.

Control

So how did Jesus' idea of the church get so messed up? Why all this stress about which church or denomination or doctrine or style of worship is right or wrong, good or bad?

As mentioned earlier, man has a strong desire born out of fear and insecurity to control his own life for his own protection. This often requires that he control others so they cannot hurt him. Whether the conflict is personal, political, or ethnic, history has proven men have a hard time getting along with each other. The two thousand year history of the fake church is filled with a similar tragedy. The sad but repeated scenario goes like this.

Someone claims to have received revelation from God. As he shares his revelation, others are drawn to it. So together they start a church. It feels good. The one with the revelation becomes important. He assumed leadership of the group because all members agreed he had heard from God. He was placed in charge, "in control." He was gracious to teach those less fortunate, sharing with them his revelation. The idea is once they know what he knows they will act like him. And everyone will be happy.

If others come along who share a new, different, or better revelation, the leader must protect his followers from them. If his followers rebel against his authority, he and the elder board will discipline them. If they remain divisively unrepentant they will be cut off from fellowship with the leader and the rest of his church. Though this is an extreme measure, the leader and the board are forced by conscience to act to prevent the rebellious from leading the rest of his church astray. All of this is right and good because the leader heard from God and because this, ours, his, mine, is the true church. In the best-case scenario this divisive abusive control is done with Christ-like humility in the "name of Jesus." How sad.

And two thousand years after the gloriously incomparable resurrection of Christ the world is filled with disputing members of "His body, the church" all claiming to be the real or true church.

Yet, man seldom looks for God, except when he is in pain. So, as long as things are going reasonably well for him in the church he is happy. Yet when the abuse or control becomes too much, he finds himself in a dilemma. Now the very thing and those he trusted to make him feel comfortable about his religious life are causing him discomfort. What to do? Hopefully, if push comes to shove, the uncomfortable disciple will cry out to God.

And every time, God will respond because He loves his children. He never tires of responding to cries for help. His goal is always the same; to heal man of his shame and guilt, and fear, and to protect man from his need to either control, or to be controlled by others. Only through God's intervention can man get reconnected to God. But even redeemed man is a funny guy. He has a tendency to mess things up, even God's intervention. As soon as man begins to feel pretty good about himself again, and begins to hear from God, he soon slides back into egotism, exalts his self-ordained security, rejects God's authority, and begins to promote his perspective as if it belongs to God.

However, I am happy to report, from my reading of Scripture, there is another wonderful theme. No matter how badly man messes up God's plan, controls and abuses God's people, and tramples the blood of Jesus under the oppressive heel of ecumenical insecurity and fear, God is always looking for man to redeem him. Consider the following from Genesis to Revelation. Genesis 3:8-9, "Adam where are you?" Isaiah 1:18, "Come let us reason together." Matthew 11:28, "Come to me all you who are weary and heavy laden and I will give you rest." Revelation 3:20, "Behold I stand at the door and knock."

The Current Church

Currently the real church is no different than it has been for centuries. Those who love God because of His revelation of Jesus Christ go quietly about the earth sharing His love with others. This they do so in spite of where they attend or if they attend weekly religious services. They may participate in communion, celebrate the mass, pray or not pray in tongues. Yet, despite their conflicting opinions about the sacraments, the Sabbath, and what it takes or what it means to be a Christian they share a common experience. Each one has encountered the love of God in such a profoundly personal way that they are compelled to demonstrate His love to others. And this alone makes them the church.

God desires so much more for us than dogmatic church attendance and doctrinal obedience. He desires that we know Him and enjoy Him by living in community with

Him. He has called us to Himself first and foremost. If we respond, run to Him, thanking and praising Him for His indescribable gift we do so because we are members of His church, functioning parts of His body, and children in His household.

The fake church has many more rules to follow. It would appear the Holy Spirit's indwelling presence is not powerful enough for to make disciples. If you listen very long usually you will hear three major themes promoted and repeated by most corporate churches. 1) What God expects you to do. 2) What God will do for you if you do what you are told, and what He will do to you if you disobey Him. 3) How you can be a blessing to our church. At best these instructions are a bit elementary, and at worst they manipulate and control their members through fear.

I have enjoyed an exciting Christian life. Over the last twenty-four years I have attended many, many churches. Preached in some, taught in others. I have visited Pentecostal, Charismatic, Anglican, Methodist, Charismatic Catholic, inter-denominational and non-denominational churches. I spent six years as a Christian college student and five years as a Christian college teacher, and I have many pastors and teachers as my friends. I have dialogued with proponents who by their own disclosure were of the tongues camp, the faith camp, the river camp, the refreshing, the second wave, the prophetic, the apostolic, the liturgical, the evangelical, the Vineyard, AG, PHC, PCA, UMC, and SBC. I have studied the writings of those from Colorado Springs, Pasadena, Kansas City, Chicago, Charlotte, Oxford, The

Vatican, and Toronto. I have worshipped to the music of 2nd Chapter of Acts, Phil Driscoll, Hill Songs, Matt Redman, La Mar Boschman, Integrity, Don Potter, Terry Clark and Terry Macalmon. And I have listened to the teaching of Hayford, Benny, Rob, Kim, TD, Crefloe, Paula, Copeland, Hagin, Hagee, Meyers, Oral, Richard, Van Impe, Lindsey, Jeffrey, Hamon, and Robertson. And read Kenyon, Lake, Tozer, Henry, Spurgeon, Stott, Packer, Williams and Sproul. And good or bad, right or wrong, simple or profound, none of these folks have given me the joy and pleasure, the peace and contentment, the empowerment and conviction that I have found in my personal study of God's Word, and my daily discipline of prayer and worship.

I believe the Word of God, the Bible, is the most priceless treasure in mankind's history. I also believe the fear, confusion, deception, and abusive control, experienced by far too many Christians is directly tied to the neglect of the most elementary and necessary of all Christian disciplines; personal Bible study. Wounded, confused, deceived Christians suffer unnecessarily due to a lack of personal exploration of the Word of God. Yet how can the faithful disciple expect to accurately assess what others say about God, Jesus, and the Holy Spirit, unless he reads the Word of God for himself?

Resolving the Conflict

As an ordained minister and Christian counselor I have listened for twenty-plus years to hundreds of sincere Christians tell their sad stories of church related control, neglect, and abuse. How they were manipulated, controlled, rejected, and lied to and about, by pastors, teachers, preachers, evangelists, apostles and prophets. Over and over they have said things like, "If it's this bad in the church where can I go for help?" And "I feel guilty about not being there on Sunday but that feels better than the way I felt when I was mistreated by the people in authority."

It would appear the church has assumed the identity of the unredeemed world. Control, manipulation, abuse, deception, denial, competition, co-dependency, divorce, and sexual harassment and abuse are as prevalent in the church as they are in the un-churched world. Churches and their administrators, world-wide, claim Christ-likeness, and yet are ego-centric, racist, elitist, sectarian, divisive, abusive, and in some parts of the world, even violently combative.

If things are this bad, what can one do? Is the solution to abandon the concept of corporate fellowship? To avoid further personal pain and humiliation must we forsake the apostles' teaching, breaking of bread, worship and prayer? Some might think so. But I say, no, of course not. The body of Christ is alive and well, available and safe. But there are many misguided impostors out there. And as Paul cautioned we must, "See then that you walk circumspectly, not as fools but as wise, redeeming the time, because the days are evil" (Ephesians 5:15-16).

There are many mature Spirit led Christian brothers and sisters attending corporate church meetings all over the globe who can love us with Christ's love. But the secular corporate model in which they dwell can make them difficult to find.

The solution to the dilemma is simple although not always easy or comfortable. First, each Christian must decide if, where, or how he/she is in the conflict. To help you do so consider the questions below and answer them humbly and honestly.

1. Am I a member of my church or a member of the church?

2. Am I a functioning member of the body of Christ?

3. What is my purpose for membership in either of these two conflicting churches?

4. Am I growing in my relationship with Christ?

5. Do I feel personally connected to Him more now than I did when I first met Him?

6. Is He a real and daily part of my lifestyle?

7. Is His will for me clear to me as I travel the pot-holed road of life?

And then ask yourself some questions about your church experience.

1. Am I happy with my interaction with the people I call my church family?

2. Do I feel loved and accepted by my church family?

3. Am I treated well, affirmed, and encouraged by those elders to whom I submit?

4. Do I look forward to meeting with and being in their presence again this week?

5. Do I enjoy the freedom to explore, discover, and grow spiritually closer to God?

Each disciple must find a balance in the conflict between my church and the church. Being a member of my church, or any church, does not make me a Christian. Attending services at my church every time the door is open does not mean I am a member of the church. Nor does such loyalty earn for me right standing with God. And not attending weekly services does not make me a "rebellious back-slider" who is ignorant of God and His plan for the church and who needs a firm application of godly correction or adjustment. It's your awareness of Christ not your attendance at a meeting that declares your membership in His church.

You can hold membership in the largest congregation or most unchristian church in your city or state and still love God with all your heart, soul, and strength. And you can worship in the most reverent church every Sunday and still be personally offensive to God because you are not submitted to the Lordship of Christ. But you had better know for sure which group you belong to. Your eternal future will depend on it.

If, however, the church you attend and give you money and time to is not a warm fellowship of like-minded disciples of Christ, you might need to seek the Lord's will. You might be called to speak out. Then again you might find it's time to move on. Your relationship with God will not suffer as long as you continue to read His Word and pray, and seek fellowship with those who do the same. Remember, the One who called you is faithful. He is your Lord, Savior, Teacher, and He is available to you right now right where you sit. He has taken up residence within you.

The Elders

If you desire the genuine church experience, look for an elder in the church to mentor you in the faith. An elder is one who demonstrates a kind, gentle, humble Christ-like attitude, and who has a happy well adjusted out look on life. It is also important that he/she possess the wisdom and the track record of one who has helped others along the way. An elder will encourage you, affirm you, instruct you, and model for you true discipleship. He will be quick to compliment and slow to criticize you. He will be as aware of his own weaknesses and failures as he is aware of yours. And He will always speak highly and often of our wonderful loving heavenly Father, Jesus Christ and His Word, and the ever present availability of the Holy Spirit.

Be wary of those "elders" offering to help you complain about all the bad things going on in the church. Be careful also if they have a grudge against the church or are still noticeably angry, unforgiving, or resentful of those in leadership. A servant's heart and humility are two very important Christian virtues demonstrated by elders.

And to those who are elders in the body as described above I say, seek those among your church who desire to know Him more. Bless them with fellowship, the breaking of bread (both a real meal and the communion meal), and prayer, in your home. Show them there are those who know Jesus personally and serve Him in loving submission, by loving those around them. Discuss their needs and pray for them. Bless them as others ahead of you on the path have blessed you. Inspire the new ones and the weak ones to get to know the love of our wonderful heavenly Father, through disciplined times of prayer and Scripture study.

Personally Speaking

As I write this essay I have been on a sabbatical of sorts for six months. Burnt out after twenty-plus years of non-stop counseling ministry, my lovely bride, Michele, and I had to "punch out" to get some much-needed rest. I spent my time in the most enjoyable study of the Word I have had in many years. And oh the thrill my study brought! Oh the nearness of my Savior! At times I felt guilty for feeling so close to God. Several times my nearness to Him produced in me a refreshing reverential fear.

Words cannot do justice to the experience. There are times when my attempt to explain what I see of God is pointless. My limited skill with the human language cannot capture Him. When I get in close to Him all my preconceived notions become dust before His refreshing wind. So much of what I thought was so important becomes pig food. My self-righteous concept of God is shattered into millions of tiny bits again and again. At one moment I feel I am standing on a concrete pad of revelation only to find it wiped away by His one simple, tiny correction that leaves me breathlessly dangling in mid-air, anticipating certain destruction, totally dependent upon Him for help, for rescue, for my next breath, for life itself.

Twenty-two years ago, as Michele and I were just beginning this journey with God, He said two things to me that I have always remembered.

1. You can have as much of me as you want. But you'll never have any more than that.

2. There are no shortcuts on the road to Christian maturity."

Over the years I have been led astray many times by well meaning teachers, pastors, elders, deacons, apostles, prophets, et al. I was confused by their ideas primarily because I lacked experience with Him. Those who are deceived do not know it. And only as He gives revelation, as He turns on His light, do I see my error of putting any teacher, any teaching, or doctrine, or style of worship in His place in my life. Yes, I have those whom I trust for their understanding of the word. I am not a rebellious egocentric. Nor do I believe I have the final understanding on any Biblical subject, including the one I write about now. I am a student, still learning. I am enjoying the process mainly because I enjoy time alone with my Teacher.

When confronted by a new revelation belonging to someone else I go to the word of God, the Bible, and to my prayer closet. I read what's written and believe it is obvious and true, not shrouded in mystery. And I am reluctant to believe anything that is not clearly harmonious with the simple truth of the Word. I find most disputes among Christians have nothing to do with enhancing their relationship with God. Quite often those disputes are merely the meowing of misinformed and fearful men who desire either to appear intelligent or righteous, or even worse, to simply control others for personal advancement.

All His children should know He is the dad, we are the kids. He is in control, even when we think we are. Peace for me rests in knowing He is in control. I bask in the freedom that His love lavishes upon me. I sleep easy every night knowing God is in His heaven and nothing escapes His notice. Scripture tells me He surveys the earth to and fro, "to strongly support those whose hearts are completely His." As His loving gaze falls upon me I know I am a welcomed son in His family, a functioning part of His body, and an eternal member of His church.

I trust dear one you will feel His love for you every day regardless of where within the family of God you choose to fellowship.

CHAPTER 13

The Forsaking Dilemma

*For where two or three come together in my name,
there am I with them" (Matthew 18:20).*

B efore we begin this discussion I wish to remind you
of something very important. You should know this
about me by now, but I want to make sure you know it.
I can only give you my opinion on any subject. I read
and study diligently, and daily. I love Jesus and I treasure
His Word. It is the greatest treasure I own next to my
relationship with Him. I search the Scriptures, and love
doing it. I thank God for calling me to this vocation,
knowing His Word and helping others know it as well.
But as enthusiastic as I am, after more than twenty years
of study, I know I do not have the final word on the
Word. I am a student. I am still learning. And as any
other self-conscious student knows by virtue of his on-
going studies, I do not know everything there is to know

about anything. So, as I give you my opinion on any subject please remember that opinion is based upon my current understanding. It is certainly subject to on-going modifications. So, be advised.

I do not want you to accept my opinion as final. I give it to you to encourage you to be strong in your faith. I expect you to be challenged to study for yourself. I am a teacher. That is what God has called and apparently gifted me to do. For many years my motto has been, "Read to learn and write to teach." And my prayer has been, "Show me your will, Lord, and empower me by Your Spirit to do it."

I do not mind teaching others and then later finding I was wrong. I see this as the normal process of learning. What I know today and believe to be true can be much different than what I believed last year. And for me such is to be expected and it's okay. Why? Because I have found as long as I teach with this attitude, I am not going to intentionally harm anyone with my teaching. I believe the one flaw among many that makes me most unlike God is that I do not know everything and especially that I do not know the future. Thus, I place great confidence and find true peace in His omnipresent omniscience.

The focus of my teaching is to reveal the majesty of God, Jesus Christ, and the Holy Spirit. My search is one of devotional passion. My purpose is that you will know them more intimately and love them more passionately. I endeavor to make Him known so all can love Him more. It is the filter through which passes all my effort. Therefore, the goal of my interpretation or discussion is always to this end. I avoid endless disputes, arguments, and hair-splitting of Scripture. I leave that to the scholars who are much more inclined to do so and certainly much more capable than me.

The Forsaking Dilemma

Now, for some thoughts on the "forsaking" dilemma. More than a few Christians have told me stories of being scolded for failing to attend "church meetings." It seems those in leadership "wondered where you were last Sunday, because you were not here with us." I have heard the guilty parties tell me that no one from the church phoned them with concern for their welfare as a result of their absence. But they did make a point to scold the truants when they returned. Interesting, huh?

In other cases Christians were told they were in sin, or being rebellious, since they broke the command to "not forsake the fellowship." As they are in rebellion to God they will be punished for this sin. I hope this is not your case. If it is your case I offer this article to correct the misuse of the Scripture to make one feel guilty for failing to appear.

To begin our discussion we must look at Hebrews 10:24, since this is the verse that church leaders most often use to make you feel guilty for your truancy. But before we begin let's remember some important rules for accurate exegesis. First, as you read Scripture always interpret it as literally as possible. It was written to inform you, not to shroud the majesty of God in mystery. Next,

225

always read a particular verse in the context of verses that precede and follow it. And finally, search the Bible to find other Scripture to support the concept or subject being discussed. Following these three rules will help avoid proof-texting and other bias. I study from The Spirit Filled Life Bible, which is the New King James translation. You may use your favorite as well. For the most part and with only relatively minor conflicts all convey the same message.

10:24 And let us consider one another to stir up love and good works, not forsaking the assembly of ourselves together, as is the manner of some, but exhorting one another, and so much more as you see the Day approaching.

The Message in Context

First the context. The letter is written to Hebrews who have become believers. It is written before the destruction of the temple in 70AD. It is written to address their fear that they may have made a mistake coming to faith in Jesus. This fear is growing because of the persecution of Christians, which is also growing throughout the Roman controlled Middle East. The theme of the letter is the supremacy of Christ, as sacrifice and priest. Over and over the writer uses the word, better, to describe Christ and the good news of the gospel. Summarizing we can say, the letter was written to encourage new believers to continue to believe Jesus Christ is truly who God says He is.

Hebrews chapter ten addresses the contrast between the limitations of the Law to remove sin and its eventual punishment, and Christ who removes the guilt of sin and the required punishment completely. From verse 11 through verse 18 God reminds believers of the supremacy of Christ's sacrifice and concludes with, "Their sins and their lawless deeds I will remember no more." And "Now where there is remission (forgiveness) of these there is no longer an offering for sin (required). The parenthesis is mine.

Verse 19 begins with the important word, therefore. My paraphrase would render it; "So brothers, since Jesus Christ removed the guilt and punishment from sin and which could have prevented us from enjoying the wonderful presence of God, lets go into His Holy Presence with confidence, and continue to believe He who promised to forgive us, has forgiven us, and guaranteed us eternal joy with Him, because He is faithful." Wow! How much more liberating can this good news be?

Now in the verses in question, 23-25, we have four major encouragements, all based upon the supremacy of Christ's sacrifice, and God's promise not to punish us or deny us access to His wonderful presence. As believers living in a culture that is hostile to our faith we are encouraged:

1. To hold fast our confession
2. To stir up love and good works
3. To continue in fellowship and in our faith
4. To exhort one another

If you have felt guilty for not attending "church meetings," notice first of all there is nothing even remotely suggestive of a command here. Thus there is no command that can be broken. So it cannot be implied from the plain meaning of this verse that there is a command that if broken will bring retribution from God. The whole passage, verses 11-25, encourages discouraged believers wavering in their faith in the face of real persecution to cling to the grace, forgiveness, and promise of God. The entrance into God's presence for those who believe is guaranteed by His sacrifice and His faithfulness, therefore, "keep the faith, brother and sister."

Clarifying the Confusion

So, why do well-meaning Christian leaders teach us that this passage is a warning to those who break the command to meet together on a regular, once weekly, twice weekly, monthly or daily basis? And my answer must be, "I don't know, you would have to ask the one making the statement." But I am sure any answer or support will be culturally or denominationally biased.

Notice Matthew Henry's comment. On verse 25 Henry writes: "Even in those times there were some that forsook these meetings. The communion of saints is a great help and privilege and a good means of steadiness and perseverance. To exhort one another, to watch over one another, and be jealous for one another and ourselves with a godly jealousy. This would be the best friendship."

I agree, regular meetings with Christians of like mind will greatly assist you in maintaining your relationship with God. After all, it's an ungodly jungle out there. As a Christian you are an alien, a foreigner, a peculiar people. And the secular world will not understand you, and just might hate you and try to destroy your faith. And you will certainly be badgered by the demons that work against anything that pertains to the truth of Jesus Christ. Consequently Christians should meet together for the four reasons stated in the text of this passage and listed above.

To extend the meaning of this passage to imply impending judgment for breaking a command has no basis whatsoever.

However, the confusion caused by this interpretation from those who want you to continue to fellowship with them or their church could be related to the verses following verse 25.

Verse 26 For if we sin willfully after we have received the knowledge of the truth, there no longer remains a sacrifice for sins.

However, this verse is not connected to verse 25 alone, but to the entire subject being discussed in Chapter 10. Verses 19-25 speak of the personal benefits afforded us by the sacrifice. And verse 26 reconnects the reader with verse 18 to continue to discussion. Read verse 18, Now where there is remission of these there is no longer an offering for sin. Followed by verse 26, For if we sin willfully after we have received the knowledge of the truth, there no longer remains a sacrifice for sins.

In view of the plain language of the text, to connect not forsaking the assembly with a punishable command is an exegetical stretch. The passage is about God's wonderful grace, not His punishable commands.

Again, the entire chapter taken in context presents a contrast between the limitations of sacrifices under the Law and the supremacy of God's grace through the sacrifice of Christ. The encouragement is meant to help terrified persecuted first century Jewish Christians to continue to hold on to the promises of God made through Christ in the face of a culture that has already destroyed many of them in the Roman Coliseum. The exhortation to maintain, not forsake, fellowship is for protection against the faith-smashing influence of the unbelieving world. Not for fear of breaking a punishable command or losing one's right standing with God. Hence, there is no hint of a command to assemble or a punishment for refusing to assemble.

To further support this interpretation read chapter eleven, the faith chapter. Unwavering confidence in the God that promised is our assurance of eternal joy. Faith in Christ's sacrificial love and God's incredible grace is our strongest weapon against the enemies of God. Faith demonstrated in the face of persecution and even death, dismemberment, and burning, is the requirement for entrance into God's eternal rest. The martyrs knew this. I pray I never experience it.

The Fellowship Factor

So then, what about the fellowship factor? Is it required? And what does it look like? My Spirit-filled Life Bible (the notes of which I recommend highly) refers the Hebrews 10:25 verse to Acts 2:42, which states:

"And they (the believers) continued steadfastly in;
1. The apostle's doctrine,
2. Fellowship,
3. In the breaking of bread,
4. And in prayers."

1. The apostle's doctrine refers to their disclosure of Christ as Savior, Lord, and God in the flesh. And the word apostle is not capitalized. Apostle, ap-os-tol-os, means one who is co-missioned by someone else. It means one who is sent with a specific message and authority. It is often taught to mean the apostles, and primarily those who were among the original 12, minus Judas, and which were eyewitnesses of Jesus. In which case it is used in a limited sense, referring only to those who saw Jesus personally, and who were commissioned by Him to write Scripture and rule the church with undisputable authority.

In a general sense, apostle can mean anyone who is commissioned by someone in authority to take his message to others. Currently among certain tribes of the church there is a resurgence of the use of the word. Apostle is used by those adhering to the current teachings of the new Prophetic/Apostolic arm of the church.

In a limited sense apostle is used to qualify the Pope. That tradition teaches only those descended from Peter by the laying on of hands, Peter being the first in a long line of Apostles, can rightly be given the office and title of Apostle. Yet there is certainly room for debate over the meaning of Jesus' declaration in Matthew 16:17,18;

"Blessed are you Simon Bar Jonah for flesh and blood has not revealed this to you but My Father who is in heaven. And also I say that you are Peter, and on this rock I will build my church and the gates of hell shall not prevail against it."

However, Paul did refer to himself as the last of the apostles. In the context of this verse (Acts 2:42) it means the ones who were commissioned by Jesus to lead the early Christian movement. The movement began with the coming of the Holy Spirit and the preaching of Peter on the day of Pentecost, and is the message found in Acts chapter 2. My point is, the apostles' doctrine (which means instruction) was the message of Jesus Christ as Peter preached it that day (Acts 2) and which he had declared to Jesus in Matthew 16:16, "You are the Christ, the Son of the Living God."

Peter's declaration, not Peter because of his Holy Spirit inspired declaration, is still the message today. All the additional religious stuff done through the various denominations and traditions, are like ornaments on the tree. For the tree is the Cross. It does not need any more glitter to make it more beautiful or powerful than it was in the beginning. In fact ornaments often detract from the beauty of the tree itself. The tree too often becomes the platform upon which men hang their gaudy decorations thinking they are making it more attractive. Modern church theatre certainly does that.

I am not saying, as some critics contend, the succession of Popes and the Anglican or Roman Catholic doctrine is wrong, ungodly, or begging for judgment. It if is, God will deal with it. The question is; Does that doctrine help you love God and love others? It may or may not possess elitist power, and it may or may not find special favor with God. However, to think that it is necessary for salvation is to say anyone who does not know it or believe it is not "safe in Christ." Which also implies that something in addition to Spirit given revelation of the Cross is required for salvation. And of course to believe or teach such nonsense would be blasphemous.

2. Fellowship means social intercourse. The early Christians enjoyed getting together to encourage each other in their faith because they were a minority. It was very difficult to be a Christian in 33 AD. One reason for this was there was no Bible to read from! Jesus shared a personal relationship with His pals. And we certainly need to follow His example today, for our benefit though, not for fear of breaking a punishable command.

3. In the breaking of bread: there is no indication that this means Holy Communion. It could mean and probably does mean both eating a meal together, and sharing in the memorial cup and bread. Again as an example, Jesus did both the night He was betrayed.

4. And in prayers: pros-yoo-khay, used here, means worship. It can mean by extension, corporate worship and or fervent prayer. But this is self-explanatory. Jesus did this often during his entire life and on the last night with His guys.

So these four items were the subjects of the early church meetings. And if you follow the life of Jesus you will see these four elements over and over. Teaching, fellowship, eating, and prayer.

Lets explore another example from Scripture.

Additional Notes on Fellowship

Acts 15 records how Paul and Barnabas were sent to the new believers in Antioch. The text tells us "it pleased the apostles, and elders, with the whole church" (at Jerusalem) to send chosen men with Paul and Barnabus. They wrote a letter of introduction to the believers, and sent instruction to correct some bad information the Antioch believers had received previously. And the new instructions?

"For it seemed good to the Holy Spirit, and to us, to lay upon you no greater burden than these necessary things:

1. That you abstain from things offered to idols,
2. From blood of things strangled,
3. From sexual immorality.
4. If you keep yourselves from these, you will do well.

How simple can you get? Why would they only require these things of believers? Because they knew and or expected these folks to be believers! They expected them to have been born again, and to desire more than anything else to live a life filled with praise, thanksgiving, generosity, patience, and righteousness, joy, and peace. Why? Because according to Paul, "the Kingdom of God is not eating and drinking but righteousness and peace and joy in the Holy Spirit." Romans 14:17.

Man has a long history of trying to make things better. In some cases church tradition has been born out of the desire to help those weak in faith to grow more disciplined and hence to guarantee their membership in the Kingdom of God, the family of God, and the church, or body of Christ. But man has another tendency. That is he often makes a mess of things with all his fiddling. At times what once began as a helpful thing gets turned into a necessary thing. And a necessary thing then becomes a imperative thing. Then by virtue of repeated use, and stressed importance over time, it is elevated to a command. And eventually the new believer that was being encouraged in his faith is now a rebellious backslider who requires church discipline, and or excommunication! And that's how spiritual abuse begins, how church splits occur, how denominations are birthed, and why religious people kill other religious people thinking they are serving God!

In conclusion, let me say this: Jesus delivered us from the need to be good and right and sinless and perfect. How? Because He was all those things for us. That is the message of Hebrews 10. And we who are born again and are indwelt by His Spirit, the same One who raised

Him from the dead, have been given the power to live liked He did. Primarily we live to love God and to love others. He commands us, expects us, encourages us and He empowers us to BE LIKE HIM. He does not desire that we STRIVE to be PERFECT. We cannot be perfect. Mature yes, but not sinless. There is only One who was sinless. He desires that we to learn to love Him totally, completely, selflessly, and sacrificially. It is a process for which we require His empowerment each day.

Loving God has nothing to do with church services at a certain time or a certain form of worship or prayer. A particular ritualistic approach to God on Sunday morning or Saturday night, with pianos, organs, or acoustic guitars or electric ones, does not impress God, or guarantee right standing with Him. All of that has been tried for two thousand years by millions of people. It does not work and will not work because it cannot work. It is impossible to please God by anything less than being His child, by loving Him, admiring Him, respecting Him, praising Him, bragging about Him, and having a heart-felt deep-down desire to be pleasing to Him in word, action, attitude, and desire. That is faith. Substance of things hoped for (promised to be delivered in the future), evidence of things as yet unseen (but which will be seen eventually). Anything less, no matter how religious sounding or appearing, is religious defilement. It is a form of godliness, yet denies the power of the grace of God in Christ, and thus it is often hypocritical, self-promoting, divisive, and in the end, it may prove to have been a terribly taxing waste of time and energy. The word futile comes to mind.

Christian Fellowship

Living in fellowship as Christians means sharing with those of like mind, fellow aliens and foreigners.

1. His Righteousness: eternal right standing with God through Christ's blood.
2. His Peace: the invincible unshakable peace, which is available only through personal revelation of His incredible Sacrifice.
3. His Joy: eternal, inexpressible and full of glory; a happiness rising from a true, personal, and life-altering encounter with Christ.
4. His Holy Spirit: in union with and available only through a relationship with God based on the revelation of Christ Jesus that comes only through the indwelling presence of the Holy Spirit.

Have you been forsaking the fellowship? If you have your lifestyle will reflect it. You will be like the unbelieving world in which you live. They are selfish, fearful, anxious, unsatisfied, and lonely. They strive to find peace and yet are stressed. They strive to find joy, yet are angry and fearful. They strive to find fulfillment and yet are never satisfied. Does this describe you? If so, and you call yourself a Christian, it is time for you to reconnect with your family, the body of Christ, the church. And we're everywhere. We're looking for you. And we will be an encouragement for you the next time we get together. We will welcome you and pray for you. We will listen to you and care for you. We may even feed you!

God does not want to punish you for your absence at church meetings. He knows better than anyone how frustrating those meetings can be. They had that affect on Him. He quit going to them. Instead He went out into the hills, and beaches, and met His brothers and sisters in the homes of His friends.

So, dear one, do it regularly. Bless me with your fellowship and allow me to do the same for you. Let's do it with love, joy, mercy, and grace. And let's do it to remind each other of His love and to encourage each other in our faith. Let us enjoy each other here and now while we patiently wait to see Him soon face to face. And lets tell others about this wonderful fellowship we have with Him and with each other.

CHAPTER 14

Ordination

"But as God has distributed to each one, as the Lord has called each one, so let him walk. And so I ordain in all the churches." 1 Corinthians 7:17

From Strong's Concordance, [1299] diatasso, dee-at-ass-so. From [1223] and [5021]; to arrange thoroughly, to institute, appoint, set in order. [1223], dia, dee-ah. The channel of an act. [5021], tasso, tas-so. To arrange in an orderly manner.

In Paul's writing above we see him following a prescribed path for his life. God has distributed to (to give or bestow upon) him a specific spiritual gifting, or skill-set. The Lord has called (called forth, commissioned) Paul into His ordained role, and Paul answered the call to use his spiritual gifts in the way God ordained (set in order). So, acting in his prescribed role Paul exhorts the church to honor and respect the divine decree with corresponding action, just as he has done. In other words, Paul's call by God into His service (ministry) includes the ordaining of others for the benefit of those they will serve, and because that is what God ordained for him to do.

Paul's act of ordaining others is a duty, which God gifted him to undertake, and called him to, and to which he has submitted. In the context of the definition, God decreed a path[(1223)] for Paul to walk upon. He chose to walk that path, therefore he was embracing the channel through which God's will was to be established in Paul's life. This sets his life in divine order and he is moving in the flow God has decreed. Thus, we can see, Paul's office in the body of Christ was a result of his relationship with God, a personal relationship built upon divine order. For us it means this; just as Paul was expected to enter the role and embrace the authority God had decreed for him, he likewise possessed the gifting and empowerment of God's Spirit to fulfill the duties of that role.

God decreed the channel through which His authority would flow. Paul embraced that channel and consequently ordained others. Therefore those who acknowledge Paul's ordained position are acknowledging God's will for his life and for their own. If Paul directs others, as he was ordained to do, and they submit, then those he ordains enter with him into that same channel of divine will.

The act of ordaining then is a biblical principle established by God for the purpose of bringing order to the (His) family (relational) business on Earth.

God is not the author of confusion. He is the supreme example of relationship, harmony, unity, and peace. He knows the best way to accomplish any task or achieve any goal. When we, His once corrupt, now redeemed, children, are brought into right relationship with Him, understand His will and make the effort to embrace it, we enter the flow of His order on earth. Not only is success assured, but the power and authority to accomplish His will is granted to those who submit to His will. For examples of this principle review the lives and ministry of Abraham, Joseph, Moses, David, Esther, Gideon, Joshua, Joseph, Mary, John the Baptist, Matthew, Peter, James, and John. God chose each of them to accomplish for Him a specific task. They submitted to His Lordship, entered into a harmonious relationship with Him, and His will was accomplished. These were ordinary men and women who did extraordinary things because they embraced a relationship with God, and through that relationship, discovered the task for which they were ordained. Doing His will may have been difficult, painful, and challenging. But it was worth the effort and pain.

The Other Side

There is another side to this concept worth considering. That is, if God called and one does not reply with obedience, the channel of divine will is broken. And the channel through which the authority, power, and spiritual gifting commensurate with the call are expected to flow, is broken. This is often the source of confusion and frustration among aspiring ministers and ministries.

God's desire is to use us through direct and constant interaction with us. Jesus is our role model for this.

It makes sense to think, given God's personal orderliness, there is a divine plan for each human life. All but the most ignorant Christian ministers would agree. And a human is never more complete or productive than when he finds and follows God's will. It also seems reasonable to think there is available through ordination a harmonizing of authority, spiritual gifting, and empowerment. God has provided each person a variety of spiritual gifts, talents, and abilities for his/her specific station in life. To be happy each one needs to know what he is destined to do and then develop his abilities in that area. One destined and gifted to be a wife and mother won't be fulfilled committing to a monastic life. A rocket scientist would not be happy working as car salesman. And one ordained for full-time ministry cannot expect to find peace and contentment in any other endeavor.

In the case of a call to fulltime ministry, the minister must not only recognize the spiritual gifting and answer the personal call, he must also find the people/organization within the body of Christ to which he is called. I believe the minister is called to both a work and to a group of like-minded workers. We work together for God's glory. Nowhere in Scripture do we see a successful minister acting solo, as an isolated super-hero. According to God's design we are family members, co-missioners, and team-mates. Jesus sent out His disciples in pairs and told them which people group to address. If the disciple is called to the foreign mission field, he won't be fulfilled teaching in a seminary. And if he is called to a Pentecostal bible college he won't be happy in a Presbyterian seminary. If called to pastor a local fellowship, he won't be happy in a third world orphanage. The lack of fulfillment won't be the result of merely being in the wrong geographical location, it will also be because the minister is not in relationship with the people and organization that share a similar vision, gifting, and desire. So, we see, by virtue of the definition of ordination, the call is to at three levels. 1) Fellowship with God. 2) A particular role. 3) A particular group of people.

Another important aspect of this concept is that of submission for accountability, instruction, and correction. To benefit from all of the above one must be in relationship with those "elders" who possess similar, (not necessarily identical) vision and gifting. As one pursues God's will the infamous learning curve will provide every disciple many opportunities for conflict. The aspiring Christian minister asks, What am I called to do? Where do I do it? Does anyone else know I am called? Who will train me? And how often does he or she struggle to find his or her place only to feel frustrated, confused, and at times used and abused by elders? Consequently, it is critical for the sake of harmony and efficiency that those called "join" those who have preceded them in a similar call. Herein lies the essence of the ordination process. To assist me in answering my call, they must have answered their call and should be successfully working in their God-ordained field. By virtue of experience, they are capable of providing me with personal spiritual oversight, accountability, clear instruction, and when needed, gentle empowering correction. In the classic case of ordination for ministry, the ordaining body should ordain those who have proven themselves to possess personal gifting compatible with the vision of the ministry. So, in the best cases, ordination is a recognition of relationship, not an invitation to relationship. Too often we find groups ordaining for ministry men and women they do not even know. No wonder there is frustration and conflict! Neither of these is God's will.

Summary: To be fulfilled I must fulfill God's will for my life, just as Jesus did. This includes discovering not only the nature of my gifting, and developing it, but finding those who possess the ordained authority and similar spiritual gifting with whom I am called to harmoniously co-labor. This then is the channel in which I am to flow, the orderly path of ordination. Therefore, according to the definition of "ordain," I can expect to find fulfillment because I am in the flow of His call, I have been set in proper order. I can enjoy a distribution of various but harmonizing spiritual gifting because I am in a mutually fulfilling relationship with the one's who have been ordained to empower others into that same call. If my relationship with others is in fact, in order, it is evidenced by similarity of vision and harmonizing of gifting, and shared trust, equal submission, and mutual accountability. And if it is then I have been ordained, regardless of whether or not I have a ordination document hanging on my wall, or a card in my wallet.

For more information on this subject see the following Scriptures. There are many others as well.

Titus 1:5 For this cause[5484, 5127] left[2641] I thee[4571] in[1722] Crete,[2914] that[2443] thou shouldest set in order[1930] the things that are wanting,³⁰⁰⁷ and²⁵³² ordain²⁵²⁵ elders⁴²⁴⁵ in every city,²⁵⁹⁶, ⁴¹⁷² as⁵⁶¹³ I¹⁴⁷³ had appointed¹²⁹⁹ thee:⁴⁶⁷¹

1Chronicles 17:9 Also I will ordain⁷⁷⁶⁰ a place⁴⁷²⁵ for my people⁵⁹⁷¹ Israel,³⁴⁷⁸ and will plant⁵¹⁹³ them, and they shall dwell⁷⁹³¹ in their place,⁸⁴⁷⁸

1 Chronicles 9:22 These¹⁹⁹² were reckoned by their genealogy³¹⁸⁷ in their villages,²⁶⁹¹ whom David¹⁷³² and Samuel⁸⁰⁵⁰ the seer⁷²⁰³ did ordain³²⁴⁵ in their set office.⁵³⁰

Act 17:31 Because¹³⁶⁰ he hath appointed²⁴⁷⁶ a day,²²⁵⁰ in¹⁷²² the which³⁷³⁹ he will³¹⁹⁵ judge²⁹¹⁹ the³⁵⁸⁸ world³⁶²⁵ in¹⁷²² righteousness¹³⁴³ by¹⁷²² that man⁴³⁵ whom³⁷³⁹ he hath ordained;³⁷²⁴ whereof he hath given³⁹³⁰ assurance⁴¹⁰² unto all³⁹⁵⁶ men, in that he hath raised⁴⁵⁰ him⁸⁴⁶ from¹⁵³⁷ the dead.³⁴⁹⁸

(Ephesians 4:1-6) I therefore, the prisoner of the Lord, beseech you to walk worthy of the calling with which you were called, with humility, and gentleness, with patience, bearing with one another in love, endeavoring to keep the unity of the Spirit in the bond of peace. There is one Spirit, just as you were called in one hope of your calling; one Lord, one faith, one baptism; one God and Father of all, who is above all, and through all, and in you all.

CHAPTER 15

Financial Success

Luke 12:34 For where your treasure is, there your heart will be also.

Now, dear ones, I want to write to you about money. I have had several conversations recently with some of you who seem unsettled about God's view of money and especially how His view of money relates to you. All of you know me. I am not a prosperity preacher chasing the "almighty dollar." So, listen carefully. I hope this will help.

I know all of you are thoughtfully generous because you have proven it to us, many times. But some of you need a little bit more information on the value, benefits, or scriptural principles of generosity. I believe what we think about money and finance is a corollary to the overall condition of our faith.

At the present time Michele and I do not possess the financial excess needed to meet our needs and the needs of others in truly philanthropic ways. However, we know people who do possess that much and I am sure you know some as well. You may be one of them. Yet, according to God, all of His children can possess more than enough as well. But if we are to succeed in this we must be determined to become living proof that God's Word is true. Yes, we must begin where we are. Some of you are in the process of overcoming the financial limitations imposed on you by your ancestors. Knowing this I want to remind you, each of us, yes every individual, sets the limits of his own achievements.

Jesus told us it was as we "seek first the Kingdom of God, AND HIS RIGHTEOUSNESS…," that all these other things will be given to us. Not for our selfish self-indulgence will they be given, but for HIS GLORY and for the benefit of those in need. Regardless of where our family of origin has forced to begin we must be faithful to pursue the vision for Kingdom Living until we are proof of it!

You will rarely, if ever, be a blessing to others if you are living in poverty. Yes, you can always find someone less fortunate than yourself to bless. But I am talking about feeding the hungry, caring for the widows and orphans, etc. in substantial ways. And yes I know, we do not need to be abundantly blessed to be a blessing. But I hope you will not use your current limited financial condition as evidence that you have reached the highest peak of God's will. Neither would I encourage you to use your current situation as an excuse for laziness.

Regarding finances and the abundant life God's Word says:

John 10:10 I have come to give you life more abundantly...

Luke 6:38 Give and it shall be given to you pressed down shaken together...

Philippians 4:19 And my God shall supply all of your needs according to HIS riches in glory through Christ Jesus...

2 Corinthians 9:7 God loves (blesses) a cheerful (hilarious) giver...

Malachi 3:10 Test Me in this and see if I will not open the windows of Heaven and pour out a blessing so large you will not have room for it...

Paul describes God as the One who can do: "*exceeding abundantly beyond all you can ask or think.*" *Ephesians 3:20.*

God's Will

Do you know He really does want you to have "more than more than enough." Do you? Jesus described Kingdom life to be "more abundant." Kingdom dwellers are God's children. God isn't pleased that His children live in poverty. Living at that level is just having life. All who draw a breath have that. Neither did Jesus say we should have abundant life. Having abundance means possessing more than enough to meet your needs. But His words were, "life more abundantly." This is a very expressive phrase. Yet if we hope to accurately compare our earth life with Kingdom life we must use terminology some folks might call lofty.

Our Father lives in a city with streets paved with gold! Gold is the most precious metal on earth. The world economy is based on it. Yet the people and angels living in God's presence walk on golden streets! Can you see how limited our defiled mind-set truly is? Remember, our understanding of any subject is truly accurate only if our perspective of that subject is harmonious with God's perspective.

To have life more abundantly is to possess more than, more than enough of everything required to enjoy happy, healthy lives! Wow! That sounds good. Is it a metaphor, a lie, a fantasy, or the truth? I believe, since Jesus is neither a poet, a liar, a dreamer, or a mythical creature, He must be stating the truth as plainly as He possibly can. He said, "I am the way the truth and the life…" Do you believe Him? He said "God so loved the world that He sent… Do you believe Him?

So then, knowing He wants you to have more abundance, why does it seem so hard for you to become financially successful? I believe our experience is limited quite often because our expectations of the possibilities is limited. Jesus said "all things are possible to those who believe." Perhaps that is why He was able to feed five thousand hungry people with a couple of fish and a few pieces of bread.

God's Word

For more on this look at Romans 12, one and two, again. Although these verses are not usually used to address financial prosperity, they will support of my point.

1 Therefore, I urge you, brothers, in view of God's mercy, to offer your bodies as living sacrifices, holy and pleasing to God—this is your spiritual act of worship.

2 Do not conform any longer to the pattern of this world, but be transformed by the renewing of your mind. Then you will be able to test and approve what God's will is—his good, pleasing and perfect will.

Notice the correlation between BODY AND MIND. Present your BODY to GOD as a living sacrifice... Do not be conformed to the world's (limited way of behaving)

But be TRANSFORMED by the RENEWING OF YOUR MIND.

So, you can prove to the world, what is the good, pleasing, and perfect will of God.

My BODY will be used for God's glory to the degree that I am transformed by the renewing of my

MIND. My body is the vehicle I use to interact with the physical world. Without my body I am no good to those in need. How many deceased persons have blessed you tangibly lately? If my body is to be the vehicle by which I demonstrate God's Kingdom on earth, including, "life more abundantly," then my mind, which directs the outward activities of my body, must function like the mind of Christ (anointed by the Spirit). I must think (mind) like Christ in order to act (body) like Christ. Why? First, because the Spirit is willing but the flesh is weak. This means the Holy Spirit desires to assist me to live on earth as well God wants me to. But my habits, behavior, mind-sets, beliefs, and family history all combine to prevent me from doing so. And second, the limit of my success is quite often tied directly to the limit of my expectations.

For those who start with nothing financial abundance usually comes as a result of hard work, careful planning, cautious spending, and wise investing. For people unaccustomed to having unlimited financial resources there is an additional ingredient. Having a positive and expectant attitude. One of the big differences between successful and unsuccessful people is successful people really do believe they can be successful. Another key to success is associating with successful people. Grumbling complainers are not usually successful. Unsuccessful people do not see opportunities for success. Instead, they are quick to point out the potential for failure.

Three Keys to Success

In addition to hard work any quest for success should also include these three elements.

1. Discovering your aptitude.
2. Displaying your power.
3. Declaring your authority.

Your aptitude is the collection of gifting that came in your package. Its what defines you. For example, you may be a natural athlete. Throwing and catching or hitting balls of various sizes and shapes may be easy for you. This means you have an aptitude for athletics. If not gifted in athletics, you might find learning math, music, or a foreign language easy. If not, maybe you have an aptitude for mechanics, engineering, counseling, medicine, or business. Discovering your aptitude will greatly enhance your chances of achieving success.

Once you discover your aptitude you must also embrace a "can do" attitude. This confidence will become the display of power needed to propel you to success. Discovering your aptitude is easy. Developing your aptitude in a specific area may be difficult in the beginning. But at some point in the learning or training process you should start to think, "I can do this." This confidence will become the driving force that empowers you to overcome any obstacles encountered on your path toward success.

Declaring your authority is a way of verbalizing agreement with God regarding your destiny. Your expectations of success, your confidence, and your determination are all rooted in the knowledge that God has destined you for a particular career or work or job. Agreement with God is an unseen spiritual element of success. Declaring your authority means telling anyone, human beings or spirit beings, that you have found your divine destiny and you are committed to fulfilling it. You feel and think you are doing what God has birthed you to do. Therefore you embrace and exercise the "authority" or divine right granted by God to succeed in this arena.

"For assuredly, I say to you, whoever says to this mountain, 'Be removed and be cast into the sea,' and does not doubt in his heart, but believes that those things he says will be done, he will have whatever he says" (Mark 11:23).

The Double Minded Man

If all three keys to success discussed above are in place and yet you feel you are marching up a sand dune with a backpack full of rocks there might be yet another hindrance. If you have been struggling for a prolonged time to increase your financial base you better make sure you are not a double-minded man (or woman). Trying to believe God's word, but doubting it to be true for you will prevent you from successfully manifesting any Kingdom principle. And doing so will definitely hinder your success in finances. Doubt and confusion is never in harmony with the mind, will, or plans of God. And God's word tells us the double-minded man is unstable in all his ways, and can expect to receive nothing from

God. How often have you heard someone say to you, "Well, make up your mind!"

If the truth contained in the Word (the written wisdom and will) of God is going to be any good to you, you must know it. You must read it to know it. You must know it to believe it. You must believe it to act upon it. And especially to act upon it before it is manifested in your life. If you do not act on it, or if you wax and wane, come and go, have good days and bad days, it might be because you do not, truly deep down in your heart of hearts, believe it. And it might be a long time before you achieve the "life more abundantly" which God desires for you. Christ-like faith is an unshakable confidence that God will do what He said He would do.

Ungodly Beliefs

Proverbs 23:7 "As a man thinks in his heart, so is he." Your behavior and the results of that behavior, good or bad, are directly and spiritually tied to your strongly held beliefs. Your beliefs show up in your behavior. If you desire to alter your behavior you must alter your beliefs. To make your experience positive your expectations must be positive. And if your thoughts are God's thoughts they will be positive but also they will be true.

Ungodly Ancestors

Many of us were not born into godly successful families. We are hard working men and women who are

255

fighting to overcome the lack and limitations imposed upon us by our ancestors. To enjoy abundant financial success will require physical energy, wise use of time and money, continuing education, etc. In God's kingdom success also requires unshakable determination to continue to believe the truth, in the face of circumstances to the contrary. We must be transformed by the renewing of ours minds. We cannot achieve success while continuing to accept, believe, think, and speak out of our mouths the fear, lack, doubt, and limitations that came down our family line.

Demonic Interaction

Yes, dear ones, demons are real. Yes, they do live here on earth with us. And yes, even though we cannot see them they have influence on all human beings. How much influence do they have? As much as man's ignorance allows! And the quicker you realize this reality, the quicker you will deal with their stuff. Are demons responsible for everything bad that happens to you? No. But they do interact with you more than you may realize. Yet Jesus, who frequently confronted the presence of demons, said, "And these signs will follow those who believe. In my name they will cast out demons." Mark 16:17 In another place He said, "Behold, I have given you authority to tread upon serpents and scorpions and over ALL the power of the enemy and nothing will by any means harm you." Luke 10:19.

If success evades you no matter how confidently and well you work, you should suspect demonic involvement.

In such a case you can use your authority as a child of God, a member of the church, and forbid demons from hindering your success. Speak to them, tell them to go away and leave you and your finances alone. Will you? If you do, they will. The Word of God says, "Submit therefore to God, resist the devil and he will flee."

Come Forth

Raise your expectations dear ones! Please do not settle for just getting by, just paying your bills, or just living "life as usual." God desires to bless you. He went to a lot of trouble, and pain, to empower you to live freely in this world, without the limitations imposed by a poverty mentality. Rise up and be determined as Abraham was. Steadfast in his faith he, "continued to believe that what God promised He was also able to deliver." And the result was Abraham became the father of all of us who believe the message of the cross. Abraham's confidence was considered by God to be righteousness! His faith positioned him to manifest "life more abundantly." And God blessed him abundantly.

Where are you right now? What do you do to earn money? Is it a job, a career, an idea, a product, a service? Do you believe it is God's will for you? Do you expect God to bless it? Are you looking for ways to make it fruitful, to multiply it, to bring an increase of, 30, 60, 100%? Are you using your money wisely, including giving to the needs of others less fortunate? If the answers are yes, then according to God, you are on the way to proving the good, pleasing, and perfect will of God. And you are on your way to experiencing life more abundantly.

If you know you are pursuing the career, business plan, idea, product or service God has for you then do pursue it with teeth-gritting determination. And pursue it with the joyous expectation that God will bless it, increase it, and to bless others because of your effort. Don't let the enemy rob you of your inheritance by telling you "you can't," "you'll never," "you'll always." He tried it with Adam and Eve and it worked. However, He tried the same thing with Jesus and it did not work. How about you? How are you going to react to his snarling curses, whispered lies, and relentless verbal assault?

Thank God often for manifesting His wonderful divine will to you. Praise Him for His persistent assistance to your efforts. Thank Him for blessing you with success. Praise Him for empowering and equipping you to live life more abundantly.

Conclusion

For years Michele and I have lived with the expectation that our wonderful, loving, faithful, powerful, ever-present Father desired to bless us, so we can be used by Him to be a blessing to others as well! How about you? Do you expect Him to bless you? Are you looking for ways to bless others?

We love you and pray for you. And we continue to thank God for allowing us to share this life with you. Remember, we're all in this together, and we're here to help.

CHAPTER 16

Fathers and Sons

Behold, I am going to send you Elijah the prophet before the coming of the great and terrible day of the LORD. 6"He will restore the hearts of the fathers to their children and the hearts of the children to their fathers, so that I will not come and smite the land with a curse." Malachi 4:5-6

It was not too many years ago that a new buzzword circulated throughout the body of Christ. It was shouted from the biggest pulpits in the world that God was returning the hearts of the Fathers to the children, and vice versa. Having previously noticed a deficit in this critically important area I looked forward to watching this new revelation manifest. Sadly I report, I watched in vain.

Some Questions

The prophet Malachi was the last prophet to prophesy to Israel and did so 450 years before the birth of Christ. In this prophecy Malachi says the appearance of Jesus Christ on the earth, heralded by John the Baptist, would usher in a time before God's judgment of life on earth, for a re-connecting of hearts to take place. John the Baptist, compared to Elijah in the text by a much later prophecy of the Angel to Zacharias (Luke 1:17), was commissioned to prepare the region (and the earth) for Jesus Christ. Then Christ came and went. Since John and Jesus successfully completed their respective missions, we must ask, "Has the time for the reconnect occurred?" If the answer is yes, then the curse associated with the lack of loving father-child relationships been erased. Then why do we see so few healthy father-child relationships in the body of Christ?

The deficit of healthy father-son relationships in the body of Christ suggests the reconnect has not occurred. Has it? So, does the prophecy and its curse apply to the body of Christ? If it does, as the Apostle and Prophets of the 21st century church claim, and the reconnect has been accomplished, then why do we see so little evidence of the new heart connection?

One last question. Was Malachi's message a prophecy intended to be fulfilled in the nation of Israel alone? Or was it meant to be manifested in the church? All of this is important if we are to properly interpret or even explain this, and any other, prophecy and its implications for you and me.

Regardless of your choice of interpretation, modern Apostles have pontificated on the subject, prophets prophesied, famous authors wrote and sold books, and the children attended conferences and seminars to learn how to be a good child to their "spiritual" father. But the espoused relationship seldom, if ever, developed. As the calendar flipped its pages further revelation came, the children ran after it, paid their fees, bought the books, and CDs and DVDs. And yet godly fathers, those who pursue and enjoy life with their children, remain as enigmatic as always. Does this mean the prophecy is not true? Or maybe it's not for today? Or, could it be, the prophecy has been anounced by God and as yet has not been embraced by His people, the fathers in His church? In other words, even though God has declared this is the day for the prophecy to be fulfilled it remains unfulfilled because fathers still do not know how to take their place in it.

After living in the Christian family, the family of God, for twenty-plus years I am of the opinion there remains a shortage of godly fathers. (What do you think?) The children are suffering as a result. Their suffering is demonstrated in many forms. Insecurity, fear, guilt, rebellion, violence and loneliness are the most obvious. Most troubling though is that their suffering, regardless of the form it takes, is a sign of the absence of an intimate connection with a godly father and hence the lack of loving nurture, affirmation, and security.

One reason for the children's suffering may be rooted in what I call a case of mistaken identity. I am sure most would agree the family of God is more sophisticated today than in years past. Pastors, parishioners, parents, and children have become dependent on technology. Cell phones, laptops, iPods, gameboys, power-point, skype, and GPS. It seems we cannot communicate, learn, entertain ourselves, or find our way anymore without the very latest electronic gadget. We are told and believe life would be better if we had more giga-bytes, more ram, more pixels, more band-width, or bits per second. The obsessive attention given to e/c-technology (electronic communication) during the past ten or so years may have covertly reshaped man's thinking about himself.

Is it possible westernized man has begun to view human life from the porch of e/c-techno-dependence, and lost the view of life as a collection of mutually supportive interconnected relationships? Are we more dependent on machines for our sense of security, peace, and confidence? If so then our method of instructing, correcting, healing, has been altered as well. Perhaps the modern church-man believes, like his unredeemed brother, that emotionally healthy relationships are so infrequently found that it is futile to continue searching for one!

This mistaken identity has occurred previously in the church. Constantine caused it with the Edict of Milan (313AD) by proclaiming the Roman Empire to be a Christian nation. So, to enjoy favor with the Emperor a citizen would, at least, not persecute Christians, and at best, profess Christ as Lord. Politically Convenient Christianity I call it. In such a society the Emperor displaces God. Just as the modern Pope does for millions of Roman Catholics.

Mistaken identity occurred again during the early twentieth century. Sigmund Freud sold the world and the church a new model of man based on his system of psychoanalysis. And the church jumped up on his wagon. It wasn't long before the church began referring its troubled parishioners to the psychoanalyst's couch for healing. Even though, for more than a thousand years psycho-therapy, soul-care (or cure), had been done by the church. Interestingly, one of Freud's contemporaries, Alfred Adler, Jewish by birth, after experiencing redemption through Christ (1932?) stated, "the man who does not adhere to the ethic of 'doing unto others' causes society all of its ills."

The latest corruption of man's identity is based on an ec-tech view of man. It suggests man and his relationships can be fixed with the right program, the right method, or some other non-living impersonal additive. The idea is expressed something like, "If he/she is still in pain simply, add, subtract, or modify this or that component, and he/she will experience more pleasure or less pain." This impersonal view of man began centuries ago as a mechanical or a medical model. The mechanical model offers a simple solution to a complex problem. Scientists and engineers pride themselves on finding simple solutions to complex problems as fast as possible. Whether the subject is human, animal, vegetable, mineral, or electronic. Unfortunately it appears leaders, the fathers, in the body of Christ are increasingly promoting the same view.

When dealing with man's spiritual problems leadership in the body of Christ often adapts an ec-tech mind set. The apostle, prophet, evangelist, pastor, and teacher see the disciple in need of tweaking. "If you think or feel anything ungodly you must pray the right prayer, accept the right revelation, buy the right book, listen to the right CD, or watch the right DVD." However, this mindset is not even remotely consistent with the concept of personally engaging the healing power of God's loving presence. In fact, unless any healing methodology, or gadget, leads to a deeper intimacy with God it might inadvertently lead to a false sense of dependency and security.

The healing and freedom God intends man to enjoy is discovered when man encounters God on a personal level through personal experience. God is the healer, and time with Him brings both revelation of man's need and revelation of God's willingness and ability to meet the need. The man that learns to sit with God and learn from Him by experience is the man most able to assist other men to do the same. It is true. You cannot give to anyone something you do not possess. And perhaps, in spite of Malachi's prophecy, this explains the continuing deficit of godly fathers in the body of Christ today.

The Father and His Son

To understand the role of fathers and sons in the body of Christ we must search the Scripture. We should look for examples of healthy God-ordained father-son relationships. We must realize though even when the relationship is God-ordained, it can be very unhealthy. As we undertake such a study from Scripture we find the full gamut of those relationships. Some are as healthy as Abraham and Isaac (Genesis 18-24). Others are unhealthy as David's was with Amnon, and Absalom (2 Samuel 13).

However, if we desire to see the perfect Father-son relationship we need to look at the relationship between Jesus Christ and God the Father. And truly this is the role model for fathers and their sons today. Any and all other role models must be judged and will be judged by this one. But bear in mind, in all that follows, the healthy father-son relationship begins with the affection, will, power, and behavior of the father. Never forget that. Proceed slowly to place your hope in anyone other than God Almighty, for He is the Father of all living things! Trust that He can be counted upon to lead you into a relationship with a godly father. But beware, for there are many imposters and posers out there. Some may be ignorant of their incapacity for parenting, but others knowingly prey on your emotional insecurity.

Study Jesus Christ and His Father and you quickly see the most obvious sign of a healthy father-son relationship; the love the two share. The Father loves His son and the Son loves His Father. How do we know that? Because their love is demonstrated in self-sacrificing action. Love is a verb. It is meant to describe the interaction of two people who are mutually affectionate. Often, I believe most often, the word is used inappropriately to describe a feeling of affection which does not necessarily manifest in corresponding action. Yet God is very serious about this correlation between professed affection and behavior.

"For I am a jealous God visiting the iniquity of the fathers upon the children to the third and fourth generations of those who hate Me, but showing mercy to thousands, to those who love me and keep My commandments." (Exodus 20:5-6). Notice He equates love with obedience, and hate with disobedience. For the one who loves, obedience is not a burdensome duty. It is an affectionate response to the Father's demonstration of love.

God tells us to submit to and obey Him because our inbred rebellion (generational sin) has and will continue to cause us (and our children) more trouble and pain than we can imagine! If you think God wants you to obey Him because He doesn't like fun and adventure, you have missed life's most liberating truth. His love and affection is the driving force behind His plan of redemption! The cross of Christ is the most incredibly selfless demonstration of love mankind will ever see!

God came in the flesh as a man because He loved humanity that much! Jesus Christ went to the cross because He loved His Father that much! He loved, ugly, fearful, shameful, violent, irreverent, selfish, humanity, just as it is today. God died for each human being that ever drew a breath to reconcile them to Himself. He did not want them to live pain-filled, fearful lives. Not one of them. He came and died for each one. You and me, and yes, even Adolf Hitler, and Osama ben Laden! (Hebrews 12:2-3).

Matthew 6:31 "Therefore do not worry, saying, 'What shall we eat?' or 'What shall we drink?' or

'What shall we wear?' 32 For after all these things the Gentiles seek. For your heavenly Father knows that you need all these things. 33 But seek first the kingdom of God and His righteousness, and all these things shall be added to you.

God asks us to love Him because He loves us. The Scripture says He is a jealous God. Yet He is not jealous of us, He is jealous for us. He knows there is no man or woman on earth who will or can love us as well as He can! His love for us, His strong affection, moves Him to protect us and provide for us in ways we never could for ourselves. Can you imagine how offensive it must be when a helpless hopeless child rejects the loving wisdom and eternal security of the best Father in the universe? Yet that is exactly what happens every time a human being refuses to believe God is not only capable but willing to meet our every need. And I must ask the question, "Why would any child act this way?"

The answer is simple. The rebellious child does not know that the Almighty Father is truly sincere. The child has nothing in his or her personal experience that indicates this Father will act any better than any human who has previously acted in the role of father. The child that refuses the assistance of the Father does so because he:

1. does not trust the Father
2. does not love the Father
3. does not know the Father

Ask yourself some questions at this point in our discussion.

1. What would you say to someone who asks, "Did your father love you?"
2. How did he demonstrate his love?
3. How often did you hear him say, "I love you?"
4. Describe your most intimate moments with your father.

Far too often the answers to these questions do not evoke memories of warm affection. As history rolls on there are fewer and fewer affectionate fathers in the world. Unfortunately, the number of unloving fathers inside the Christian ghetto is similar to the number outside of it. Why is that? If you haven't had one it will be very difficult to be one. Jesus had One and He is One.

Therefore, we must begin to see this sad situation cannot be corrected by reading a book, listening to a CD, or sermon, or watching the latest Christian TV show or DVD. Love is transferred from God to man through personal interaction with God.

Fathers, Sons, and Fathers

Godly fathers are sons of godly fathers. If you, as a dad, struggle to be a good father, there's a good chance you do so because you didn't have one. That's right. It isn't your fault. No one modeled for you the healing power of Father's unconditional love. No one touched you at the heart level with affection so powerful as to heal your inbred misconception of father.

If this is your case then can you really expect to be a good father? Is it any wonder why people who want to know a godly father, do not confidently place you in that role? Perhaps they don't trust you. Perhaps they have not been convinced you are who and what you say you are. You may be a pastor with rebellious sheep. Their rebellion is a sign of an inability to trust. I remember one frustrated pastor who told me he had teeth marks on his heart. When I asked for further information he added, "sheep have teeth, and they bite!"

If you are a father take a long look at the relationship you shared with your own father. What do you see? Did he instruct you in the lessons of life? Did he tell you about sex, money, marriage? Did he explain what it meant to be a father and husband? Did he tell you about providing for your wife and children, and especially providing protection for them? What method did he use to instruct you? Was he calm and affirming? Was he tolerant of your mistakes and failures, supporting you because he knew you were just a kid? Was he slow to become angry when you did something poorly or something wrong? And when you made a mistake did he correct you harshly or violently?

If the memories of these situations are not happy ones, then the answers to the questions are not complimentary of your father. And unless you overcome your anger toward him and the sadness or pain which caused your anger, you will probably find being a godly dad rough going.

Are you a dad that's doing a pretty good job? Ask your sons and daughters to speak truthfully with you about this. They might be reluctant to do so at your first invitation. So, give them time to think about it and then follow up with them later. I'm not trying to stir up trouble. However, I have always thought the best opinion of my claim of loving someone would come from the one I claimed to love. I can tell you, "I love my wife." But you will get more accurate answer by asking her.

Do not despair though if you had a less than godly relationship with your dad. There is a solution. You can become the kind of father sons will be drawn to. You have two sources to pursue for instruction on this subject. There are some good godly fathers out there, I am sure. But they are very few when compared to the number of men who have successfully impregnated women. My friend, and good father, Bob, says there is a big difference between being a father and being a daddy! So, be careful when searching for a godly spiritual father.

Many men especially those in Christian leadership positions will tell you all about the role of fathers and sons. That is one of their primary purposes as "ministers," whether or not they know it! Yet, their instruction alone will not make you a godly father or a godly son. This is never the case. Personal experience, not instruction, is the best teacher. Therefore even if the pastor instructs us regarding the security that is ours by "submitting to leadership" we may find it difficult to do so unless he demonstrates unconditional love for us. I sure am glad my father didn't simply give me a book to read when I asked him to teach me to drive a car!

The Love of the Father

You must understand this; a godly father is one whose love for the child exceeds the child's ability to understand. The child does not learn the depth of his father's love by listening to the instruction. He learns the value and depth of his father's love by experiencing it! That's right. He feels his father's love by being in his father's presence for extended periods of time, in many different scenarios. The child watches and listens to the father all the time! He watches father interact with his wife, his children, the people in his community, at church, in the hardware store, employers and employees, etc. He feels comfortable hanging out with dad. Just being in his presence is enough to make the child feel secure, protected, provided for. The child might not call this sense of security love, but it is a primary emotion related to love.

Knowing dad is here and in charge feels good. There is no feeling as warm and fuzzy as knowing whatever happens daddy will take care of it. Trust is created automatically in such a comfortable environment. "Ahh, daddy's home." In too many cases the thought of "daddy's home," creates insecurity, fear, and panic! And in other cases many children cannot imagine what it's like to have a daddy in their presence! However, a loving father will create feelings of security and trust as a result of his presence, not his instruction. God is the most trustworthy example of Father, and yet people who receive weekly instruction about Him and from Him for years do not trust Him! Why? Because they do not spend enough time in His presence.

Many pastors want their "spiritual children" to trust, honor, and obey them because they believe this is the will of God for pastors and sheep. And many well-meaning but very wounded sheep agree. Being fearful of more ill-treatment from "another father" sheep will often rebel against the pastor's desires and/or demands for loyalty, submission and obedience. Their rebellion can cause the shepherd to feel insecure, frustrated and even angry when they do. Yet if you cannot trust him how can you honor and obey him? To do so would put you in harm's way. So, even if you want to trust, honor, and obey your designated and ordained spiritual father, you may reject his authority in order to protect yourself from a repeat of the pain you experienced previously with a another untrustworthy father. When you reject his authority his insecurity clashes with your insecurity, and separation or divorce is the eventual result.

A godly (loving) father, biological or spiritual, will not become insecure by your rebellion. Neither will he become harsh or demanding. Why? Because if he has received his concept of love from interaction with either his biological father, his Heavenly Father, or both, he will not be threatened by your rebellion. He will honor your loyalty, but he will not demand it. He knows you will benefit by his authority because he knows his authority is godly. Yet the security he receives from his relationship with his Heavenly father empowers him to understand your fear and to continue to love you in spite of your insecurity. As he does this he demonstrates to you the godly father's love and if he does it long enough you will eventually become secure in his love.

Experiencing Father's Love

So then, how do we, I, or the church, bridge the chasm which exists between fathers and sons? What can be done to heal the wounds received from the rough hands and snarling mouths of unloving fathers? Can one who has not known the love of a godly bio-father truly find it? Is such godly fatherly love available, in the body of Christ?

The healing power of God's unconditional love is discovered in two places. First it is always available, 24-7, in the presence of Almighty God our Heavenly Father. And second, it can be found in the presence of a man (or woman) who has been a recipient of The Father's love. Sadly though my experience in more than twenty years of circuit riding among the family of God has revealed very little demonstration of it. Does such love even exist? Yes, of course. But it can take years for an insecure or abused child to learn to love God confidently and to love others appropriately.

The real important question is; have you experienced unconditional love from anyone claiming to be ordained by God to full-time ministry? Your experience is always a more important consideration than the statistics and stereotypes promoted by researchers. Personally, it matters little what the latest poll says about God, men, women, money, etc. Your life experience is the most powerful teacher.

The healing I have received has not helped you one bit, has it? That is, unless I am your pastor, brother, husband, or father? Why? Because those who interact with me on a daily basis are the ones most directly affected by the love I have received from God. They are the ones who will report to you most accurately my capacity to love. You see, what I am speaks so loud most people don't hear what I say. Its true for all of us, actions speak louder than words. My behavior is a reflection of my belief system. What I think about God, money, sex, men, women, wives, husbands, and fathers is demonstrated in my interaction with each of them. In the case of father, what I believe is demonstrated by my performance in the role. In all cases however, if I say one thing and do another it won't be long before people quit listening to me. In the pastor's case, the sheep may only appear to listen. While they sit submissively outwardly, inwardly they may be "standing in rebellion."

The same principle is true for apostles, prophets, pastors, evangelists and teachers. If they have been recipients of unconditional love they will be carriers of the same. If they have not received they cannot give it to you, no matter how hard they try to convince you! And maybe that's why they "instruct and correct" you rather than love you. They simply do not know how to love you any more than you know how to love them!

The ec-tech model says, "Do what I say not what I do." I see it so often I think it is the (unspoken) rule, not the exception. "Even though I can't teach you to swim because I don't know how, I feel it is my duty to criticize your attempts to swim." Confronted by such misguided instruction even a conscientious person would rebel!

Yet if healing is to come, if children are to experience the loving leadership God intends leaders must first experience the father's love. In the case of leaders who did not receive their biological father's love, they must find a spiritual father who can love them unconditionally. Is the one right now demanding your submission, submitted to a spiritual father? If he/she is not in a healthy relationship with a healthy father, should you confidently depend on him to give you the loving leadership both of you desire.

Confused Priorities

Many leaders know they have wounded the sheep because of the pain of their own wounds. And healing for them will come only as they sit in the presence of God. However, the percentage of men in leadership who spend more time with God than with other men is quite low. Most men, leadership or not, are wounded, angry, insecure and as a result, they are shameful, fearful, and controlling. In addition they are either deceived to the extent of their personal pain and its effect, or they deny the incessant need to cover up their guilt and shame. And yet they find time for everything but for sitting with God. Seminars, conferences, lunches with important people, sports, TV, even internet porn, are given more time than God. And you ask, "What's wrong with this picture?"

You might be surprised by the number of ministers I have heard say things like, "I don't trust God," "God isn't fair," "God did this to me." And you might also be surprised to know how many men in church leadership feel isolated and lonely.

Years ago as a Bible college teacher I asked my incoming students to complete a "Personal Spiritual Survey" I had designed. The instructions were simple. "Take your time, think about each statement, and then answer honestly." The answers were amazing and support the opinions in this article.

Men and women who had recently met Christ felt called to the nations, to plant churches and other ministries, to become apostles, to prophesy to generals and heads of state. There were other similar and lofty ministry aspirations as well. People who spent less than an hour a week in personal bible study, and even less time in personal prayer wrote that they felt called to change the world, to advance the kingdom of God on earth, etc. I was shocked! I was happy they had such high aspirations but unless they changed their lifestyle I knew disappointment was waiting in the wings.

My own experience as a bible college student (age 39 when enrolling) affirmed that many students under the biological age of thirty, redeemed for a few years at most, held similar views. In both scenarios I envisioned the blind leading the blind.

My point in sharing these two stories is to point out a very popular but dangerous misconception shared by aspiring ministers. Far too many of those destined for leadership direct too much personal effort on preparing for the role of minister and far too little on pursuing their role of child of God. As a result of this, verified by more than twenty years as a Christian family counselor, people in ministry positions are deeply wounded individuals who cause or add to the existing wounds of those they work beside and those they have in their charge. I have met more than a few ministers who were not even born again! They had no relationship with God. None! Can you imagine?

Only as a wounded child of Almighty God learns to sit with God does he discover the power God possesses to heal all wounds. There is no other way to learn this. History has proven this time and again in the lives of countless famous, powerful, successful human beings, even ministers! We say, "What a great work he or she accomplished!" Yet we see a trail of wounded individuals bobbing in his or her wake. Yes, he accomplished a great deal while here on earth, but he was married four times, estranged from his children, self-centered, egotistical and emotionally detached from everyone.

Do you think God is pleased by his accomplishments? What do you think He thinks of the way the mighty man of industry, entertainment, or ministry neglected those of his own household, or those he crawled over to get to the top, or those he pushed to the side to accomplish his noble goal? Is this the type of man or woman you want to be your spiritual father or mother?

Time alone with God experiencing His love brings the swiftest healing. It also develops an incredible and indelible appreciation of true love. You would think Christians and especially those educated in the finest

Christian colleges and seminaries would be taught this spiritual discipline. Yet, as difficult as it is for me to admit, many among the counseling/inner healing ministry community are promoting this dangerous methodology.

The E/C-Tech Healing Method

Remember my phrase, ec-tech (ektek), used several pages ago? Due to the love of technology (electronic communication) churches have begun gravitating toward a new method of inner healing. The modern (westernized?) church is becoming more sophisticated, high tech, and detail oriented. In fact, if physical appearance is any indication, it appears to be using its secular counter-part as a role model!

In their desire to see the bride of Christ get free of all the "spots and wrinkles" churches in general, and healing ministries specifically, might be unknowingly circumventing God's preferred method of healing and restoration. I am sure they are not malicious in this. They are sincere and committed even to the point of being self-sacrificing in their dedication. However, their ever-expanding techno-theology suggests there is some, as yet undiscovered, power in the spiritual realm that exceeds the healing power of God's presence! I feel certain they would disagree with my opinion, and that they would defend their newest revelation. And they should, as defense (apologetics) is a natural reaction to criticism of revelation any conscientious Christian claims to have received from God.

Is it reasonable to believe or to suggest that further need of healing is the result of incomplete revelation? Or is it possible every method of inner-healing however sophisticated, theologically speaking, is lacking the most important element necessary to end man's suffering? God's loving presence.

The Gergesene demoniac (Matthew 8:28) certainly received all that was necessary. And he did so without faith, without extensive lists of generational causes, specifically worded prayers, or fasting. He, in fact, was touched by the healing power of God's love operating through His Son, Jesus Christ. The power manifested by Christ was most certainly a by-product of His relationship with God.

Inner healing ministers should carefully consider the method of healing they embrace. For if the technique displaces God's incomprehensible love, by stressing agreement with certain words, lists, prayers, actions, behaviors, etc., it could actually be hindering God's power and willingness to heal. Perhaps the academy of inner healing practitioners well intentioned as they (we) are should re-visit the original source of healing to experience the power of God personally before offering new theories and creating dependence on new methods for helping others remove their own plank.

I wonder if we (ordained ministers of healing like myself and my colleagues) strive to find further revelation for healing because we feel so inadequate to bring healing to others. Are we trying to manifest God's willingness and power, and yet choosing a method that actually limits displays of His power?

What place does God's principle of suffering play in the healing process? Isn't there a benefit for trials and tests? And isn't there a place in the human condition for man's, and more specifically ministerial, inadequacy? Doesn't need create dependency? Doesn't demand create supply? Do we need more methodology or more of God's power? Do we depend on our wisdom and intellect or on God's presence? Are we hungry for more of God's love? If we are and we ask Him, I am convinced He would supply it.

Scripture teaches us that we are not like Christ yet. We still "know in part, and prophesy in part." Compared to Christ, we are like little children. Yes, we desire to grow into the fullness of Christ and are even destined by our Heavenly Father to do so. But even the most confident Christian among us would agree, we have not arrived yet. I saw a bumper sticker recently that read, "When you begin to feel perfect, try walking on water!"

If the man with a new or further revelation does not sit with Father God allowing Him to heal the wounds suffered by the dysfunctional relationship with his bio-father, he may be too easily led astray. If he does not yet trust the simple invitation offered by God in Scripture, ie. "Adam where are you?" "Come let us reason together…" "Come to Me all who are weary and heavy laden…" and finally, "Behold I stand at the door and knock…" can he honestly proclaim to have been given a new, better, and more necessary revelation? Or is he an unwitting victim of the ec-tech perspective of man's identity?

As always, God our loving Heavenly Father is our nearest and most reliable source of healing. We must seek Him first in repeated times of intimate communion. We must desire to know Him more intimately than we know any other human being. We must learn to love Him more than we love anyone. And when we do we will trust Him more confidently than we trust any other living being, to love us, to empower us to love others, and to heal the wounds received from our dysfunctional relationship with our biological father.

Conclusion

All men struggle to overcome feelings of shame, guilt, and the fear associated with being neglected by a biological father. The symptoms are specific for each individual and they vary greatly. And Christian men, including pastors, feel neglected by God. While the neglect from bio-fathers is to be expected, God Almighty has never and will never neglect His child. Regardless of the source of the neglect and subsequent insecurity, the treatment for all symptoms is universal. Most of us cannot go back to our bio-dad to receive his loving affirmation. He may not have any more now than he did then. Or he may no longer be available. But healing is still available from the eternal source. God. If man desires to be healed so he can be the father to his sons God destined him to be, then man must spend more time with his father, God. There he will encounter the personally intimate, emotional, and spiritually uncompromising, unconditional, and eternal love of God. And he will experience the promise of Scripture that states, "perfect love casts out fear." In his time with God he will find that His love truly does "cover a multitude of sin." And in the end he will be empowered by that incredible exchange of affection to meet the challenges of fatherhood confidently.

There are godly fathers out there in the body of Christ. I am sure of that. So, if you are looking for one, don't lose hope. However, you may want to raise the standard by which you assess those competing for your loyalty. And in the mean time I encourage you to increase the amount of time you sit with God. Turn off the TV and the computer, and the cell phone, and the iPod. Go to a quiet place and learn to sit with God. This may be difficult if it is new to you. But boy, oh boy is it worth it!

Godly fathers are sons of godly fathers. A healthy son is the product of a healthy relationship with a healthy father. And only a healthy son can become a healthy father to his own sons, biological or spiritual.

There are no shortcuts on the road to godliness. The Holy Spirit told me a long ago, "You can't shorten the distance of your journey, but you can increase the speed at which you travel." May God fill you with the wonderful peace of His presence as you go about the earth finding, following, and fulfilling His wonderful will.

I John 3:1 Behold what manner of love the Father has bestowed on us, that we should be called children of God!

"As the Father loved Me, I also have loved you; abide in My love (John 15:9).

CHAPTER 17

The Fellowship Model

John 14:23 Jesus replied, "If anyone loves me, he will obey my teaching. My Father will love him, and we will come to him and make our home with him.

God desires to share a relationship with man. That is the reason God made man. Man is the only entity in the universe made in the image of God. God is the father from whom every man on the planet gets his name. Genesis 1:26, John 15, John 17:3.

God did not design man to be religious in the sense that man must perform religious rituals to be pleasing to God. God made man and loves man. And above all God desires man to know Him and to love Him. God desires man to experience the joy of living in relationship with God. In fact, it is God's love for man that allows God to tolerate man's continued rebellion toward God, his continued violence toward other men, and especially his continued disrespect for the weak, ignorant, and infirm.

Man lives in an imperfect world. This is not the world God desires man to live in. Man's world, the planet earth, and everything in it, is corrupted, dangerous, and ruined, by man's original rebellion against God and man's continued rebellion. This corruption makes life with God, lived in harmony with God's love, very difficult. So difficult in fact that many men do not know God, and do not experience the joy available from living in loving relationship with God. This sad condition is even experienced by those who claim to know God. Unfortunately the majority of men alive today remain unaware of God's absolute eternal unconditional love. Nothing could be more pathetic.

Love is the most godly of all human qualities. Love originated with God. It is an eternally constant quality of His character. With and for His love God created all that man can know, see, hear, and experience. Even though man's world is broken as a result of his rebellion, evidences of God's work surround man and witnesses of His love abound.

Man is intuitively, yet unknowingly, driven to see, hear, and experience God's love. He is unconsciously compelled by a silent insatiable hunger to find or produce fulfillment, peace, and rest. However, man's primary need is to be reconnected with God's love. Until man does reconnect with God's love, he remains disenfranchised, lonely, and hopeless to find peace and rest.

No other relationship can fill the void in man's life. No other pursuit, pleasure or accomplishment can provide the joy and peace found in a relationship with man's loving father, God. Sadly, man continues to settle for momentary pleasure, and transitory fulfillment. Only at the end of his life does he come face to face with the utter worthlessness of all his accomplishments. Only when his heart quits beating does he finally realize the years and energy he wasted in selfish pursuits. Too late, he sees the magnitude of his failure.

Why does he continue to fail? Because the joy and peace found in God's love is found nowhere else. It is available from One source. It belongs to God, it originated with Him, thus it is supreme, absolute, and incomparable.

What must man do to experience God's love? How can he find lasting peace?

The most profitable event in man's life is his encounter with the truth regarding Jesus Christ. This truth is not available as information one can read in a book. It is not the result of hearing, reading, or reciting a prayer. According to Jesus Christ this life-transforming event occurs as the Holy Spirit, the Spirit of Truth, reveals to man the truth that Jesus Christ of Nazareth is, "...the Christ, Son of the Living God." This powerful encounter with the Truth changes the way a man thinks about God, and the way he thinks about his life and his world. Jesus calls this event the act of being "born again." Jesus said unless one is born again "he cannot see..." or "enter the kingdom of God." John 3. Jesus believed this principle so strongly that He came proclaiming, "Repent for the Kingdom is here!"

Jesus also made this remarkable statement. "I am the way the truth and the life. No one comes to God except through me." John 14:6. That is a very bold statement requiring no interpretation to be understood. There is no hidden meaning, no mysterious metaphysical truth, nothing which can be twisted through fanciful interpretation. Jesus Christ is who He said He is; the way to life with God, the Truth about man and God, and the only means by which the life of God can, once again, dwell in man.

When a man is "born again from above by the Spirit," his interest is drawn to the things of God. He is drawn to knowing more about God and God's opinion of the world, life, death, eternity, etc. As (if?) he pursues this knowledge through study of God's word, the Bible, and through prayer, a strange and wonderful thing happens. The Spirit of God reveals more and more of God and His perspective of all things to man. That is His mission. Just as Jesus' mission was to live a sinless life and to die for the sins of all mankind, the Holy Spirit's mission is to take the things of God and to disclose them to man. This occurs as man studies God's Word and develops a prayer life. This is how a tangible relationship with God is established. And this is the process wherein man becomes a lover of God.

The Fellowship Model Concept

The fellowship model has steps or levels that are encountered as man learns to value the presence, availability, and wisdom of the Holy Spirit. For the purpose of this discussion consider the following progression.

1. Time
2. Knowledge
3. Experience
4. Love
5. Obedience

This model suggests it is only through Time spent in Word study and prayer that the born again man receives from the Holy Spirit accurate Knowledge of God. Such Holy Spirit imparted Knowledge becomes experiential as man applies this knowledge in life. As his Experience with the Holy Spirit continues his Love for God continues to expand. This is because he becomes more familiar with God through repeatedly applying God's revealed truth in life through experience. He begins to think, see, and hear from God's perspective. He begins to desire the things God desires. He begins to react the way God does. The result is confident, yes loving, submission to God. This is Obedience, the only obedience, God desires.

The concept is that Time with God leads one to Obedience to God. It is based upon God's self-disclosure that He is a jealous God who believes love is demonstrated through obedience. Who calls disobedience an act of hatred. Exodus 20:5. Who says only love endures the trials of life. 1 Corinthians 13. Who says loving God and loving others fulfills everything written in the law and spoken through the prophets. Matthew 7:12, and 22:40. Revelation 22:14.

When man misses this point, that God desires man to share His love, man fails to develop the relationship with God, which God desires. For centuries man has mistakenly tried, and failed, to appease God by his obedience. Entire civilizations have been built and have crumbled as a result. Wars have been fought by those zealous to force others to conform to their interpretation of God's commands, laws, and rules. Millions have tried, and are still trying, to be good enough to earn God's affection. Millions more are still living in fear of falling short of the mark, breaking a rule or command, and in general placing more value on Obedience than on Love. The truly pathetic outcome of centuries of this is that highly educated religious leaders, pundits, pastors, priests, rabbi's, and Sunday school teachers continue to promote this impossible, non-loving obedience, as the way to safely avoid God's wrath. Perhaps even more horrible is the idea, coming from many religious authorities, that man can't do anything to appease God other than believe he is a worthless sinner saved by grace!

Such religious teaching focuses attention on the disciples behavior, not on God's love. These dogmatic instructions typically highlight the furiousness of God's wrath, and teach us how to appease Him, so we can find safety. Man cannot appease God's wrath, not for one minute. Man does not contain the power, or the purity needed for such a monumental task. Yet because God's love is unconditional, He appeased His wrath. God came in the flesh, Jesus of Nazareth, and took care of the wrath of God issue.

Any religious philosophy that encourages ritual as the pathway to relationship misses the main point. That is; God loves man so much that He died on a grotesque Roman cross so He and man could live happily ever after in a love-filled, personally intimate, relationship. God did it! Man did not do it, and he cannot do it. It is impossible for man to enter into this most important of all relationships through any other means, but the cross of Christ.

The Fellowship Model Process

1. Time

Time is a funny thing. Time is the intangible continuum in which man experiences life. His progress through life is a process through experience. As one experience wanes another waxes. As one season ends another season begins. Man moves not through time so much as he moves through experience. And time has value only as a way of tracking progress as man moves from one experience to another. His life is a collection of past and present experiences. He lives, moment by moment, minute by minute, hour by hour, day by day, week by week, month by month, year by year, decade by decade, century by century, one experience at a time.

How long must I boil the egg before it becomes solid? How long must I refrigerate the water until it becomes ice? How long must I attempt to walk upright until I do so without falling? How long must I ride my two-wheeler with training wheels until I no longer need them? How long must I love my wife before she ceases to doubt my love? I have two days off this weekend, how should I spend my time? How much time do I have before I die?

The truth is, the more time we give to pursuing any activity the more accomplished we become at doing it. There is nothing you are doing well that you have not been doing a long time. Energy expended repeatedly in any pursuit equals experience. Repeated experience rewards the pursuer by enhancing the quality of the experience.

Developing a loving relationship with God requires time.

Time with God is the most essential and yet most often missing ingredient in a born again man's new life. It appears modern man does not have time in his schedule for God. As a result he allows others to hear from God for him, and report what they hear. He appoints others and even pays them money to spend time with God for his benefit, while he pursues life in the kingdom of men. He has built a system, a religious one, which allows him the freedom to pursue his life in the world of fallen men and yet reserve some time with God on the weekend. That is if it's not too inconvenient.

Is it any wonder man does not understand God? Is it any wonder that man does not know God? Is it any wonder man is deceived by other men who have no relationship with God and yet claim to hear from God? Is it possible that even though man claims to know God, God might disagree? Matthew 7:20-23. John 5:41-43. Titus 1:16. 2 Thessalonians 1:7-9.

2. Knowledge

The pursuit of knowledge begins when man desires to obtain information he has not yet received. The purpose of information is to inform or to make previously undisclosed knowledge available. Read a newspaper, college textbook, or the Bible. Surf the internet, visit wikipedia, a chat room, or blog. Much too much information is available. And most of it is neither, verifiable, practically beneficial, or particularly trustworthy. We live in an information-saturated age. Some wise guy once said, "Knowledge is power."

Is the quality of your life really better because of all the information you have collected? Will you live longer, happier, or more peacefully? And when you die, will all the time and effort you give to experience an informed life produce any enjoyable eternal results?

Time given to the Holy Spirit-assisted study of God's word increases accurate knowledge of God. Prayer and meditation on the things of God, with the Holy Spirit as a trusted guide increases accurate knowledge of God. But unlike information, the knowledge the Holy Spirit brings is in the form of a life-giving power encounter. God's self-disclosed information is actually alive! Hebrews 4:12. As the Holy Spirit grants access man can begin with a desire to receive intellectual information and end with an experiential revelation. Revelation has the power to change lives. Information does not. Information needs to be applied for change to come. Revelation, by definition, includes an element of divine life force wherein the knowledge God possesses is granted to man via spiritual experience. This explains why so many men claiming to possess saving knowledge of Christ and the cross live as if they never received it. They have information given them by other men, not revelation granted to them by God through personal spiritual interaction with the Holy Spirit. Information is received by the intellect, revelation is received by the spirit. Many misguided souls have embraced a religious philosophy but have yet to encounter the truth experientially. Jesus likened them to, white wash tombs filled with dead men's bones. Matthew 23:27. These are those whom Paul spoke of to Timothy when he said, such men hold on to a form of godliness and yet deny His power. 2 Timothy 3:4-6.

Information will not save you from God's wrath. Demons believe Jesus is the savior of the world and they tremble in fear because they know such knowledge cannot change their future. James 2:19.

Time spent in His word will eventually, if not immediately due to the conflict with old habits, mind-sets, and religious rhetoric, produce revelation of God. Revelation is experiential via the involvement of the spirit. Information is not. As the spirit of man is immersed in an experience with the self-revelation of God man becomes more god-like. He will in fact begin to "experience" God.

3. Experience

Man has a problem. He is trapped in space. He has a damaged physical body which is limited to experiencing life on a physical plane. Yet in his purest form, as designed and created by God, "in our image," man is a spiritual being. His once flawless physical body is no longer capable of functioning in his former "God-like" condition. God is Spirit and those who worship him must do so in Spirit and in Truth. John 4:24. Herein lies man's greatest challenge. How can man relate to God who is Spirit while being trapped in the limitations imposed upon him by his corrupt physical body? Must he somehow leave his physical body and travel through space, to have fellowship with God at some distant place in the galaxy? And how can man comprehend the infinitude of God with the finite limits of the intellect, the mind?

Fellowship with God begins as man explores the things of God intellectually yet with the assistance of the Spirit of God. Man can experience God spiritually, on the unseen, non-physical level of experience. He can do this as he learns to rely upon repeated interaction with the Holy Spirit. Doing so regularly teaches man the value of interacting on a spiritual level. And doing so empowers him to apply more and more of his spiritual experience to his physical experience. As man learns, through experience with God, to think about life as God does, from God's perspective, he will quite naturally begin to respond to physical life from a spiritually accurate, or godly, perspective. In fact, a miracle, which by definition circumvents a physical process, is a case in which God bridges the gap between the spirit and the physical.

Therefore as man spends time reading, praying, and meditating on the Word of God, the Holy Spirit empowers him to encounter God. It's a beautiful thing indeed! Jesus said, "If you continue in my Word you are my disciples indeed. And you shall know the truth and the truth shall make you free." John 8:31-32. The encouragement is this; if you desire to know God, truly to know Him experientially, you must spend time getting to know Him. To know Him you must spend time in His Word. And if you do spend time with Him He will continue to reveal to you more and more of Himself, His Spirit and His Truth.

4. Love

Time leads to increased knowledge. Increased Knowledge translates into intimate experience. Intimate experience produces love. To know God is to love Him. To encounter experientially the magnitude of His love, its depth and breadth, intensity and completeness, its unconditional and eternal availability, is to truly be transformed from physical to spiritual.

Jesus Christ is the supreme example of a man consumed by the love of God. He was and is a man. Born through the birth canal of a woman. Yet he was conceived in her womb by the Holy Spirit. He is "the last Adam," the new man, the "first born among many brethren." 1 Corinthians 15:45, Romans 8:29.

Jesus Christ is the victorious, sinless, faithful, loving son, obedient to the point of death. He is man's role model for real life, for life with God. He is the quintessential example of intimacy with God and of the benefits of that intimacy. He attributed his miracles to his Father. He claimed it was His Father who did those wonderful things. John 5:30, John 8:29.

Jesus Christ was tempted to rebel against God just as every other man born to a woman is tempted to do. Yet he remained faithful. And it was not easy. If you think it was you have much more reading to do. His life was a constant battle from the moment he was conceived until the moment he died on the cross. He resisted every temptation, every day of his life. The more He matured the more intense His battle became. The final victory was achieved as He declared, "Father, forgive them for the do not realize what they are doing." Luke 23:24. He proved His love by His obedience to die on the cross. Hours before He had spoken to His friends saying, "Greater love has no man than this, that He lay down His life for His friends." John 15:13.

So, what was His secret weapon that empowered him to succeed where every man before had failed? His love for God. And how did he develop this all consuming love? Through fellowship with God. From early childhood, He diligently developed and maintained a loving relationship with God. God and God's truth and will was more important to Jesus Christ than any other thing, even life itself!

Paul said men are dead in their trespasses and sins. Colossians 2:13. Men arrogantly walk the earth eating, drinking, procreating, conquering, boasting of their accomplishments, their power and wisdom, and yet God considers them dead men! Why? Because all men are dead men until they experience intimacy with God. This is the reason they live. This is the purpose of their lives. This is why they were created by God in the first place.

Until man experiences the love of God man does not live. He remains less than who and what God desires him to be. He is a ship without a helmsman destined to sail the vast expanse of sea without a plotted course or destination. In the case of the religious man, he is a vain actor, a hypocrite, portraying a role to the best of his ability but always lacking the sparkle of authenticity.

The religious man is trained by other religious men to be good. He attempts to please God by accepting and submitting to a godly moral code. He is connected intellectually and behaviorally to the rules for kingdom living but remains aloof to the joy and peace available to him in the loving benevolent presence of the King. He has received but failed to respond to the invitation of audience with the King.

Jesus said, echoing God, "If you love me you will obey what I command."

John 14:15, 24. Please note true obedience is a result of true love. Obedience is not a substitute for love. It is not the ticket to peace with God. Obedience is the response of love. Obedience will not and cannot parry the wrath of God. 1 Corinthians 13. If this were possible the Law would not have been replaced by Grace. Obedience to the Law was an inferior method for bridging the chasm between God's love and man's rejection of that love. Galatians 2:21. The obedience Jesus proclaims He also demonstrated. He was able to obey perfectly. We cannot. We need not even try. Why? God desires our love, not our obedience. According to Scripture if we try to have peace with God by obeying His commands perfectly we will fail, every time! Yet if we learn to love God by patiently, persistently, developing a relationship with Him over a prolonged period of time, we will delight to obey Him, to the best of our corruptible ability. And as He promised, love will cover a multitude of sin. 1 Peter 4:8. We will no longer fear falling short of obeying. Perfect love casts out fear. 1 John 4:18. God has not given us a spirit of fear. Romans 8:15-16. 2 Timothy 1:7. God does not want us to fear breaking His commandments. He wants us to rejoice in His unconditional love. Deuteronomy 10:15. Deuteronomy 30:19-20. Deuteronomy 7:12-14.

5. Obedience

Regardless of how faithful man is to obey God's rules if he has no desire to know God, God is not satisfied. Matthew 7:21-23. Isaiah 29:13. For in fact God gave rules to men so they could benefit from His loving grace in the face of their rebelliousness. He communicated with them for their benefit. He pursued them. He desired them. He promised their love for Him demonstrated by obedience would bring blessings into their lives. Their obedience to His benevolence would be evidence of their love. That is, if they had love in their hearts for Him they would respond to His love with obedience.

The nation of Israel is the most glaring example of this concept. They wanted the benefits of living in harmony with God. But they did not want to know Him personally. They attempted through their sacrifices and rituals to appease God's wrath. Isaiah 1:14. However, and as incredible as it seems, they had not made the connection that He desired their love. He wanted to be known to them personally, intimately, as their Father. But they wanted to know Him from a distance, as their ruling magistrate. Deuteronomy 9:13, Isaiah 29:13, Matthew 23:37, Luke 19:41.

Jesus Christ taught the disciples to know God as Father. He said, "When you pray say, Father…" Matthew 6:6, 9. He thought of God as his Father. And he dialogued with God using the title Father, not "oh high and lofty unknowable God … etc."

For the one who loves God obedience is no longer a duty. It is a privilege. It is an honor.

This man is a child of God. John 1:12-13, 1 John 3:2. He believes God is the good Father Who delights in giving His children the Kingdom. Luke 12:32. Obedience is a demonstration of willful surrender. And surrender is the shortest path to fulfillment. Our Savior taught us to pray "thy will be done, on earth as it is (ordained to be done) in heaven." If these words are prayed from the head, the intellect, they are the vain rhetoric of a religious man. Yet if they come out of a heart consumed by and surrendered to the love of God, they are the most liberating words spoken by man. If these words are spoken by a man who is passionately in love with God, they are spoken by a man who knows God intimately. This man is one who answered when God called to him from the cross. This man knows God intimately because he has spent time with Him. He has found Him to be kind, gentle, and generous. He has learned by personal experience to love God passionately and to obey Him joyously. This man is not a servant in God's stable but a child at God's table.

Conclusion

How about you? Do you know Him? Or do you know about Him? Do you have a religion or do you have a relationship with the One True Living God? Are you trying to be good enough to please God? Or are you enjoying the benefits of God's love? Do you feel closer now to God than when you were first born again? Would you be willing to die to prove your love for God? These are weighty questions. But they must be asked. God is very serious about things like love and obedience. But He is always gracious to those who approach Him. He is always willing to begin again. Revelation 3:19-21.

Addendum: An 8 Stage Love Development Model

Every loving relationship is developed slowly over time. Two individuals grow closer one stage at a time as they accumulate the amount of time they interact with each other. The following is an example of the 8 stages of growth every relationship will pass through on the way to becoming a loving relationship.

1. Attraction: Meeting for the first time we decide if we desire to meet again.

2. Appreciation: As we meet often we begin to appreciate the individual's impact on us.

3. Affection: More time leads to a heightened desire to be in one's presence more often.

4. Intimacy: We share the private secret details of our lives and previous experiences, good and not so good. We become vulnerable to each other. We are happy to be in one another's presence. And we are sad when we are forced by circumstances to be separated.

5. Conflict: If we have not conflicted before the intimacy stage we will during it. This is due to the personal vulnerability created by intimacy.

6. Resolution: Only as we learn to resolve conflict quickly and graciously we will learn to value conflict as it moves the relationship to a deeper level. If we refuse to serve our lover, if we refuse to resolve the conflict, any further development of the relationship comes to a screeching halt. As conflict is resolved repeatedly, it occurs less frequently.

7. Intimacy: Resolving conflict successfully strengthens the relationship and simultaneously moves it to a more intimate level. Resolving conflict causes the relationship to move on into a new realm of intimacy many people never experience. In the Greek this level is called agape.

8. Love: Agape Love is not an emotion, not a feeling. The word, love is often used to describe a feeling. The

word is properly used when describing a permanent bond of loyalty, confidence, and support. True love is proven by a self-sacrificing commitment for the good of the beloved. Therefore, in most cases, it cannot be achieved or shared without intense conflict. To love is to surrender one's concern for self in favor of concern for another. It is during the conflict encountered at an intimate level that love is discovered through surrender. John 15:13, Mark 12:31.

Christ at the cross is the supreme example of true love. His strong affection for God caused him to ignore the pain and suffering, the humiliation and shame of the cross. His loyalty exemplified His love. He did not love in word only but in deed. He loved so much that when he was asked to die for the sins of humanity, so God and man could be reconciled, he did it. He did not do it begrudgingly. He did not do it with "an attitude." He did not do it because he "had to," or because he was forced to. He did not do it "to be obedient." He went through the humiliation, shame, and pain of the cross because he loved God. His attitude was one of confident submission to God's will knowing if God desired it, it was good. This then is love, self-sacrificing service to the beloved.

Are You Paying Attention?

Matthew 24:3 Now as He sat on the Mount of Olives, the disciples came to Him privately, saying, "Tell us, when will these things be? And what will be the sign of Your coming, and of the end of the age?"

Preface to Chapter 18

This article was written several years ago. I am including it here because I feel it is even more relevant today. It is presented just as it was written in August of 2005.

Please allow me a little space to share my thoughts with you regarding the signs of the times. I believe I have been prompted by the Holy Spirit to do so.

A couple weeks ago I was afforded the opportunity to spend some much needed, and much desired, time alone with God. While Michele was away visiting her mother, I tool five days to fast and pray, and spend time soaking in the Word and in His presence. Much of this time was spent in silence. It was an enjoyable time, to say the least!

I was seeking to hear clearly from God regarding this new season Michele and I feel we are entering. How are we to minister? Where are we to minister the healing power of His love? And to whom are we to minister? You might think the answers to such questions are clear enough from a casual reading of Matthew 5, 6, and 7. But I wanted to know the specific details of all of the above. We have been asked to minister in various places and to various people literally all over the world. Invitations have come from England, Sri Lanka, Singapore and New Zealand, as well as from various groups in several states in the US. We are thankful for these opportunities and blessed by the confidence of those making the requests. But with so many opportunities coming to us we want to be sure we go as He leads and do as He wills.

Yet for all my time alone with Him during my fast He surprised me by speaking on another subject. One day as I was soaking and listening, He asked simply, "Are you paying attention?"

I responded, "Paying attention? To what?"

And He said, "To the signs of the times."

I replied, "Do you mean, tsunamis, earthquakes, forest fires, famine, wars and rumors of war, AIDS, SARS, terrorists, the US judicial system, abortion, gay marriage, pornography, sexual immorality, sin in the church, etc?"

"Yes indeed, those signs, and the signs in Israel as well." He answered.

You know me, some of you, very well. I am not a Bible scholar nor am I very wise on the subject of last-days prophesy, eschatology, or apocalyptic Scripture. Neither am I an alarmist, extremist, or band-wagon jumper. So, I pondered His comments carefully. And since that encounter with His Spirit two weeks ago I have been intently studying all of these subjects again in the light of Scripture. And now, at His urging, I want to ask you the same question.

Are you paying attention? We are living in perilous times. Especially since September 11, 2001. The world has become a dangerous place, and it appears to be becoming more dangerous by the week! Immediately following the horrible tragedy of 911 I sought the Lord in prayer. As the media moguls were racing around spouting opinions and trying to make sense of it, I was prompted to keep silent and pray for discernment. In the days that followed I kept asking, "What do you want me to learn from this, Lord?" I believe I finally heard Him say two things. First He said, "I have been telling you that you are living in desperate times. Now you know it."

And next He reminded me of this chilling fact. "No one who died that morning knew they were going to die that day except the terrorists. All were going about their business of living life as usual. You were as well. Yet everyone that died that day was placed into one of two categories. They either had a relationship with me or they didn't. If they did have a relationship with Me, September 11 was a truly wonderful day for them and they are with me now. If they did not have a relationship with Me they are not with me now, and they will never be."

That morning despite their differences, Jew, Gentile, Arab, Muslim, Caucasian, Hispanic, Asian, Native American, African American, Republican, Democrat and Independent, all were put into one of two categories. There are only two.

What is it that is consuming your time and attention? Where do you spend the majority of your free time? To what cause or purpose are you directing your energy, and your reserve finances? Whatever it is, if it does not include keeping up with the events in the Middle East and the events described in Matthew 24, Romans 1, 2 Peter 3, and Revelation 6, you might not be paying attention.

I am not sending a warning, a judgment, or a criticism. I am merely doing as I was instructed to do. I pray His Spirit will lead you and guide you into all truth in these desperate last days. Jesus Christ is coming again soon!

Blessings,
Mike

CHAPTER 19

A Morning Walk With My Father

Genesis 3: 8-9 Then the man and his wife heard the sound of the LORD God as he was walking in the garden in the cool of the day, and they hid from the LORD God among the trees of the garden. But the LORD God called to the man, "Where are you?"

This morning I accepted an invitation to go for a walk with my Father. We walked through His garden following a well-worn path. Though the scenery was new to me it was obvious I had not been the first to walk this way. Many, perhaps very many, had walked this path before.

Just after starting out I heard a rooster crowing in the distance. A little further along I saw a goat standing in a field. He bawled at us once. As the path twisted and turned I heard the chirping song of various birds in the trees. We ducked under a low-hanging branch and I heard the buzzing of bees of a nearby hive. The horses in the pasture looked up briefly greeting us with wide-eyed gazes, and then went back to their grazing.

As we drew near a gurgling stream I was reminded of the first time I heard His voice. The sound became more forceful as we approached and the cacophony of its rustling timbre and tone began to sound like a symphony of intermingling voices. A more majestic chorus I have never heard.

The morning path led us up hills where the breeze caressed my face and the bright sunlight caused me to squint. And then down again we went into the shady creek side grotto, cool and refreshing. In the grotto we passed a pile of rotting fruit. Flies buzzed. A curious little black fly left the pile and landed briefly on my neck, tasting my flesh. Just as quickly it flew away, feeling victorious, angry, or disgusted, I do not know which.

Rounding a bend in the path I heard the sound of something growling fiercely in the bush. It startled me and made my heart stop for a moment. But I kept walking with God. The growling was punctuated by a snort, and followed by a rushing sound through the leaves of the garden bushes. As the ominous sound approached I became frightened and considered bolting away for safety. However, I did not know where I would go. I looked quickly around me. Where could I go to find more security? There was no place to hide; nothing to protect me. But then I remembered, I was walking with God. As the vicious dog charged me snarling with the intimidating voice of hatred and violence I shuddered, anticipating the imminent force of his crushing weight against me. As he closed for the kill I was assaulted by the foul odor of his breath.

However, just before he lunged, a strange thing happened. He abruptly stopped his charge. He stood still staring defiantly, seething with rage, his muscles flexing, poised to strike, his eyes glaring. Yet in only a moment those glowing yellow eyes caught sight of something that seemed to perplex him. He twisted his head from side to side as if he was trying to understand. In an instant the thing he gazed upon calmed him, turned his rage to fear, and then cowering quietly, he turned around and quickly retreated into the bush from which he had emerged only moments before.

When my breathing returned to normal I noticed Father's reassuring smile. And we continued on our way along the path. I reflected on the number of animals I had seen thus far. There was such variety of size and sound and appearance and color. It was truly amazing and I complimented Father on His work, saying how much I was enjoying our walk in His garden.

As the path began climbing again our foot-worn course crossed a gravel track. We turned onto it and walked along listening to the crunching sound of our feet against the pebbles of the road. It widened as we went along, until it became broad enough that five men could walk abreast without touching. We climbed higher and approached the crest of the hill. My ears perked up to the faint rumble of what sounded like motorized machinery moving on the gravel ahead of us. As I listened I could tell the machine was coming toward us. It sounded as though it was moving quite fast.

Father touched my shoulder firmly and I stepped to the side of the roadway just as the large metallic machine came roaring up the hill in a cloud of dust. Rumbling and rattling it whizzed by me throwing pebbles to the side of its spinning black wheels. I had just enough time to briefly see the determined steel-eyed gaze of the man at the controls, before it was past me, charging down the hill. Immediately I was engulfed in the dusty cloud trailing behind in the wake of the noisy foul smelling beast.

I coughed, closed my eyes, and covered my mouth and nose with the collar of my shirt. I stood still waiting for the cloud to dissipate.

Father patted me gently on my shoulder, and once again He smiled. I was reminded how secure His presence makes me feel. Yet, as we resumed our walk, now through the lingering haze of dust, I could not help noticing the contrast between the animals I had seen earlier along our path and the man in his noisy machine.

I soon dismissed the intrusion and concentrated once again on the beauty surrounding me, and on the gentle comforting grip of Father's hand on mine.

I am continually amazed by the variety of adventures we share as I walk together with Father in His garden. So often each walk, like each day, feels new and different. Though each day shares similarities with the one before it, they are unique, occurring only once. One might not be as easy or as much fun as another and the track we follow one morning may be more difficult than the previous day. At times I lag behind Him, and when I do I get side-tracked easily. It's not difficult for me to wander off on my own for a while. Usually the trails of my solitary adventures remind me how much I miss walking beside Him. But when I return to the path I always find Him waiting patiently for me. He smiles when our eyes meet, extends His hand once again, and asks me to tell Him all about it. And then, with His hand once again in mine, we walk and talk and continue to celebrate the unfolding, ever-expanding beauty of His garden.

Beyond the Veil
Mike Green
2008

Take me through the veil, dear Lord,
That separates me from You
Even though I know You are here with me,
I long to be there with You.
Take me through the veil, O Lord
To the place where You reside
To hear and see and touch you Lord
I lay this flesh aside.

Take me through the veil, my Lord
Consume this robe of flesh.
Open wide my spirit, Lord
To know Your holiness.
Take me through the veil O Lord
And never let me go.
Remove from me this filthy shroud,
To let your glory show.

I worship you, O Lord Most High,
I praise Your matchless grace!
My God and Savior how I rejoice,
To feel Your warm embrace!

www.ingramcontent.com/pod-product-compliance
Lightning Source LLC
Chambersburg PA
CBHW031235090426
42742CB00007B/212